my Better Half and Me

2010

Moray

Happy Days

JOSS & ROSEMARY
ACKLAND

My Better Half
and Me

A LOVE AFFAIR THAT LASTED FIFTY YEARS

Joss Ackland

EBURY
PRESS

3 5 7 9 10 8 6 4 2

Published in 2009 by Ebury Press, an imprint of Ebury Publishing
A Random House Group Company

The Random House Group Limited Reg. No. 954009

Addresses for companies within the Random House Group can be found at
www.randomhouse.co.uk

A CIP catalogue record for this book is available from the British Library

The Random House Group Limited supports The Forest Stewardship Council
(FSC), the leading international forest certification organisation. All our titles
that are printed on Greenpeace approved FSC certified paper carry the FSC logo.
Our paper procurement policy can be found at www.rbooks.co.uk/environment

Mixed Sources
Product group from well-managed
forests and other controlled sources
www.fsc.org Cert no. TT-COC-2139
© 1996 Forest Stewardship Council
FSC

Printed in the UK by CPI Mackays, Chatham, ME5 8TD

ISBN 9780091930615

To buy books by your favourite authors and register for offers visit
www.rbooks.co.uk

To our family

PREFACE

Towards the end of the Second World War, fifteen-year-old Rosemary Kirkcaldy started to keep a diary. She kept it, intermittently, over a period of fifty-eight years – a diary with which she communicated, in a matter-of-fact, dispassionate manner, the events of the day. During our long partnership, the thought never crossed my mind that I might read it – nor did she suggest it. It was only towards the end of her life, suffering motor neurone disease, when she needed my help to hold her pen that I read any of her words. I found the cool, laid-back approach to an extraordinary life of fun, poverty, success, tragedy and excitement, both touching, and at times very funny. When I asked her if I could see about getting it published – unable to move or speak, she smiled and nodded her assent.

For six years after her death I spent all my free time copying and editing the multitude of words, from diaries of various shapes and sizes. I wrote about a great deal of our life in an autobiography which was published in the early eighties, so I now have included some experiences from her point of view, and to fill in the gaps when she was too desperate or too busy to write.

The changes that have taken place on this planet in the fifty-eight years since Rosemary started her diary are greater than at any time since man first walked the earth – even the years after the Industrial Revolution. Class distinction has evaporated, equality of the sexes is nearer and homosexuality is generally accepted. Racism still exists, but only with the fading minority. However we are still primitive creatures, and today we have such colossal powers of destruction that once the wrong button is pressed we could be back where we began. We are still immature, and if we are without morals and faith we are liable to self-destruct. We know nothing of the moment before we emerge from the womb – and nothing after we leave the door at the end of life.

Our faiths have multiplied, and these faiths usually depend on the piece of land that we inhabit. Sadly this has often led to violence, hate and war. All religions can create some balance of self-discipline. As long as they advocate love of fellow man they can guide us. We exist for a purpose, but what that purpose is no one knows. Throughout the ages there have always been exceptional leaders to drive us forward. During the last fifty years Martin Luther King, Nelson Mandela and others have led the way in removing racial prejudice. To go forward it is important to have faith – but to despise or reject those whose faith is different is a dangerous arrogance. With the constant threat of war and terrorism, in spite of all our scientific and technological advances, we are still very primitive creatures. We exist for a purpose but no one knows what that purpose is. Rosemary followed the Christian path, and whatever path she took – I knew I should follow.

It is very important that the world progresses forward from one generation to another. These days, once the young reach their teens, it is not easy. When Rosemary and I grew up, you were a child and then you were an adult – there was no period in between – no time to balance precariously on that tightrope of uncertain confidence. Today there are few apprentices and no mentors, and very few of the young have any conception what we were like at their age. We are totally different creatures. There are times I feel I have landed on Mars; but then I realise that I am the Martian.

Rosemary started her diary in 1945 at her home in Malawi in the heart of Central Africa, and I was in London training to be an actor. This was six years before we met, and our love story began.

And it *is* a love story. In those days there were no nuptial agreements – no preparing for divorce a before joining together in marriage. And sixty years ago – less was considerably more – the joy of the first kiss, the pleasure of touch, the longing for the unobtainable – and when the unobtainable was obtained more was considerably more. Then two hearts really could start beating as one.

And it was not long before our two hearts did beat as one. We became soulmates. It was not a generous act to see our partner happy. Our satisfaction was achieved from the other's pleasure. We loved each other more than we loved ourselves. When I was working abroad without Rosemary, I could not find real joy and satisfaction in any location until I returned with her beside me.

Our lives have not been ordinary, but Rosemary always accepted everything with a calm detachment. One minute she would be doing household chores and picking up the children and the next popping off to Rio as if she was nipping round the corner to buy bread. She coped with disaster and trauma with patience, cool stoic acceptance and enormous courage. Even when our house burnt down, with no one else able to help, she ran through the flames, and saved our children.

Today I do not have the confidence to return to the theatre, because Rosemary and I always worked together tackling a play, and it was always her strength and her calm quiet assurance that energised me, and moved me forward.

By the time Rosemary developed motor neurone disease, unable to speak or move, it was only with her diary with that she was able to communicate, and so I have included these last two years in more detail.

EARLY DAYS

In 1945, when she first started her diary, Rosemary and I were at the opposite ends of the earth. She was in Nyasaland – Malawi – and I was in England. Our backgrounds were very different. I was one of three children. My father was Norman Ackland, an Irish journalist, who, after seducing his parents' maid, had been sent over as a remittance man to England to stay with his aunt Annie, in London. There he seduced his aunt's maid, Ruth, and so my older brother, Paddy, was born.

Ruth then spent her life living in rented basement flats. My father went off to war in 1914 and when he returned, he married her, and then went off again. Once in a while he would drop in, and after six years my sister Barbara was born. He was next around seven years later and then I dropped from the womb. I was due to be born in Saint Mary Abbott's Hospital in Kensington, but there had been a confusion of babies – two mothers had been given the wrong child by mistake – so my mother fled from the hospital in her nightdress, in the middle of the night, and I was born in our basement flat near Ladbroke Grove.

In 1939 we moved to yet another basement flat in Stoke Newington where, at the age of eleven, I was due to start senior school at Dame

Alice Owens, the only school where I had managed to pass the entrance exam. Before I started school there, we had a chance to see the sea for the first time when we boarded HMS *Innisfallen*, en route to a two-week holiday at my mother's brother's place just outside Cork. But while we were there war broke out, and the *Innisfallen* was sunk. We stayed in Ireland for three months and then, after travelling by rail to Dublin, we zigzagged across the sea to England. By this time Dame Alice Owens School had been evacuated to Bedford. After saying farewell to my mother I picked up my gas mask, got on a train and was billeted there – until my mother gave up the flat in London and rented a flat in Bedford.

At the outbreak of war both my brother and my rarely seen father joined up. I didn't see my father again until he arrived at our flat looking tired and worn. He had come straight from a boat that had picked him out of the water at Dunkirk. He lay on a bed and, for the first time ever, he listened intently as I told him the story of the film I had seen the day before, *The Wizard of Oz*.

It was some time before our forces returned to France. But when they did, just after D-Day, my brother Paddy was killed. He had a wife and child. They went to the United States, but we have remained close to this day.

In 1944 I left school before taking my matriculation exam, because I knew I would fail my Latin. In those days Latin was essential. When I told my headmaster that I was going to be an actor he told me that it was a bad idea because I had never managed to get into any of the school plays – not even into the chorus of *Cyrano de Bergerac*. He delicately warned me against becoming an actor. He said, 'I have just been measured for a suit, but the tailor took far too many measurements – there are a lot of people like that in the theatre.'

So I worked in a brewery, worked backstage in the local theatre, worked in a dairy and finally got to the Central School of Speech Training at the Albert Hall. I got in because there were two hundred and fifty female students and only three men. I could not afford to pay, but as they were desperately in need of male students they took me in. Even though it was against the rules I managed to subsidise myself by painting walls for the American troops at their club in Knightsbridge. While Rosemary was starting her diary on the other side of the world I stayed at a flat with my sister, who had just come down from Oxford.

I was streetwise in a bombed city, and the war was on. Rosemary was an innocent, away from civilisation, far from the turmoil of war, living in a white colony in black Africa – in another world and with a very different background.

Rosemary's grandmother, Louise Ryall, had left England in 1898, the first white woman to travel alone to Nyasaland, so that she could join her missionary husband. After many weeks at sea, she arrived at Chinde, where she was transferred in a basket to a small river tug. Two weeks later she left on a river steamer, in very primitive conditions, up the Zambezi, a journey which she described as follows:

> I thoroughly enjoyed the trip – stopping at different stations for firewood, and the paddle steamer getting stuck on sandbanks very often. How cheerful the natives were, jumping in the river, getting us off by using long poles, and singing native songs all the while. There was no rush or hurry – patience was a great thing.

There were quite a number of crocodiles on the banks, and lower down the river, near Chinde, many hippos. We did not travel by night unless there was a bright moon. We tied up by the side of the river. A fortnight later we arrived at Chiromo. We managed to get as far as Katungas – the foot of Cholo Hills – approximately 350 miles from Chinde, and then I was carried off by machilla to Blantyre. At first I was a little nervous, being sent off in a machilla with sixteen natives. I was a little afraid of running into game. However the natives were a wonderful team, and their songs, as we went plodding along, made me forget my fears.

Strong and determined, Louise Ryall was a true pioneer. She strode through life with a simple optimism. Life was hard and there were many conflicts between rival tribes – and in 1915 a native rising – but in time, the small town of Blantyre grew. After her husband died, she opened Ryall's Hotel, which eventually was known as the 'finest hotel north of the Zambezi'. She had two children: a boy and a girl. After the First World War, her daughter Phyllis married Robert Hunter Kirkcaldy, a Scottish soldier, who had served in Africa. He became a successful businessman and eventually was elected Mayor of Blantyre. They had three children, Robert, Catherine and Rosemary Jean, who, on 15 January 1929, was born into a world where the small population of white people continued to live as if they were back in Britain – only now they had black servants. And to be black in that day and age was to be subservient to their white masters. While there was no official apartheid the segregation of black and whites was considered natural. But it was never natural for Rosemary, for she was closer to Effie, her black nanny, than she was to her busy parents. Rosemary's brother, Robert, was far away fighting in Burma, and Rosemary could only gather news in snatches – from the wireless and from old newspapers.

Rosemary began her diary in Malawi, which, until independence was restored, had been renamed Nyasaland by the white settlers. The diary is not continuous – some years were lost – some destroyed by fire – and there were times when life was either too hard, or she was too busy, to write more than bare details. I have included some of these scraps because the public life of an actor and the private life of family are a cauldron of hard times, laughter, success and tragedy.

When Rosemary started her diary in 1945 she was only fifteen, but what remained constant was not only her lust for life, but also her energy, compassion and quiet determination, which helped us live through so much personal disaster, excitement, poverty and tragedy.

Meanwhile the world was changing fast as we lived through the rise and fall of fascism, the Holocaust of the Jews, the McCarthy trials in America, the racist problems in the fifties, the collapse of Communism in the USSR, the Berlin Wall coming down, the end of apartheid, pointless wars in Korea and Vietnam, a bizarre war in the Falklands, Iraq, the Middle East, drugs, Aids, George Bush – and for most of those years with the sword of Damocles dangling above the planet.

Rosemary started celebrating New Year's Eve at home in Blantyre. Her life begins for us – on the first day of the last year of the war – with every paragraph a different day.

1945–1946

We had a lovely party and I danced a lot with Bill – so I got questioned! I went first footing till half past three in the morning.

In the afternoon went to ballet practice, and I had a devil of a row with Mr Whitehouse. It was most annoying – but I enjoyed it. Saw Bill at the flicks and he winked at me. Oh gee!

I went to the dress rehearsal in Limbe. I saw Bill, and he knocked the footlights over. Got home, and Dad was in a terrible temper – he didn't care whether it was my birthday or not. There was a terrible row in the house – I nearly fainted; poor Mum was very upset too. She slept with me in the end, and I was so glad.

Got up at six, and rode Gypsy, and then took Peps out to the foals to be crossed with Buster. Unfortunately nothing happened!!! Saw Bill – but my thoughts on him were shattered.

Woke up with a hell of a throat, and I felt dreadful. Mummy called the doctor, and the silly fool confined me to bed for a week. I was livid!

I'm feeling better, but the school train left Limbe minus me. I was given a letter from Bill. He asked me to be his girlfriend, but I don't know what to answer!!

It was a horrible, horrible day. I wanted to go on the mail-train but, as luck would have it, Mum kept me in bed. So I stormed around the house, and my temperature went up ten degrees. There was a row tonight, and Dad told Mum never to come back from Salisbury.

Here we are on the train, and it's rocking so violently that I can hardly write my diary. [The train from Limbe to Salisbury took three days and two nights, and even when she was a very young child, Rosemary had travelled to Salisbury and back on her own many times. However, this time her mother was with her.] The journey so far has been a bit trying, and oh! I've just been bitten by a ruddy tsetse fly – ouch!

I was sick all the time on the train, but felt better by the time I arrived at Salisbury, although my eye was swollen by the bite. Straight to school. I was voted convener of the Dramatic Society.

I spent, without exaggeration, the whole day doing concert practice. I'm simply dead tired, my feet are throbbing, my back's aching and I haven't done a spot of homework or written a line of a letter. God please help me. I am sure I must have been made to learn to endure hardships. I shall one day be happy though. I shall make and produce a great Russian dance to Hungarian Rhapsody No. 2. No less than thirty dances.

The bishop took the 7 a.m. service, and although it was interesting, I just about fell asleep. [Rosemary was not Catholic, but her school was a convent, and her teachers were nuns.] In the hall it was announced that I was vice captain of St Louis Bertrand. It is a great honour.

Today was a dreadful one, so I'd rather not talk about school.

Trudy was rushed to St Anne's to have her appendix out – just like I was. She was very brave.

Went to the seven o'clock service, and I gave sixpence in collection, as it was a special day. After our walk tonight, on our way back to school, it poured with rain and we were stuck, but a handsome young man gave us a lift.

The first allied aircraft have flown over Berlin. I got up at a quarter to four, but was sent to bed again. I worked very hard, and finished before supper – yippee!! This evening there was a flick. It was ever so spooky, but I enjoyed it very much. After lights went out, Joan and I ate apples in bed.

It is Robert's twenty-first birthday. I went to Holy Communion. The service was rather drawn out, and personally I felt like having a wee snooze! I rested after lunch, and Maggie, Joan and I apple-pied all the beds!

Oh dear! What a ghastly day. Why, of course – it's the thirteenth. I got news today that Robert had been wounded in Burma. Sister Kevin told me in parlour, and I couldn't stop sobbing. However I tried to be brave, so I washed my face and went to night study.

For the last few days Jean has been horrible to me. She won't even speak to me civilly. We are going to have it out tonight. I can't stand being treated as if I don't exist – I feel like crying.

Germany has been bombed for the twenty-seventh night running. Last night nine hundred planes went over, and only twelve were missing.

Last night we had a midi [midnight feast]. It was great. Cherry got in bed with me. We had sandwiches, boiled eggs, doughnuts, chips, fruit, cakes, sausage rolls, etc. This morning Clemi found out, and was she wild – and how!! I got a letter from Granny saying Robert had leave. Yippee!

This evening I received a letter from Mummy with wonderful news about Robert. He is not as badly wounded as we might have expected. He was shot through the arm, and they got the poison out with leeches, but, oh, he is so brave, and I am so proud of my big brother.

Dad arrived this morning. I didn't go to meet him. Berlin has been bombed for thirty-seven nights, and there is very hard fighting in Burma. In the afternoon we went to see the flick *This Happy Breed*. We all enjoyed it very much. Came back to school this evening, and then on to Saints to see Mozart's opera acted. I loved it.

The Russians are getting near to Berlin. I never went to church, but saw Daddy off. The train left an hour later. Daddy gave me five pounds – yippee. I also got a letter from Mum, with three pounds inside – doing well, what!

Today was quite nice in school. In our hygiene lesson Sister brought up the subject of VD. Last night I started my period, and got a big patch on my sheet all soiled. What shall I do, I wonder?

President Roosevelt died tonight at a quarter to nine from cerebral haemorrhage. He was having his photo taken when he fainted. The doctor said he would not live long. My spots are much better today.

The Americans are going into thirty days mourning for their president. Harry Truman has taken his place. He is very quiet and serious – a little like Lincoln was.

The Americans and the Russians are nearing each other, and they are not far from Berlin. I got a letter from Mummy today, and a suitcase, full of clothes and soaps and tuck, for Inyanga. Now I wish I was going home with her, but I'm glad I won't have to hear Daddy getting cross with Mum. We had a dance with St George's this evening. Boy oh boy!!! I got Keith Green as my first partner. He danced with me nearly all evening. And we were always the first on the floor. Talk about exhibition!! How everyone teased me about Green.

The Russian and American troops have linked up, and Mussolini has been captured. This afternoon Joan and I went downtown and bought two records: 'Chicka Chicka Boom Chick' and 'Hawaiian Memories'.

We left by train early this morning, arriving at Rusapi at two o'clock and then took the bus for Inyanga. After a terrible bus journey for seventy miles, we arrived at the guesthouse, and I found I had a room to myself. Mussolini and eighteen generals have been shot.

We went down to the river this morning and fooled around on the rocks. In the afternoon we went to see the old native church. It's a funny little place, with mats to kneel on and pews to sit in. Then we saw the valley of a thousand hills – a gorgeous sight. Himmler has offered a new peace treaty to Britain, America and Russia. Later we listened to request night on the wireless.

I went with a crowd of people to Inyangombi Falls. I got ever so sunburnt. We shot a dika, but lost it, unfortunately.

Hitler is supposed to have died of a cerebral haemorrhage. In the afternoon I went for a long walk by myself, and thought about what career I should choose. I decided that I should either be a journalist or take up dancing.

Hitler and Goebbels are supposed to have committed suicide. Gran rang me up and told me that Robert had just won the Military Cross for gallantry. I'm so terribly thrilled.

Everyone's sitting around the wireless, waiting for news of peace. Rangoon has surrendered, and one million Germans have been captured. How exciting. This afternoon Jo and I went swimming, and how cold it was.

VICTORY DAY IN EUROPE. Oh, this is wonderful. I listened to Churchill's speech, and the description of scenes at Buckingham Palace, Whitehall, Trafalgar Square, Scotland and Belfast, etc. This evening we had a bonfire on top of the hill and songs. Then we listened to the King's speech. Today was a whole holiday.

Ten million Commonwealth prisoners have returned, and there have been four hundred planes over Japan. In the evening we went to a braevlae [barbecue]. Oh, what a super time we had. We sang songs around the fire, and cooked a whole sheep. How I long for Rob and Cath to be with me. It was sad to think of war still in Burma. I have decided to always try to be sensible and serious. This has been a grand day.

Knitted squares for the Yugoslavs all morning. I was a waitress all afternoon. I am sleeping with Mrs Nolan tonight – because a priest went to my room.

Hitler's death has been sorted out. He was injected with poison, and then burnt!!! We went to communion, and knelt on grass mats in the Native church, and listened to Churchill in the evening. He wishes to resign. Mr Loads threw two glasses of water over me!! – and so Jo and I apple-pied his bed.

Jo, Meryl and I climbed to the top of Kopje! Gee! It took some work – climbing over rocks to reach the end of the waterfall! We saw a buck and two baboons up there. What a lovely day it has been. At present I am reading *My Son My Son*. It isn't a very decent book. I think Howard Spring, the author, is rather awful. Himmler has committed suicide – but Hitler seems to still be alive!! I had to sleep with Mrs Nolan once more!!!

After lunch I decided to wash my hair, but by mistake I left the tap on, and the basin flooded. What a mess. There was water all over the steps. Maggie and I spent ages mopping it up!!!! It was so funny – we laughed and laughed.

I went to the eight o'clock service. Then to the Presby church. In the afternoon we all went up to a garden party at St Georges that opened with a Benediction for Thanksgiving. The RAR band played, and I danced on the lawn with Keith Green all afternoon. Today I have been to three different churches. Quite good, eh!

This evening we all went to listen to some man speaking on Shakespeare. Oh, it was painful! He babbled off pages and pages, and everyone was practically asleep. Nothing exciting happened today. In fact I'm rather sick of school life. Yesterday Flora was called up in front of the whole assembly and gated, because she wrote to boys.

What glorious news I received this evening. I got a wire from Robert, saying, 'Arriving approximately tenth of June'. I don't know what Sister's going to say to my maths – but who cares, Robert's coming home. I'm so happy.

Japan is being bombed nightly. I woke up at 4 a.m. as Mum and Gran are here. We were all terrifically excited, and went to the station to meet Robert. He looked grand jumping off the train, and I shall never forget that moment we were reunited. How proud I am of him.

After the exam we all went downtown to view the Victory Parade. This afternoon I swatted Virgil and Cicero Gee!!

This is a memorable day in my life. Today was the first time I have been in an aeroplane. I flew from Salisbury to home to spend half term with Robert dear. I loved it in the plane. It's grand to have Robert home here – although – so far, it seems rather strange.

Hitler has landed in Mexico. We went to a dance tonight at the club, and I had a wizard time. Peter Dean got fresh with me, and I was terrified!! But Campbell said he would look after me!! I think Bob Bowie is super.

I began my period today. I am a week late. I was a bit worried at first, but I think the flu had delayed it.

I wrote letters – one to Sam Goldwyn – and swatted all afternoon. I must do really well in the Cambridge.

No homework because we went to see *The Merry Wives of Windsor*. It was glorious, and I enjoyed this Shakespeare play to the full. I must be an actress and go on the stage one day. It is my greatest wish.

We were all terribly excited this morning, waiting for the results of the General Election. At five the results came out. Atlee was Prime Minister, and the Labour Party won. Churchill resigned. Everyone was mad.

I got a letter from Mum today. She seems rather upset about Robert being engaged so young. I think she should be glad instead. We are waiting for D-Day in Japan. I went out with Robert once more. He had been at a party all day, and was a bit 'pocki'.

Oh what a magnificent day. Catherine is back. [Rosemary's sister Catherine returned home after spending the war years at boarding school in Scotland.] I went to the station. At first I didn't see her, but then I saw the most beautiful girl walking beside Dad. It was Cath, and what a lovely accent she has got. We got back, and talked until after midnight. Daddy seems so proud of his elder daughter, and so do Gran and Uncle. Russia has declared war with Japan.

An atomic bomb has been dropped on Japan.

Japan has offered surrender terms. Today is the first in six years that our family has been reunited. It was great. I had my first day playing baby sister again, and had my third plane ride. This evening we went to a dance in Limbe. It was okay. Cath flirted ever so much, and she drinks quite a bit too.

I went riding with Robert early this morning. We went through the bundu. Riding back through the town, we saw it was all decorated. We guessed it was VJ day. AND HOW it was!!! We all went to the store, and between fifteen of us, opened eight bottles of champagne. Mrs Whitehouse got tight!!! We then went to Zomba, to the officers' mess to dance. Oh, I had a glorious time. I never sat out once. Harry Pratt asked me to wait two years for him!!! Boy oh boy!!! Cath went home early, but I went home at 4 a.m. with Bob, Rob and Dad. Oh, how I loved today.

I slept until half past ten, trying to recover from our hectic celebrations. Then I got up and had a cold bath and did some washing. I quarrelled with Cath all night.

In the afternoon we went riding. Then we went down to the station. On the platform we had a grand party, with champagne, to see Rob off. He went off very happily. Mum, Cath, Dad and I were ever so cut up about him leaving, and we shed buckets of tears. Catherine doesn't seem to like me much; she is always grumbling and grousing. She groused all the way back in the car – and all night – it was painful.

This afternoon we went to see *National Velvet* with Elizabeth Taylor. How I love this flick! Mum came home feeling very ill, so we put her to bed. The doctor said she had malaria, and gave her an injection. Dad was in an awful temper. I went for a ride this afternoon.

Mr Ellis taught me some archery. I managed to get three arrows on the target. Dad was in a temper this evening. I went for a ride on Gingerbread.

This afternoon I went riding on my own, and then went to the hotel to see Uncle Denver, because the family was SO sociable!!! This evening we went to Stan's party. It was a bit boring. I danced a lot with Tich – he really does seem nice. Bill was there too. I am sick of him. In fact, I don't like boys at all.

This morning I sat by the wireless, and read *Silas Marner*. Then I rang up Tich on the phone, to apologise for Cath's behaviour. He was ever so nice. We stayed talking on the phone for twenty-five minutes. He didn't like me calling him Tich, so now I call him Tarzan. He prefers that. He wears a tooth around his neck – like Sabu does! Oh gee!! I went riding this afternoon on Ginger.

This afternoon the rest of the kids from Nyasaland arrived. It is lovely being back at school with all my books and pals. We went to bed early, and I dreamed of Cicero! I got a lovely letter from Tich today. He said he couldn't stop thinking of me!

I must work really very hard and do ever so well in the Cambridge. I will too, I know, because my God is going to be with me, and help me do very well.

I had a long talk about varsity with Ma Rose. She thought that a kindergarten schoolteacher would be a much more suitable career for me than dancing. I wonder which I really should do – I'll ask Mum and Dad. I have an awful cold today, and my nose is all bloody.

I am rather worried because I started my period yesterday – it's not time yet. It's a gorgeous day. When I woke up the jacarandas were all in bloom, and the world looked so lovely.

Sister Pretiosia died today. What a pity. Still, I suppose she is happy. Got up at 5.40, and swatted history for a test. I got eighty per cent. I'm so thrilled.

It was lovely last night being Halloween Eve – we all got up at midnight, lit a candle and, with our heads veiled, went to the mirror to see our future husbands. We saw nothing but the street light in the glass.

We had our dress rehearsal this afternoon. I did my dance and the girls said they loved it. After the dress rehearsal I heard that I had won the Gordon Milne prize. Yippee.

At midday I saw General Smuts. I was so thrilled to see him – he looked so sweet. OH BOY the Cambridge is over, and am I happy? – AND HOW! Now for a sleep.

Tonight we went to the leaving school dance. I had a simply wizard time, and didn't sit out once. Everyone ended up calling me 'Bright Eyes'. Why, I don't know!!!

We got up at six, and went to the station to see the Nyasaland girls off. There was a band on the station to welcome the re-pats [repatriated prisoners]. I saw Bill, and was browned off with him. I said goodbye to all the nuns at the convent. They were exceedingly nice to me.

I got up at 5.30, and had my bath. I then flew home by plane. There was no one at Chileka to meet me, but eventually Dad and

Cath turned up. It was good to see them – but I was sorry to leave Granny. This afternoon Tom Mason arrived. He is good-looking, but rather a drizzle. We went to the sundowners' dance. There were a lot of KAR [Kings African Rifles] and we had a grand time, and I got to bed at 3.30 a.m.

I've done nothing today but loaf!!! This afternoon I went for a ride. Ted rang up tonight, and sang 'Rose Marie' over the phone – but loves Cath! Mrs Smith came to take Cath and me over to Zomba, to the Fancy Dress Ball. Mum didn't want us to go, but eventually we went as two gypsies. It was great. Bob and Ted drove us home. I got in the back of the car with Ted. He kissed me several times.

We all went to Ryall's for the dance. Ted told me he wanted to marry Catherine! I think it is a great joke, because he is already married! We got to bed about four o'clock

This afternoon I went for a long ride – I just adore riding. I heard this morning that the Women's Residence wouldn't accept me in Cape Town. Oh, I am unlucky – these things always happen to me – I wonder why I was ever born at all.

Dad took Cath for a driving lesson, and Cath drove us into a bank! Dad got tight, and all night we had to humour him. We played the piano, danced and sang until past midnight.

This evening Dad wouldn't let Cath and I go to the pictures, and there was an awful row. We all ended up in tears.

Ted, Peter and all went to play rugger in Limbe – I went for a long ride, I galloped all the way – but it was fun.

[Despite her fears, Rosemary successfully passed all her exams. Her convent days are over.]

1947

[The year 1947 begins as the independent seventeen-year-old is at university at Cape Town in South Africa. Initially she studied medicine but she soon transferred to the theatre course.

Meanwhile, in England I joined the Stratford-on-Avon Shakespeare company playing very small roles so badly that a member of the company took me aside and advised me to give up. The following year I didn't get one day's work.

However across the sea in Africa Rosemary's theatre studies were going well.]

I flew to Salisbury and stayed with Granny.

After a very hot and dirty trip, I arrived at Bulawayo. I went by plane to Cape Town, and then taxi to Spes Bona. The taxi cost six shillings! I've got a room to myself.

I was given the role of Rebecca in Thornton Wilder's *Our Town*, and a part in a radio play.

Communion this morning, and then I had my first lecture in make-up. I heard today that I won the bursary. I'm so very thrilled.

After lectures I wrote to the Governor. Then I had great fun recording at the broadcasting studio.

Got up at five – waited five hours. It was a most wonderful day today. I saw King George Vl and Queen Elizabeth, and Princess Elizabeth and Margaret Rose. They arrived in South Africa for the first time in history. This evening I saw *A Woman of No Importance*, and ushered officers of the Vanguard to their seats.

I went with Lionel to a dinner and dance at Rotunda this evening. [This is her first mention of Lionel, an acquaintance of Rosemary's family – young, pleasant, good-looking and wealthy.]

I went to Communion, and then rehearsed *Our Town* at the Little Theatre. Miss Birch said I did Rebecca very well. Went to Clifton with Lionel and then went with him to a symphony concert. It was very good.

Went and taught for the first time at Zonnebleum College. I opened my post office account with the tickies [sixpences] I have saved. I met the second officer this afternoon. We had tea together, and then I practised the castanets. There was a performance tonight of *Our Town* for the coloured group.

Spes Bona Dance – but I went to the flicks with Garth.

I went to the ex-servicemen's dance at Barbican Plaza with Lionel. He was very serious about me, he said. He gave me a beautiful bunch of red roses again.

Did Greek dancing all morning. This afternoon I auditioned for two different parts. After supper I went for a walk with Lionel.

I went to the demonstration, and got drenched in the rain. After rehearsing *Antigone* I bought gloves for the Royal Ball, and put five pounds in my saving book. I received another bunch of roses from Lionel. First night of *Antigone*. Wonderful.

Walked absolute miles up the mountain with Lionel, and got back at 3.30 p.m., without breakfast or lunch. Later I went to the Civic Ball, for Princess Elizabeth's twenty-first birthday party. The princess looked radiant, and gave a lovely speech. I got home at 2 a.m.

I was up early, and went to varsity to see the Queen being cupped. She said 'Good morning' to me, and chatted to the girl next to me about her varsity blazer. Then the Queen said to us, 'What a happy atmosphere up at varsity,' and then she passed on. How thrilled I am, so I went to bank and drew out sixteen pounds – spent one pound for Wellingtons, and two pounds for Mum's present.

This morning I went to Communion, learnt poems and rested, and then went for a walk with Lionel. He sent me a huge bunch of red roses yesterday. After rehearsal I demonstrated at St Cyprians and then Spes Dance this evening. I invited Lionel. It was rather nice.

I'm not feeling good at all. I have a bit of a cold, and there are matinee and evening performances today. The critics were not at all helpful – and I'm feeling terrible.

Mrs Taylor made me stay in bed all day. I have flu. Miss Van de Gucht came up to fetch me. I had to perform with a raving head, and a terrible cold and sore throat – oh goodness knows what, and got a terrible letter from Mummy saying that Catherine had fallen in love with Mr Johnson, a married man with four children. Oh God, please help us. Cried – good and proper.

Lionel took me for a drive to Constantia, and then round the peninsula – he told me he was in love with me. I came back and worked all evening. Sent wire to cancel bookings. I've decided to stay in Cape Town for vac. Pray God I've done the right thing this time. I got a sad letter from Mummy. I wonder if I should go home – I'm so worried.

I taught at Zonnebloem. Philippa got a fine for parking, so we went to the Chief of Traffic to get let off. Rob [Rosemary's brother] got married at Tillicoultry in Scotland to Elizabeth Anderson. I sent them a wire – thought of them a lot – and wished them all the very best. I performed in the Greek Ballet. David walked home with me. [David Lytton – a young South African poet and writer.]

I drew out eight pounds – paid five pounds for glasses, and two pounds for a twin set. Gosh – money flies – and how! David took me to the flicks, and bought me a box of chocolates. We came home in a hansom cab. Lionel sent me a bunch of roses.

Everyone has gone on vac. Now I am the only girl here. I did some washing, read *King Lear* and slept. David rang up this evening.

Tonight we opened *The Valiant*. It went very well, and we won hands down with a hundred and seven votes. The other plays got three and eight votes respectively...

This afternoon I went to Weinburg, and spent the afternoon with David and his old lady, and then had supper there. Everyone congratulated me on my part in *The Valiant* – said I played with perfect restraint, and was very good. David signed contract for me with SABC [South African Broadcasting Corporation].

After rehearsal, David and I went out to Sea Point and walked along the beachfront. He said he was in love with me.

I spent the afternoon with David. He played *Hamlet* for me. This evening we went to the Hofmeyer Theatre to see *Claudia*, which was very well done. Afterwards we went backstage, and I was introduced to all. David took me home.

I worked on Racine's *Phaedre*, and this evening David and I went to listen to Moiseiwitch. It was lovely, and Albert Coates conducted. We came home in a hansom cab – great fun!

David and I spent the whole day together, walking up the beach. It rained and we got wet, but all the same it's been a grand day.

This afternoon I spent with David, talking. I went to the theatre. Bust-up with Lionel.

This afternoon David and I spent together, and this evening we acted *The Valiant*. Oh, I feel as if this is a wonderful dream. We won first prize, and Philip Wade [a well-known English director] said I was the star of the evening, and did some first-class acting. Everyone said I was excellent. I feel wonderful.

Varsity reopened. I taught at Zonnebloem. In the evening I saw *Pink String and Sealing Wax* at the Hofmeyer. Brian Brooke asked me to join the company.

Met David and we spent the afternoon together. I went to the audition for *The Adding Machine*, and was given the leading role, Daisy. I am so happy. This evening I went to a symphony concert.

We all towed out to Worchester. This afternoon saw *Scheherazade*. Lovely – I'm longing to dance. This evening we performed at the Nande Theatre, and won hands down. Half the audience was weeping, and it went off beautifully. Celebration. Philip Wade gave me a broadcast audition, and said I was 'the tops', but I cannot take the lead in the play he offered me, because of *The Adding Machine*. I am very disappointed.

I rehearsed *The Adding Machine* all afternoon. This evening a rehearsal for *My Sister Eileen* – but Costa was annoyed that I was doing two plays at once, so I walked out.

Last night was the opening night of *The Adding Machine*. We had lots of technical hitches, but the Cape Times and *Die Burger* gave me quite a good mention.

After Greek dancing I went to see *The Lost Weekend* – acting superb. I met David, and had coffee with him – and then supper. The last night of *The Adding Machine* went off very well. Afterwards we had a wonderful party. I got home at 1.10 a.m. and was gated.

I played Maria in *A Man about the House* with the Brian Brooke Company, met Francis Brett Young and was offered the part of Alice McNeill in *The Best People*, but I had to refuse it, because Miss Van de Gucht said I was doing too much. I'm very upset about it, and feel I've missed my opportunity.

Spent the day with David on the beach. He asked me to do Juliet and Cordelia in their tour. I'm too busy. I looked for men to cast in *The Mask*.

Started Plato's *Republic*, and then saw a very good but terrifying film, *Dr Jekyll and Mr Hyde*. This evening I went to Communion at the Presbyterian church – lovely service. Then I went to a dance at the Zionist Hall with Don Howie – it was okay.

We left tonight for Bloemfontein – the train caught on fire. We travelled through the Karoo. It was hot and dusty.

After arriving back in Cape Town, I went to a political demonstration at Oakhurst. This evening I saw the ballet. Alexis Racine is wonderful.

After Greek dancing, this afternoon I lay in the sun and relaxed.

We played *Goose Play* tonight. It went off very well indeed. It was an amazing audience – they whistled when I went onstage. At the end I was handed a huge bouquet of flowers.

This afternoon David took me to see *The Winslow Boy*. Peter Mathews wanted to take me out, but I wouldn't go. I made up dances all night.

Exams are over. I feel lost with nothing to do. I went to National Theatre audition. It is Princess Elizabeth's wedding day. It has been a bloody awful day – everything has gone wrong. I feel like quitting the course.

I have passed all exams. Tonight Victor took me out. We went to see *Great Expectations* – a lovely flick.

I went to see Vic off on the Athlone Castle. After rehearsal for *King John* I came home and packed, and then spent the afternoon at Sea Point with Ruff. This evening Roger came to see me.

I left at nine on the Rhodesian train. It is quite a pleasant journey, but my eyes are still sore with the dirty soot.

I slept practically all day. We arrived at Bulawayo four hours late.

Arrived home.

1948–1950

NO DIARIES SURVIVED

In 1948 Rosemary matured fast. Towards the end of her last year at university in 1947, she had spent her spare time teaching drama at Zonnerbloom College in District 6, which was then the poor quarter inhabited by the black servants of the white city dwellers. I recently discovered a letter written by Rosemary; here is an excerpt.

In 1948 there was a general election and General Smuts was replaced by Dr Malan, and changes took place overnight. The very next day, as we students ran for our train, we were segregated by posters saying, 'Whites' only'. My friend Rica and I joined the 'Non-whites' with fellow undergraduates who were not white, and refused to move. Then at the university, at the post office and on the benches, buses and trains we joined the non-whites. We were well aware of the poverty in District 6, and that many children were not able to afford school, and were playing in the streets. So we devised a way to get them away from the poor quarter by having them act in *A Midsummer Night's Dream*.

By calling it a University of Cape Town production, they received permission to perform for two nights at the City Hall. The all-white audience was astonished and confused, and many very angry to see Shakespeare performed by black actors.

Rosemary was surprised when she was invited to the farm of Dr Malan, the South African President. During the afternoon he asked Rosemary to walk with him in the gardens, and very quietly informed her that she was undermining the prestige of the Europeans, and that she would have to surrender her passport. So Rosemary was unable to return to Blantyre for the holidays. However, later, when she applied for a job escorting white children back to their homes in Rhodesia, she managed to get a temporary pass. Once she had delivered the children safely in Salisbury, she took the train to Blantyre, where she applied successfully for her British passport, because she had persuaded her parents that she should try her luck in England.

Having spent all her life in Africa, the long sea voyage to England was to be an adventure for an attractive young woman, travelling alone, pursued by various amorous crew members – but this was mild compared with what followed.

As soon as Rosemary arrived she decided to visit Vienna, stopping en route in Paris. As she had to pass through the Eastern bloc she had acquired a special visa. But early one morning she was noisily awoken from her Paris bed by three gendarmes, and taken to the Palais de Justice. Because of student riots it was a nervous time in Paris, and Rosemary's passport with an Eastern bloc visa, plus her inability to speak French, caused grave suspicion. Unfortunately the British Consul was away for Easter. For three days and nights she stayed behind bars in the Palais de Justice, until she was released and put on a plane back to England. It would be forty years before she finally managed to get to Vienna.

In London Rosemary took a room in Regent's Park Road. The house was owned by Mary Pitcairn, an intelligent woman in her sixties, who kept a friendly, protective eye on the determined young actress. Rosemary was soon successful. At first she did any work that came along – during one period she rode an elephant in Bertram Mills' Circus. But it was not long before she was able to go from one repertory company to another. After a season with André van Gysegham's company at Nottingham Rep, she played Ela in *Charley's Aunt* at the Piccadilly Theatre in London, followed by a long tour. She was given the leading role in a major British movie, a great opportunity for a young actress – but the director became far too amorous so she walked out, and left the picture.

As for me – in 1949 and 1950 I only worked spasmodically, doing short stints at various repertory companies, but with very little light at the end of the tunnel.

Then in 1951 Rosemary was invited to go to New York by Clare Tree Major to do an American tour, and before that to play J.M. Barrie's *Mary Rose* in the very first season for the Pitlochry Festival in Scotland. Rehearsals were not due to start for four months so she decided to return home to Africa, to see her parents and to meet up with Lionel again.

Her sister Catherine had married Kenneth Robinson, an Irish tobacco farmer, in Nyasaland. They were on leave in Belfast, where Rosemary joined them at Christmastime.

1951

Ken, Cath and I came down to Dublin. Dinner at the Green Cockatoo, and had bananas and real cream!!

I went to see the American Consul – regarding working in the USA. I've definitely decided to go home first. So I cancelled doing any more plays at Nottingham and arranged my passage. Leonard Schach took me to the opening night of *The Madwoman of Chaillot*, and then on to the Caprice. Lovely evening.

Raining. Hey ho – for the rain it raineth every day. I left my suitcase on the bus. Damn! I took Ken and Cath to see *The Little Hut*. The King, Queen and two princesses sat just below us in the stalls. A letter from Lionel – and so to part – such is love! I have little faith in men. [I have no idea what he said that turned her off.]

Sailed on SS *City of Canturbury* for Cape Town. Cath and Ken were very surprised to see me on board. I sent *Rubaiyat* back to Lionel. Lovely to be out at sea, but I feel a little in the way of Ken. Cold and cloudy. I am cheesed off. I feel exhausted and a little lonely.

Arrived at Tenerife – and walked up to the gardens, accompanied by the beautiful smell of bamboos and glorious bougainvillea plants.

I arrived in Cape Town. Rica and Andy [another student] came to meet me. Andy took me to Blauberg and asked me to marry him.

Flew to Salisbury. Came down at Beaufort West, Kimberly, Joburg and Bulawayo. Pilot had me in the cockpit. [She joined him at the front of the plane!] Granny and Uncle met me. This evening went to dinner at the Grand Hotel – missed Lionel.

Flew home with Granny, and sat in the cockpit on the way up. It's wonderful to be home. Had dinner – Dad made speeches!!

Started for London. Flew over Lake Nyasa to Tanganyika and landed at Dar-es-Salaam. I stayed the night at the New Africa Hotel. Got up at 5 a.m. Took plane to Nairobi.

Arrived in Nairobi at 9 a.m. and then left at midday – flying over Sudan and Abyssinia to Khartoum, and then flew to Cairo. The next day took off for Malta, and arrived at 4.30 a.m. Arrived in London at 3 p.m. Went to bank, to book on Swissair.

Left for Geneva, and took train to Lausanne. Lionel met me. We went to dinner and on to a nightclub until 4 a.m. Switzerland is a lovely country. Lionel and I are going to be married.

I left Switzerland and had to return to London to re-pack and get ready for Pitlochry. I miss Lionel.

I went to Pam's for tea. She told me she was sleeping with a married man. I was shattered.

Rehearsal in London with Pitlochry Company. We started work on *Mary of Scotland*. A wet cold day.

This was the day that Rosemary and I met. On my way to rehearsal I bought new shoes, which cost me thirty shillings, because the ones

I wore had holes in them. This made me late, and I was the last of the large company to arrive. As I entered the room I saw this beautiful young girl cross the floor, perch on a window ledge and I fell in love.

During the next few days, after much persuasion on my part, we spent a great deal of our free time together, and went to the theatre many times. The first time, when we arrived at the box office, I was embarrassed to discover that I did not have enough money to buy the tickets, and so she saved the day with a traveller's cheque. Later she told me that a lawyer friend had bought several pair of tickets for the two of them, and then had been called away on business, and suggested that she should 'make use of them anyway'. So she did, and it seemed only natural that I should go with her.

By taking in lodgers, my mother had been able to rent a flat in Marloes Road in Kensington, near the Albert Hall, where I had trained. As Rosemary was playing Mary Rose and I was playing her husband, Simon, we spent our free time rehearsing there. It was at the flat that I first tried to kiss her – only to be put firmly in my place. However the next night we were out together at the theatre again. We were both very moved by *The Consul*, the Menotti opera, so beautifully acted and sung. After the curtain came down we walked hand in hand to the bus, without speaking. After a brief smile, and a kiss on the cheek, I left her near the house where she was staying, and returned home.

I rehearsed with Joss all day. This evening went to *The Consul* with him. It was a magnificent production. I wrote home to Mum and Dad about Lionel and I being engaged.

Started packing for Pitlochry, then rehearsed with Joss all afternoon.

Went to church with Pam, and had lunch with her. David came this evening [David Lytton had come from Cape Town to see her], and we sat and chatted until midnight.

First rehearsal of *Mary of Scotland* – without scripts! After writing home to Lionel I went to *Cosh Boy* at the Embassy Theatre with Joss. Wrote home to Lionel again.

After rehearsal had photos taken at Jos's flat, and rehearsed *Mary Rose* till 11 p.m.

Rehearsed *Mary Rose*. Went to Hayes Rep. to see Martin Tiffin [a friend both Rosemary and I had worked with – so we went together].

I received a letter from Dad with fare to America. I returned the cheque to him. This evening I went to Jos's for supper, to select photos.

Met Jos and went to see *Tales of Hoffmann*. Very enjoyable.

After seeing *Tales of Hoffmann* I noticed Rosemary's engagement ring for the first time. When she told me she was going to marry someone else, I fell into a deep depression, and Rosemary told me I was acting like a child. From that moment on, she avoided me, until the morning that we arrived in Perth, en route to Pitlochry.

I left London for Pitlochry at 7.30 p.m. We all had sleepers. We arrived at Perth at 3.30 a.m. and had breakfast at the Salutation Inn.

I managed to sit opposite Rosemary at breakfast, and things thawed a little when she discovered that I could not eat the whites of eggs, and she was not fond of yolks – so we shared.

Arrived at Pitlochry at 10.30 a.m. It's a warm sunny day. We went over the new theatre. It is in a tent! – but it looks wonderful. I lay in the sun. Joss said he wanted to marry me.

Rosemary does not mention her reply – 'I wouldn't marry you if you were the last man on earth' – but I see she did manage to spell my name correctly for the first time.

We rehearsed *Mary Rose*. I went for a long walk this afternoon, and then wrote to Lionel, and received letters from home and from Lionel.

Problem – Rosemary playing Mary Rose, and 'the last man on earth' playing her husband, but fate planned that we both had one play off – the same play – and we were both staying in the same house, together with a few other members of the company.

Rehearsed *Macbeth*, and went for a walk alone up Ben-y-Vrackie. Wonderful. I hit my head on a tree. I climbed Craig Gower with Joss this evening.

Went to church. Walked to Pass of Killicranckie with Joss – a seven-mile walk of fascinating countryside.

Rehearsed *Mary of Scotland*, and afterwards went for a long trek. Joss says he is in love with me. It is very difficult.

Opening ceremony of the Festival Theatre. I avoided Joss. Wrote to Mum and Dad and Lionel. Opening of *Mary of Scotland*. It went very well.

Rain and mist. I went for a walk alone, and wrote to Lionel.

Photographs in all the papers. Good write-ups. Joss is being a bit too persistent – I didn't sleep.

Tonight – first night of *Macbeth*. Ah me – Life is *very* difficult – and I long for my love to come to me. Joss gave me flowers. Wonderful sunshine.

Rehearsed all day. This evening went for a long walk with Simon [I was Simon in Mary Rose] across the fields.

Opened *Mary Rose*! Wonderful opening. Loads of flowers from everyone.

Went for walk with Simon. My contract from New York arrived.

I am very confused. This evening sat up late with Herbert and Joss talking.

J. and I hired cycles, and rode to Killicranckie.

Joss and I have lovely times together

Mary Rose – a wonderful evening.

Just before lunch, on a sudden whim, Joss and I hitched a ride to wherever the first car to stop was going. We thought it might be a few miles. We went all the way to Ullapool, opposite the Summer Isles. We spent the night there. WONDERFUL!!!!

I AM TERRIBLY HAPPY. Joss and I left Ullapool. We hitched to Tar Bridge, via Inverness. Had row – I was going to leave Joss – made up.

Returned to Pitlochry. It was a heavenly weekend. Joss asked me to marry him – I accepted.

In fact, Rosemary did not accept immediately. Then she read a letter from her mother telling her to stop wasting her time fooling around onstage, and to settle down with Lionel, and security. After reading the letter, Rosemary turned her face to me, and said, 'Joss, will you marry me?' And that was that. So then she wrote home to tell her family.

Over the next few days Rosemary managed very few words in her diary, but I wrote the following letter to my mother, and which I discovered by chance a few days ago. I must confess I have always been remiss at letter writing – so finding this took me by surprise.

Wednesday, 27 June 1951

My dear,

There is so much to tell you, and I will try to set it all out as clearly as possible.

You must have gathered by now that Rosemary and I have been getting on more than well together. We gradually have discovered that we are completely alike in all respects. In fact, we might be one person. Never have I felt so completely at ease and relaxed with anyone. We have the same tastes, the same thoughts, and can pretty nearly always tell what the other is thinking.

Naturally things like this are bound to bring people together. Fairly early in the season I discovered that not only was I *in* love with Rosemary, but also that I loved *her*, and I told her of my feelings. This disturbed her greatly, and she told me that it was hopeless because, as I knew, she was engaged to Lionel, the man in Switzerland. However I found it impossible to keep away from her – and she liked being with me, except on various occasions when she had an emotional impact within her, which told her to keep away from me. It was after one of these occasions that she told Graham Crowden she was in love with someone in Switzerland, and would he ask me to keep away from her. He did so, and I complied for a time. Then we were brought together again by consistent contact with *Mary Rose* rehearsals, etc – and we slowly developed a very deep friendship.

After a while the friendship ripened into love.

This Rosemary would not admit for a while, and was undergoing a severe strain, especially as she was receiving one letter – sometimes two letters – a day from Lionel. However to cut a long story short – and also cutting out a lot of very relevant matter because I cannot go on writing indefinitely – Rosemary at last confessed that she loved me, and she had not known what it was to really love someone before.

Now I will try and set out her background, and the place that Lionel holds in the story.

Rosemary's father has worked himself up to becoming a rich man. Her grandmother was the first white woman to travel alone to Nyasaland, and her son-in-law has built up quite a large business there. He has literally hundreds of acres of land, and was mayor for some time, and if you compare the size of the British Isles with that of Nyasaland you will realise that he is quite an important man there. From the start he gave Rosemary and her brother and sister everything he could, but at the same time he was very strict. Apparently he and his wife have not got on well together, and I gather Rosemary's mother is very narrow-minded – while her father, although conservative, was always a little mad. Rosemary has always confided in her father, and he with her, but neither of them with her mother. However, in Africa they had twenty-three servants and Rosemary was given the best education her parents could attain for her. After she went to university she developed her love of theatre, and studied ballet in South Africa – while her parents thought that she was studying medicine. They have no knowledge of theatre, and obviously are a little old-fashioned with their ideas regarding it.

Rosemary has nothing in common with her family – she knows that – but the fact that they did so much for her has had a very strong effect on her.

She met Lionel in Africa several years ago. Within two weeks he asked her to marry him. She – hardly eighteen – laughed and said no. However he kept on seeing her, even when she came to England. He was very much the family's choice, a very pleasant, quiet young man, with several degrees, and was brought up in Central Africa. He asked her to marry him again in England, and once again she refused. She did not see him again for two years, and he went off to Switzerland to study hotel keeping.

Meanwhile Rosemary was carrying on with the theatre. When she had come to England it was without her parents' knowledge, and she wrote them from London to tell them she was here. That is typical of her – there are not many places in the world she has not been now. She was not happy at home, and I gather they never appreciated any of her theatrical lean-ings, and always thought her more than a little mad.

But I was telling you what happened two years after Lionel went away. Rosemary suddenly developed a depression about the theatre – she had had a couple of unpleasant experiences – and feeling a little homesick went home to Central Africa for two weeks. But when she was back home she realised how out of place she felt there so when she left she was only too glad to leave. Still depressed, Rosemary went to Switzerland to see Lionel, and when, once again, he asked her to marry him she agreed, although she hardly knew him – having seen him only for short periods at various intervals over four years. He straight away asked her to give up the theatre and go and live in Africa when he had finished his course and had a hotel there. Then she came back to England to start rehearsing for Pitlochry – and two days later we met.

Early during the season Rosemary realised she could not give up the theatre, so she wrote and told Lionel so. He said he would get a hotel in Cape Town, and she could carry on acting in the rep there if she wished. You see he does not understand that half the charm of the theatre is the consistent moving on. Rosemary said she did not want this, and he replied that, in that case, he would give up his career and do something else as he had various degrees. At first Rosemary was willing to accept this, but later she realised how terrible it would be for either of them to fit themselves in with the other. By this time we had fallen in love and she was in a very difficult position. Her family were overjoyed at her engagement, because what it really meant was her going back to the life she had escaped from. They sent her various cuttings announcing her engagement – and she received congratulations from all over Nyasaland. All this made her the more miserable. She wrote less to Lionel, and slowly let him know that she was not sure about the two of them, and later that she did not think it was possible to go through with it. She told him she had been offered the American tour for nine months – and she was going there before she did anything – to which he replied that he was sure she would change again because she was enraptured by the surroundings. She wrote and told her parents how happy she was here – to which her mother replied that she had no right to be happy when she was away from Lionel. Then her mother wrote to say that she was flying over to Pitlochry, because she was worried about her. She arrives in a month, and will possibly stay until September. It is possible that Rosemary's father will come as well. Lionel arrives on Sunday with his father for a week. I expect he will bring an engagement ring with him, and Rosemary has to tell him it is all off.

Now, my dear, for the big shock. We have had plenty of time to think carefully about everything so we have made no rash statements. For some time we have discussed the possibility of marriage for Rosemary and myself when she came back from New York, but yesterday I asked her would she definitely marry me, and the sweet thing said yes.

There is no doubt now, for she promised not to say anything unless she was absolutely sure. In fact, today Rosemary wrote off to her parents in fuller detail, and told them that she was going to marry me. She also told them that they could come over and see us if they liked, but she knew her own mind and she knows what she is doing.

Well, my love, I have explained in detail as best I can – I hope you are pleased. I must get busy very quickly. Rosemary flies to the States from Scotland on 30 September and I expect we won't get married until she gets back. There is still the vague possibility of my going as well, but I doubt if the money will be enough to make it practical.

I have enclosed two letters Rosemary has sent me. [Sadly neither letter was ever recovered.] The first is one she sent me early in the season. The second is one she sent me later. As you can see, quite a lot has happened since then, but I have sent them to you, because they might help you see what sort of a girl she is. Please keep them confidential, because I should hate her to think I had let anyone else see them. Please return them when you have read them.

We have told Herbert, and he is thrilled. He asked me to tell you that he thinks we are perfect for each other. It is a wonderful thing to sit down and look forward to growing old with someone.

Rosemary did not want me to tell you yet because, until she has broken it off next week with Lionel, she is embarrassed at being engaged to two people, but I felt I had to tell you, and I thought you would be so pleased – but Rosemary does not know I have written you. She wants to have loads of children, and hates the idea of contraceptives – so we will have to be very careful for a while after we are married. The whole point of her going to the States was to be alone to think things out – and she is so sure in her mind now and does not want to leave me – but her passage is booked.

Last Sunday Rosemary and I left the hostel at 11.15 a.m.to hitch north for the weekend, as neither of us was in the play, *Brief Glory*, on the Monday. The first car that came along was a huge chauffeur-driven limousine. He stopped – sat us in the back – covered us with rugs, and we lay back in the padded seats. He asked us where we were going, and we said we just wanted to go north. He said he was going two hundred miles – just beyond Ullapool, which is off the Hebrides right at the top of the country. He was going to collect his boss – and would that be all right for us? As you may well imagine we said yes. So off we went.

The first sixty miles was through the rugged upper highlands, with al the glorious purple and red mountains surrounding us. We saw loads of highland sheep and cattle, and a few wild deer and ponies. The next forty miles was the prettiness of Inverness-shire. We stopped about twenty miles beyond Inverness for lunch – and he insisted on giving us some of his. Apparently he always has extra ham sandwiches, etc, with him, and an extra flask of coffee, because whether he was alone on the road or not he would stop people and ask them to lunch with him. Then on we went to Garve and Rosshire. It is thirty-four miles between Garve and Ullapool and the most fantastic thing about it is that in those thirty-four miles there is not even a village or a hamlet. Nothing but rugged, tough hills in awful, glorious country with sheep straggling everywhere. In fact, during the thirty-four miles we saw only two houses – and both in the distance. Then we drove along the side of Loch Broom, with its magnificent waterfalls, until suddenly we found ourselves looking down on the lovely little harbour town of Ullapool. He drove us five miles beyond the town, and left us standing on the seashore you can see on the postcard with the 'Summer Isles'. And the time was only 5 p.m. It was almost unbelievable. We thought about getting a boat, and wandering about the desolate Summer Isles, but there was nothing on them, so we decided against it. We then walked over the hills, and got a lift back to Ullapool, and found heaven. We got digs for the night at a very clean little private hotel run by a Viennese woman, had supper and went for a walk along the beach. There was a glorious salty, fresh tang in the air – for it is there that the fishermen salt their herrings. Then we saw something that neither of us had ever seen before. In front of the little harbour town, on the beach, with the waves lapping around their legs, and chewing seaweed, were sheep with their little lambs. When I said how fantastic this was Rosemary said, 'Nonsense – they are entitled to a holiday as much as anyone else.'

The next morning – after breakfast, we got a hitch all the way back to Inverness where we had lunch and tea. Afterwards we hitched to Carrbridge, and went into a tiny private hotel to stay the night. When we got inside we were terrified what they would charge us, because it was beautifully arranged – lovely rooms with some excellent etchings and Peter Scott paintings hanging beautifully, and specially lit. Also a Lady Goddard and a Brigadier were staying there, and other characters that looked as if they had come straight out of an E.M. Forster novel. However, as well as our lovely room they gave us a delicious supper and breakfast for only fourteen shillings. The next morning at 11 a.m. we got a bus for the remaining miles. This cost us seven shillings and three pence each – which was the sum total for travelling well over 400 miles.

We arrived back at Ascog at 1.10 p.m. just in time for lunch, and at 2 p.m. Rosemary went off to understudy rehearsal at the theatre.

You might realise from this that it was the most glorious weekend imaginable.

Well, my love, I must conclude what must be the longest letter you have ever had – and it has not taken me very long to write it. Either tonight or tomorrow I will ring you. There are many things to be decided and arranged within the next fortnight, and I will let you know all later.

Herbert sends his love – Rosemary doesn't because she does not know I have written. Keep well, my love. Enclosed are postcards with details on the back, the two private letters of course, and a snapshot of Graham Crowden and Phyllida Hewitt, who also seem to be getting on uncommonly well together.

Will send some more money on Friday.

Lots of love, Joss

Meanwhile Rosemary briefly continued briefly with her diary

Worried.

Mummy flying over. Lionel arriving tomorrow.

Lionel arrived in Pitlochry. I spent the day with him.

The situation is very strained. Lionel is still here. A terrible day.

Lionel is still here. Matinee and evening show of *Mary Rose*.

And Lionel came to see it. Rosemary had broken off their engagement, but deliberately had not mentioned our relationship. However, we thought, when he sees us, together in the play, he will understand. After the curtain came down, he went backstage. 'What did you think of it?' Rosemary asked nervously.

'Not bad, I suppose.'

The next evening he came to see *Susannah and the Elders*. During the course of the action I had to rush to the wings for a very quick change of costume from one scene to another. Rosemary and Graham Crowden, who was playing a guard, sauntered across the stage in order to cover my change while Sibelius played in the background. Graham would give Rosemary a quick peck on the cheek, and, once my costume had been changed, they would make their exit. However on that particular evening, I got caught up in my toga, and Rosemary and Graham had to fill the gap with a passionate kiss. After the show Lionel went backstage once more. 'I understand all,' he said, 'you are in love with that guard.'

Lionel is still here. Joss is very sweet. Depressed – it is so difficult. [By this time, I had, secretly left my single room every night to join Rosemary in her bed, and each morning we would rise up together, and I would walk with her to the Green Park Hotel, and leave her there to join Lionel for the day.]

I went to Perth with Joss, and on to Dundee. It's lovely being together. Phyllida Law and Graham Crowden got engaged.

I spent the day with Lionel at the Green Park Hotel. Raining. I said goodbye to Lionel.

Lionel left. Joss and I announced our engagement.

It is all about our engagement in the papers. 'Mary Rose to marry her Simon'. Lionel had only got as far as Edinburgh – saw the papers. He came back with his father. He wished me luck.

And so God loved the world – a wonderful sunny day. Very happy.

Longing to get married. Joss and I are so happy.

I'm worried. Mum is coming – I hope she agrees to the wedding.

Mummy arrives from home. She approves of Joss. I am terribly happy.

Rosemary and Herbert Roland switched rooms so that Rosemary and my rooms were adjoining. Early one morning, three weeks before the wedding, Rosemary's mother visited the house, and went to her daughter's room to wake her. She pulled back the sheet – and kissed Herbert Roland on the head. So later that day Rosemary—

Packed. Moved to the Green Park Hotel with Mum.

Was up at six, and left for Edinburgh to buy my wedding dress – Mary Horne is ill – so I have to play Susannah tonight – I am terrified. Mrs Ackland arrived.

Busy with wedding preparations. I had to play Susannah again, and I enjoyed it. Highland Ball at Green Park hotel. Got to bed at 5 a.m.

Got married at Holy Trinity Church, Pitlochry – VERY, VERY happy. Reception at the Green Park, and then Joss took me to the

Spittal o'Glenshie, to Dalmunzie House. Wonderful place. I'M SO HAPPY.

We had breakfast in bed, and then Joss and I went for a walk. This evening we went over Devil's Elbow for dinner.

SO VERY HAPPY. We walked in the lovely countryside, and picked wild flowers.

We moved into a cottage 'Drumchorry', on the third tee of Pitlochry golf course. It will be our first home together.

I was very sick this morning – went to the doctor. We wonder.

We packed. The doctor told us we were going to have a baby. Joss and I very excited. The baby is due next May – on the fifteenth.

Rosemary and I left Pitlochry for London. The fifties were grey and bruised – damaged by the aftermath of war. We still had rationing, and there was very little in the shops. The decade was about to produce other problems – a wasted war in Korea, and the start of the Cold War. The world held its breath when the Soviet Union produced the atomic bomb and challenged America by threatening us all with mass destruction, with both powers holding aloft the sword of Damocles. A dark decade and, without work, it was an effort to survive. What gave us the courage to battle on was Rosemary's calm determination and strength of character.

We arrived at Mrs Ackland's flat in Marloes Road. I wrote to Clare Tree Major telling her I couldn't do the tour. We went to *Carousel*, and then to Lyons Corner House.

We saw Mum off, and then went to the Labour Exchange to sign on. We had interviews for Salisbury Rep.

Signed on at the Labour Exchange, and this evening we were given tickets to see Kirsten Flagstad in *Dido and Aeneas* at the Mermaid in St John's Wood. It was a small crowded room, and we had to leave while she was in the middle of an aria because I about to be very sick. We had to force our way through the audience, stumbling over them, and only a few feet away from Kirsten. I left my coat behind –and I will have to collect it later. I was so embarrassed. The doctor told me to stay in bed for three days. Joss had to leave for Salisbury.

Wonderful having Joss back, but he has to return tonight to Salisbury.

Went to International Artists, and then met Michael McNeill regarding going to Durban to join his Repertory Company. It sounds interesting.

I went to Queen Charlotte's Hospital, I packed and came to Salisbury. It's wonderful being here with Joss. We are staying at a glorious hotel, The Grange. It is heaven being together again.

I watched *Hamlet* rehearsal. Joss is Claudius, and I'm going to be Ophelia. This evening I went to see Joss in *Young Wives' Tale*. I fainted, and had to come home.

I started rehearsing as Ophelia – it's lovely to be working again. Went to bed early.

Rehearsed all day. It poured with rain, and I got soaking wet.

Very ill. Doctor came. I have to stay in bed. Damn – there goes Ophelia!

Stayed in bed. The doctor came. Joss rehearsed all afternoon and night. He came in at 5 a.m.

I'm still in bed. Doctor came again. Joss at rehearsal all day. He opens in *Hamlet* tonight.

Rosemary was so ill she never managed to play the role. It was some time before Rosemary recovered, and very few days were touched in the diary.

Feel much better, so I went to see *Hamlet*. I enjoyed it very much.

I went to Queen Charlotte's for check-up, and then took Muz [my mother] to a flick and then to dinner at Chicken Run. Michael asked me to play Mrs De Winter in *Rebecca* opposite Joss as Maxim.

Rehearsed all morning. Packed. Moved things to Crane Lodge, and then Joss and I took the train to London. Muz left to visit her relatives in Birmingham. We sat up late doing Christmas presents.

I fainted. The doctor came. He told me I must take to my bed, and I was not allowed to return to Salisbury. I was ill all day, so I remained in bed, and Joss looked after me wonderfully.

CHRISTMAS DAY: Joss filled a stocking for me. I had to spend the day in bed. Joss left for Salisbury.

What Rosemary doesn't mention is that because I had to rehearse that night, and play on Boxing Day, I had to leave her, very sick, without food – not that she could eat – and all alone in the house on the first Christmas Day of our married life.

BOXING DAY: Stayed in bed.

1952

For the next eighteen years there are no surviving diaries. They were either lost or burnt or – with the pressure of coping with life's challenges – left blank.

Once the season at Salisbury ended life was hard. Rosemary's prenatal problems continued, and I was unable to find any work. However in May I managed to get a non-speaking role in a second feature movie, and I was filming in a small boat off the coast of Brighton, when our first child, Melanie, was born in London in Queen Charlotte's Hospital. It was a long difficult birth, and I was not there.

Rosemary was a devoted mother, but we were on the breadline, and no matter how hard we tried, all our efforts to obtain further work failed. Then, when Melanie was a few months old – Eureka! – both Rosemary and I managed to get into a big West End production. *Pagan in the Parlour*, which, after a short tour, was due to open in London and then go to New York. It was James Whale's first production in England, since he had directed the original production of *Journey's End* back in 1929 after which he moved to Hollywood, and directed big productions such as *Frankenstein* and *Showboat*. He arranged for Rosemary and I to be together, even sharing the same dressing room. I was the juvenile lead, and Rosemary understudied my girlfriend. However on the first week of the tour at our digs in Bath it was a portent of things to come, when a very old woman guest opened her handbag and asked us if we would like to see her teeth. Then she threatened to burn the house down and, some time later, she crept into our bedroom in the middle of the night and tried to strangle Melanie, who was asleep in her cot. It was a bizarre week, which somehow ended with our travelling on the train back to London, with Stan Laurel and Oliver Hardy.

As for the play – it flopped. We didn't even get to London. So – back to the breadline.

1953–1954

The huge success *South Pacific* was on at the Theatre Royal in Drury Lane. I heard that one actor was leaving the show – it was not a bad part, and the actor was getting sixty pounds a week – to us a small fortune. One agent had been friendly in the past, but when I went to see him, he wouldn't take me on and said I was far too young for the role. However Rosemary and I were finding it difficult to survive, so out of desperation I pencilled circles under my eyes, Rosemary cropped my hair and I talked my way into an audition, joining most of the American and Canadian actors in London, to read for the part. The next day I actually received a phone call from the management offering me two seats to see the show, and a second audition. Over the next two weeks Rosemary and I saw the show three times, and I attended four auditions. By the time the last audition came along, there were only four of us left, and Mary Martin, the star of the piece, was to make the final choice. Rosemary came with me, and waited in a café by the theatre. The four remaining survivors read, and then there were just two of us left. Once more I walked to the middle of the vast stage, and once more I read for the role. After discussion in the auditorium, the other actor was offered the part. I joined Rosemary in the café, took her hand and, without a word, we left Covent Garden and, in order to save the fare, walked all the way back to Marloes Road.

Throughout the year the bad luck continued, but eventually I joined the company at the Theatre Royal, Windsor, and we moved with baby Melanie to a converted horse stable, on a farm near Maidenhead. Rosemary was unable to work in the theatre, because by this time she was expecting our second child and in the afternoons, after rehearsals, I ploughed fields to earn extra money. After the season closed, and another period of unemployment, we moved up north, to Chesterfield, where I joined the local repertory company. I had to go in advance, because Rosemary was back in Queen Charlotte's, giving birth to our son Paul. Three weeks prior to the birth we had moved back to Marloes Road, because my mother said she would look after Melanie while Rosemary was in hospital. The house was full with lodgers, but somehow we squeezed in.

When her contractions began, Rosemary was busy organising our trunk to be sent to the Civic Theatre in Chesterfield, because we had nowhere booked to stay. She insisted on carrying on, until the pains grew intense, and it was only then that she let me call the ambulance. Halfway between Marloes Road and Queen Charlotte's, the pains stopped. Rosemary was embarrassed at raising a false alarm, so she decided to pretend that she was still in pain. She bent low, as I helped her from the ambulance, moaned, gave me a wink and whispered, 'I'll be back in the morning.'

That night I slept well, rose late and was in the process of shaving, when I thought I should phone the hospital to ask when I should collect

Rosemary. A nurse answered. 'Your wife gave birth to a ten-pound boy a few minutes after you left last night.'

The following day I had to leave for Chesterfield, where I found digs, rehearsed and searched for a home for our family. Back in hospital, Rosemary played for time, and persuaded the doctor to allow her to remain there for a few more days.

On the outskirts of Chesterfield I found a sad, colourless stone mining cottage, with no curtains, no linen, no light bulbs and no carpets on the cement floors. Not a welcome sight for Rosemary, coming straight from hospital. She arrived with me unable to help, because, as luck would have it, I had to return to London for the first work I had been offered for months – a precious day's filming on a documentary, at the same time as Rosemary left Queen Charlotte's. She got a cab to the station, and with Melanie and the newborn baby, travelled by train to Chesterfield, and we passed each other on the way. When I arrived at the studio it was to find I had gone on a wild goose chase. No film – no money.

The cottage was so cold it was like living in a fridge, and we were reduced to covering ourselves with newspapers at night, because we were short of blankets. With two babies it was not a happy time, and at work not a happy theatre. After a few months it seemed we were saved by the bell, when Frank Hauser came to direct the Christmas pantomime, and asked me to join his company at the Midland Theatre in Coventry – the city that had been so badly bombed in the war. There was a waiting list of ten thousand for any sort of accommodation; and to get on the list you had to have been a resident for over three years. The actors and technical staff had been allocated a house to share, but there was no room for relatives, and so Rosemary decided to stay on in Chesterfield until I found us somewhere in Coventry.

Every morning before rehearsal, every lunch hour and every late afternoon after rehearsal, I spent either with estate agents or with the new Lord Mayor of Coventry – a theatre fan – desperately trying to find anywhere for us to live – but always to no avail. Eventually Rosemary was forced out of the cottage by the Chesterfield Company's new director, Gerard Glaister.

My mother's flat was crammed with lodgers, so Rosemary took Melanie and Paul from one friend to another, pushing their pram from place to place until her hands froze to the handle. The weeks were going by – our only contact was by telephone, and we had to limit our calls to three minutes, every other day. One evening Rosemary called me at the theatre and told me that they were in Bournemouth. A small hotel for parents with young babies had just opened, and the young proprietors had taken pity on Rosemary, and allowed her to stay at the hotel, and in return she worked in the nursery. We were separated, and it was months before we could afford her travelling to Coventry with the babies, and it was only for one night. They sneaked into my room, but had to go back to Bournemouth the next day.

Only a few years before, the carefree, ambitious young girl had the world at her feet with a great future before her. Since we married she had faced poverty, disappointment and a bleak future with resilience and without complaint. Now all she could do was help her children survive. We had reached the point of no return.

Rosemary's mother and father were on leave in London, and one evening when I phoned Rosemary she said, 'We can't go on like this.

We need a re-think. Maybe I should take the kids back to Africa for a while. Dad says he will pay my fare.'

I broke our three-minute rule, and pushed another ninepence into the slot. The clanking of the coins sounded, ominously, like our marriage breaking up. The only alternative was to give up acting completely and leave the acting world.

'I'll come with you', I said.

The cheapest form of transport to Beira was on the SS *Umgeni*, an old cargo boat, carrying animals, cargo and very few people. There were only three weeks before she sailed, and Rosemary was in Bournemouth, and I was in Coventry. I was playing in *Crime Passionel*, but Frank Hauser agreed to release me in the middle of the run, 14 May. On the morning of the thirteenth, I received a phone call at the theatre. Rosemary's father had died suddenly.

So it was a day earlier than anticipated that I travelled by train to Bournemouth. Rosemary was sitting on her bed. Behind her were two cots with our sleeping babes. When she saw me, Rosemary's face lit up with that flowing, joyous smile that always made my heart leap – but not this time. I took her on my knee, held her tightly – and broke the news, as she sobbed her heart out.

Before we left I had applied for work in Nyasaland, on a tea plantation at the foot of Mount Mlanje, which Laurens van de Post described in his book *Venture to the Interior* as the furthest point from civilisation in the world.

At first we were refused, and were told to apply again once we reached Malawi. It was some time later that we learnt that for three months the tea company had been desperately trying to find a field assistant at Lilongwe. The last assistant had left after only two weeks, the previous assistant had to leave when his wife got black water fever and before that the assistant broke his leg and had to be shipped home. It was a blessing for the tea company when we applied for a Mlanje job in London. We were travelling out anyway – so they did not have to pay our passage.

The voyage to Beira took seven weeks. We stood at the stern and thought we were watching our old world disappear. Were we facing a brave new world, or just looking for security without problems?

But it was a long, fascinating voyage on the old cargo boat, and gradually the tensions of the past months evaporated. When the heat became unbearable we slept on deck, because our cabin, being the cheapest on the vessel, was right next to the engine room. There were many pauses on the way – sometimes for days at a time – while cargo was unloaded and new cargo lifted on board. On one occasion when we docked at Durban, we visited the theatre, where we met Michael McNeill who had previously offered us work there. When he repeated the offer we were still so bruised that we fled, and ran back to the ship.

At last we disembarked in Beira in Portuguese East Africa. From there we made the long train journey across the Zambezi River, sleeping under mosquito nets, and every so often the train would stop and the driver and his companion would jump off and chop down trees, to stoke up the engine. Finally we arrived in Blantyre. After staying with Rosemary's family for a few days, we packed two trucks with provisions, a duck, some chickens, a giant hunting dog for protection; and together with a cook, a night watchman and a houseboy, Rosemary and I set out for the Likanga tea estate in Lilongwe. For the last seventy miles, we travelled over rough, uneven roads, until the grey-blue myste-rious mountain Mlanje came into view, and then on through jungle and dense brush along a concealed path. Suddenly there was a clearing, and in the middle was our new home: Nachilonga bungalow.

Life at Likanga was quite different from the one Rosemary had growing up in Blantyre. It was very different for her – perhaps even more than it was for me, because although I had no experience of Central Africa, I knew what to expect – after all I had seen Tarzan movies, and *King Kong*!

For the first time in our married life our family had security. Life in the bush was primitive, but always exciting. Ants, building enormous anthills, destroyed a spare bedroom, and we had to put the legs of the children's cots in tins of petrol, to stop the ants crawling up and chok-ing them, which had happened to the child of another planter. The house was infested with snakes – two black mambas made their homes in the eaves of the nursery, and we had to call in the witchdoc-tor to get rid of them. There was a time when we had to stay inside for five days, because one night our night watchman woke us and we dispersed a huge line of ants as they headed straight for the house, which they then surrounded. One night our hunting dog, Scamp, disappeared, and we thought we had lost him. Three nights later we heard a scraping on the khonde. Scamp was lying there. All four of his paws had been slashed with a knife, and were hanging from his legs. We lifted him on to an armchair, and Rosemary covered them with anti-septic, stuck them back on and bandaged them up. He lay there for four days, and then jumped down, fully recovered. Sadly, a few months later, a leopard took him.

After many adventures we decided to return to England. We were concerned about the children, and it was Rosemary who said, 'We have had a break, now we should lift ourselves up, and try again.'

But before we left we had an experience that was to have a great influence on our lives. It was in the middle of the night. Rosemary and I were in the centre of sleep, and lying face downward. We suddenly woke together, and both of us were sweating – a strange cold sweat. The room glowed with a white light. Our hearts seemed to stop beating. There was something in the room – something outside the mosquito net at the bottom of the bed. We could not turn our heads. Neither of us moved. Neither of us breathed. We were both experiencing the same emotions: fear; joy; elation – and something else – a sensation so rich and full, that it was beyond our understanding. We knew that, at that moment in time, we were complete. Rosemary breathed the words, 'What's happened? Have we died?' The light faded. The air grew warmer. We gazed into each other's eyes. We held each other tightly. We felt serene and strangely confident – and we were together.

I cannot explain, but our lives were never quite the same again.

1955–1961

We had planned to return to England, and stopped off in Cape Town for two weeks. But when we arrived, Brian Brooke asked Rosemary to join his company at the Hofmeyer Theatre, and then when one actor left, I took his place.

We stayed for two and a half years. At the same time as acting in the theatre, I became a disc jockey. One of the programmes was *The Bovril Family Show*, which Rosemary and I presented, assisted by Melanie and Paul (aged four and three). Eventually we were earning over a hundred pounds a week, and we had a car and professional stability. We also had three children, because our third child, Antonia, was born in Cape Town. But apartheid was at its peak, and we found ourselves skating on very thin ice. If we stayed we knew we would have to choose between apathy and prison. One day, when we were staying in Johannesburg, young Afrikaans police invaded our flat. They searched, and then confiscated one book – *Black Beauty* by Anna Sewell. I had just been playing the horse on the radio.

Typically, there was no mention of this in Rosemary's letter, written at that time, to my father.

Sleepy Hollow
P.O. Rivonia
Johannesburg

13 October 1956

Hello, my dear,

Well, here we all are in this metropolis – surrounded by gold mines and millionaires. Joss flew up here, and a few days later, I got my driving licence, and packed the three children in our newly acquired Volkswagen Beetle. I tied a water bag on to the front, and set off from the Cape over de Toits Kloof, through the Karoo, and arrived in the Rand the following evening, having driven a thousand miles! Practically my first drive without the instructor! When I arrived in Jo'burg, I suddenly realised that I didn't know Joss's address. It was Sunday evening! So I drove the infants to the Carlton Hotel, ordered a meal in a private room and proceeded to make inquiries. I discovered, after a time, that Joss was at the airport meeting Moira Lister. About 9.30 p.m. he turned up at the Carlton, and we all piled back in the car, and drove out here – twelve miles from the city. This is really lovely – and ideal for the children.

Joss is doing wonderfully well in *The Sleeping Prince*. The *Sunday Times* quote, 'Ackland, a newcomer to the Johannesburg stage, has all the trimmings for a matinee idol – perhaps the first in this country'. We feel Joss deserves another chance to break into the West End, and so we are returning to London next June, or near that time. I do think Joss has done particularly good work lately, and would really get to the top – given the break. How about you and I running a little pub, just for security, if Joss has long resting periods – a nice wee pub, with chickens in the backyard – a fresh egg for breakfast each morning, and a steady wee income! Nice – eh?!!! We must talk about it. Is London the same as we left, or more difficult? I think I'll bring a Zulu back with me! Take care of yourself, Dad –

Best wishes to Maureen – tons of love,
From, Joss, Melanie, Paul, Antonia and Rosemary

But our departure was earlier than Rosemary expected. We heard that my mother was ill and we brought our plans to leave forward – and by this time we were living dangerously. Many friends were in prison, or had had to flee the country. I had to go on ahead, while Rosemary stayed with the children, fighting with the authorities over baby Toni's birth certificate and passport. We were told it would only take a few days, but it was weeks of confusion and frustration before she broke through the bureaucratic web and returned to England to join me in my mother's flat in Marloes Road. We had found security in Cape Town for the first time in our married life, but now we were right back where we had left off three years before – with no work, and no sign of light in the tunnel ahead.

My mother was diagnosed with brain cancer. She fought hard, and had several operations, but to no avail. After she died Rosemary and I could not afford to buy the Marloes Road house. My mother did not even own the top half in which we lived – it was never possible – she had even had to struggle to pay the rent. It had always been the same, wherever we lived, but never once did I hear her complain. Rosemary and I had saved just enough in Africa for us to mortgage a house in Madrid Road in Barnes, on the other side of Hammersmith Bridge. So we started from scratch – but not for long.

It had been three years since we went away and we came back to a vastly changed world. England had lost face over Suez, and the power this small island had possessed for so many centuries had disintegrated. *Look Back in Anger* opened, and John Osborne, Arnold Wesker and Harold Pinter changed the face of theatre. French windows went out, and the kitchen sink came in. Most of the actors and actresses with whom I had worked had been washed away with the tide; Rosemary and I weren't washed away, because we were not there; we were catching our breath in Africa, and we came back with the new tide.

Soon we both joined the Oxford Playhouse Company – and once again I was working with Frank Hauser. Then in 1958 I was asked to join the Old Vic Company on a six-month American tour. It was an agonising decision, because by this time Rosemary was pregnant with our fourth child, and wouldn't be able to travel, even if we had the money to pay the fare. But this was the big opportunity we had been seeking for so long. We had been through rough times during our seven years of marriage, and the worst had been when we were separated. Rosemary had no doubts. She insisted that I went. She would have the baby, and then take in lodgers to pay the mortgage. She was adamant. 'This is what we have been praying for – you have to go!'

I had persuaded Rosemary to marry me, which resulted in her not going on her American tour. Now the situation was reversed, and I was racked with guilt. But Rosemary put her foot down and the contract was signed. Off I went, and our fourth child was born when I had reached San Francisco, and just a few hours before our very first performance in America. Rosemary called the baby Penelope, because, as in the Greek legend, she was awaiting my return.

We have been asked many times in our lifetime why – when life was so hard – did we had such a big family, and the question was always difficult to answer. We have always believed in swimming with the tide no matter how high the waves. We loved children, we wanted children, and as far as Rosemary was concerned it was very important that we had children, and that was enough for both of us. If you worry too much about the strength of the current that carries you it won't carry you, and the stronger the waves are that face you, the stronger you become in return.

Rosemary was left alone with the children – only now there were four of them. But this time they did at least have a roof over their heads. She took in lodgers and, for the first time, my father kept contact with her, and was a regular visitor.

Six long months later I returned and, after a brief tour of the Soviet Union, Poland and Ireland, I stayed with the Old Vic, in London, for two more years.

Rosemary went through another pregnancy, but lost the baby boy four months prematurely. Then her doctor gently informed her that she could have no more children. We tried for another, but without success. Eventually Rosemary went to the fertility clinic. She was told that her tubes were blocked, and she should telephone the clinic and make an appointment ten days after her next period. She did so, and they unblocked her tubes – temporarily – and said that if she wanted to conceive she would have to have intercourse in the next twenty-four hours. But I was working in Scotland. Undeterred, Rosemary rushed to the station – took the night train up to Glasgow and collected me. We raced off to Pitlochry – lay by a stream in the woods – and our daughter, Samantha, was conceived.

THE SIXTIES

The sea of life had calmed and we were floating along on a calm tide in 1963, when Samantha was a year old, and Rosemary five months pregnant, when disaster struck, and once again our lives changed.

For the past two years, after leaving the Old Vic in 1961, I had joined Bernard Miles at the Mermaid Theatre, working long hours at the theatre as artistic director. This involved my casting, acting, directing and choosing plays, four of which had transferred to the West End. Long days and not much money for the long hours, but we coped. However, one day – because our cheque had bounced – the electricity in our house in Barnes was cut off. Rosemary went to see our bank manager, and asked him why he had returned the cheque.

'Because you would have been overdrawn by twenty-three pounds', he replied.

'But my husband is working, we have five children. I'm five months pregnant, and so you allow our electricity to be cut off simply because we shall be overdrawn by only twenty-three pounds!'

'I'm sorry,' said the bank manager, 'but you have no security.'

'We have a house, for God's sake'.

'That is not security. Your house could burn down at any time.'

Rosemary's temper snapped. 'And you could drop dead at any time', she said and swept out.

The next day our house burnt down and a week later the manager dropped dead in his office.

On 24 June 1963, after giving two performances that day as Galileo and then staying behind for a quick drink to celebrate a member of the company's birthday, I arrived home at Madrid Road by taxi at 12.45 a.m. When I reached home, the street was full of half-dressed people, and the dark sky was lit up by a strange unnatural light. I was aware of fire engines and glistening torsos. I looked up at our house, but it was not there. Just a mass of smouldering wood and bricks. Then that smell – that bloody awful smell. I stepped out of the taxi, people rushed towards me and flashlights exploded in my face. After that moment my memory catches only vague shadowy recollections. I was in a hospital, and Rosemary, five months pregnant, was there on a stretcher, with her face and hands burnt and blistered, and her hair like straggly charred wire. She saw me and gave me that warm open smile that has lifted me up so many times.

'Do you know what the matron said?' she murmured. 'She said she did not want that burnt herring here.'

Then I was back at Madrid Road with the children confused and wide-eyed. They slept on a neighbour's chairs and couches, and I lay next to them and held their hands. There was little sleep for any of us that night, just confused numbness, and at dawn I stood in the rubble of what had been our house. I had no sense of loss, only of desolation and relief. We had nothing left, but the family was all alive – that was all that mattered. In a short space of time I had learnt that material things mean nothing. When the crunch came – life was all.

I learnt what had happened. That night the family had all gone to bed early. Soon after midnight Paul got up to pee. As he made his way to the loo, he heard a low heavy rumbling noise, and a faint mist filled the air. He went into our bedroom, and with difficulty woke his mother. Rosemary took baby Samantha in her arms, woke Melanie, aged ten and, still drowsy from the fumes, made their way downstairs. Rosemary opened the front door, handed Samantha to Melanie, and, after telling her to keep away from the house, went back inside. Smoke filtered out from under the door to the sitting room. Rosemary opened the door and there was a tremendous explosion. Glass shattered everywhere, and the house became an inferno.

With her hair burning, Rosemary ran up through the sheet of fire that engulfed the stairs, her only thought being to reach the other children. People ran in from the street but could not get through the flames. Upstairs the four bedrooms were divided by a landing with two bedrooms on either side – Toni and Penelope's room and Paul's room on one side; Melanie's room and our room with a cot for Samantha, on the other. Rosemary took a while to find Penelope, who was unconscious behind the door of her room. When she did, she carried Penny and Toni across the landing into our bedroom.

Below in the front garden neighbours and bystanders were calling out for Rosemary to jump. She threw the unconscious child down to outstretched hands twenty feet below, and the four-year-old was safely caught, but Toni aged seven was not so easy. She was naturally reluctant to make the long leap and, crying, clutched her mother desperately, until she too was thrown and caught by the people below. 'Now jump!' they called. But Rosemary thought that Paul was still in his room; so she ran back to try and cross the landing to reach his room but the landing was a mass of flames. Hard as she tried, she could not fight through, and her mind became numb and confused as the cries 'Jump! Jump!' were being called from the crowd below. It was only instinct that drove her back to the bedroom, and at last she leapt from the window, but by this time the fire was so intense and the smoke so thick that no one could see her and, with her child inside her, she plummeted to the ground and lost consciousness.

Despite her injuries, neighbours had to pull her away from the house because the lead from the pipes had melted and was dripping beside her.

By a miracle Paul was safe. When the house exploded and the flames rushed to the top floor he was in his room. Luckily there was scaffolding down the back of the house. We had just had an attic built, and the following night some of the children would have been sleeping there. Paul climbed down the scaffolding to safety, but when he realised the rest of the family was still inside, the nine-year-old broke into the rear kitchen window, cutting his leg, in order to get up the stairs. Neighbours pulled him back and carried the naked boy round to where his mother was lying in front of the house. By now Rosemary was semi-conscious and convinced that Paul was dead. Even when neighbours brought him round to her, she could not believe it. She thought she was dreaming. Fifteen minutes later the house had gone.

Rosemary was on the danger list; and everyone assumed she would lose her baby straight away as she was five months pregnant. She refused any painkillers and, when they were forced on her, she poured them into a flower bowl by her bed. She had no feeling from the waist down. If she survived the doctors thought she would never walk again, and her burns would leave bad scars. Her back was broken, an L1 fracture, and her burns were very bad. The general consensus was that if Rosemary survived, she would be scarred for life. But after a few days Diane Lasselle, a faith healer who lived a few doors away in Madrid Road, visited Rosemary and offered to help. Rosemary said it would be no use, because she did not believe. Diane said she didn't need to, and moved her hands over the large blisters and burns.

The next day Rosemary's skin had completely healed, without the trace of a scar. After the fire the Actors' Charitable Trust helped, and the children were sent to a place by the sea. Only Samantha stayed with me. Then Maureen Mitchell, whom I had never met, lent us a house in Barnes, and the children returned home, and were given piles of clothes by friends and strangers.

From Putney Hospital, Rosemary was moved to Stoke Mandeville, where she remained for the next eighteen months, with occasional remission, and allowed home for weekends to a temporary home in Roehampton, and then I managed to find a Norwegian girl to help with the children. At Stoke Mandeville it was initially thought extremely unlikely that Rosemary would ever walk again. Less than four months later with the aid of a cage, relentless determination, plus great encouragement from the head of the hospital, Ludwig Guttman, she was able to stand.

Guttman was a hard taskmaster who positively bullied his patients into discovering their full potential and conquering their disabilities. If someone had six months to live, Guttman would say, 'You have six months of wonderful life – now live it.' Sadly he could not always succeed. In the next bed to Rosemary a young woman who had been in a car crash in South Africa could not accept her disability. Her husband would sit and hold her hand and talk sympathetically but the fight had gone out of her. After two weeks she died because she did not have the will to live.

Guttman was thrilled with Rosemary. After concentrated physio-therapy and sheer determination she was able to walk. She had achieved the 'impossible', and was temporarily released from hospital. She could only move by wearing heavy calipers on her legs. But all these months in hospital had institutionalised her. She was determined to get back to her family, but by now she was shy and apprehensive about being with the children. After coming out of the hospital we both went for a quiet meal and then to the movies before returning home when the children were asleep.

Two days later Rosemary and I went off to Venice where of course she had to walk. We were determined that she get back to normal. Then we sent for ten-year-old Paul to come and join us. Paul was now a weekly boarder at Highgate School. He had longed to go there, but we felt that he had suffered a great shock with the fire, and he was lonely at school away from the family, so he came out and joined us for the last few days of our holiday.

When we got back home, Rosemary's concern for her children gave her even more determination to conquer her injuries and she steadfastly fought her way back to normality. On 23 November, I was working at the Mermaid, when the news came through that President Kennedy had been assassinated. Within seconds Rosemary phoned me at the theatre. 'Have you heard – Kennedy has been – ouch!!' There was a moment's silence, and then she said, 'I think the baby is about to arrive'.

Our sixth child was born, a few hours later, in Queen Charlotte's Hospital. Naturally, because of the paralysis, there was concern about the birth, especially with Rosemary having little control of her muscles. However Kirsty leapt effortlessly from the womb. After much persuasion, Rosemary was allowed to breastfeed her at home for six weeks, before going back to Stoke Mandeville. With a new babe, she was more anxious than ever that our big family would not have to cope without a mother.

At that time Stoke Mandeville was a hive of activity. Margot Fonteyn's husband, Roberto Arias, was flown in from South America, with Margot at his side. He still had bullets inside him and his temperature was so high that Guttman had to encase him in ice. 'This man must not die,' he said, and Arias recovered enough to leave the hospital. Also in the hospital was the composer Sir Malcolm Sargent's secretary who, while rushing to her employer, had been in an accident and broken her neck, a C3 break. In time she was able to type by blowing through a pipette, with the power of each breath creating a different letter. Below her neck she could not move one muscle. Strangely, it was usually the people who had attempted suicide that were unable to accept their injuries. Nothing was going to stop Rosemary conquering hers and, like a determined terrier, with non-stop exercises, she fought her way back to normality.

When she finally returned home, Rosemary was the first person ever with those particular injuries to walk out of Stoke Mandeville. She was termed a walking paraplegic. She came home – and in 1966 – despite our being told it could never happen – our second son, Toby, was born.

I left the Mermaid Theatre, and concentrated on television and the theatre – just as long as the theatre was in London. After playing

Professor Medlin in *The Professor*, and Jorrocks in David Heneker and Beverly Cross's musical *Jorrocks,* I went into *Hotel in Amsterdam* by John Osborne and *Come As You Are* by John Mortimer. These were long runs that took me to the end of the decade, so that I was able to spend time at home with Rosemary and the children where she recovered her strength, and disposed of her calipers. The paralysis was permanent, and never again would she be able to run. Standing still was also difficult, but except for having a slight limp, Rosemary always managed to give the impression that everything was normal.

We moved into Ravenswood House, a huge old property on Kingston Hill, which had once belonged to Earl Haig. The owners took pity on our situation and our large family and let us have the house for two-thirds of the asking price. They even lent us money to help pay the hefty mortgage. Ravenswood had a minstrel gallery and fourteenth-century double doors from his Scottish estate, and a lovely garden for the children. Luckily for us, halfway through the sixties big houses were difficult to sell, and very reasonable to buy. The country was going through a transition stage. It was the era of 'little boxes' when everyone seemed to want small houses – to keep everything to a minimum. There were even castles for sale for two hundred pounds, because the upkeep would be too much. However, after losing everything in the fire, and as we were starting again, all our friends thought we were crazy. They all said we would not last there for more than a few weeks.

However, with the aid of a hefty mortgage, and constant employment, we managed to keep going.

The sixties was an extraordinary era of change – good and bad. In South Africa apartheid was at its worst and peaceful protests such as at Sharpeville were met with brutal force and massacre, Nelson

Mandela was jailed for life. The wall went up in Berlin. In America the Civil Rights movement broke through the US segregation with peaceful protests. They were led by Martin Luther King, Jr, who was later assassinated. Jack Kennedy and his brother Bobby were both killed. Changes were fast and furious. This was when youth came to the fore. Elvis Presley had led the way that the Beatles now followed, and so confident teenagers were targeted by marketers, and drugs became easy prey, and part of the tenor of the age. Meanwhile in the adolescent USA the young were sent abroad to fight a futile war in Vietnam.

Back home, life was full. Rosemary, in spite of her limp, was a bundle of energy. Apart from helping the children with their education, she spent her time chauffeuring them to schools, music lessons, swimming lessons and boating lessons – as well as teaching English to Japanese students at our home. Often she would often say, 'Let's have a few friends around' and a few hours later, twenty or thirty people would sit down to a delicious meal, which she prepared with what looked like little effort. These impromptu dinners and lunches became well known in our small literary and theatre world. Our children happily provided well-drilled assistance, as Rosemary smiled and calmly made magic.

Before we met both Rosemary and I had been gregarious loners. We enjoyed company, but always kept our independence. Once we met we became part of each other, and our lives became completely interwoven. We still had good friends – but our family was our world, and Rosemary has always been my best friend. We had chums who would visit us or we would visit them, but we would never dream of going away on holiday with other couples. A powerful strength of relationship seems to have passed on to our progeny who have always remained a very tight unit. As a child I had very little rapport with my cousins, but today our thirty-two grandchildren and all of our great-grandchildren meld instantly the moment they are together.

THE SEVENTIES

Luck was on our side back in the seventies, because our children were all still at school and, after the fire, it was important to try to stay together, and so I returned to the theatre, but always in London. It was fortunate that the plays I played in this decade were all successful. When *Come As You Are* finished I was in *Collaborators*, another John Mortimer play, and then *Captain Brassbound's Conversion* (Shaw), *A Streetcar Named Desire* (Tennesee Williams) and the musicals *A Little Night Music* (Sondheim) and *Evita* (Tim Rice and Lloyd Webber). The only time I played in the provinces was for a short tour of *The Taming of the Shrew*. The same rule applied to television – I did the series *The Crezz*, (Clive Exton), *Tinker, Tailor, Soldier, Spy* (John le Carré), *Access to the Children* (William Trevor) and *King's Cross* (John Mortimer). *The Three Sisters* (Anton Chekov) and *The Lie* (Ingmar Bergman) were also performed in London. The only exception was *The Canterbury Tales*, when I spent my time on horseback in the New Forest. And even though I played in twenty movies, they were mostly supporting roles – and all local. Our children were still at school, and with so many it was important that we remained a strong family unit – as much as possible.

It was a rich, full, hard-working decade, with family holidays in Greece, and concentrated studies at school, and university.

But I'm ahead of myself. Back at Ravenswood life was a flurry of activity, and life was full and fast.

By the seventies both Rosemary and I were in our forties. So much had happened in our lives, there was little time for us to take in how the world had changed. The popular music of the day showed that romance had not faded, although solo artists were gradually being replaced by groups. There were still a few theatres – even though many more had gone. Now audiences stayed at home, and repertory companies were replaced by soaps and serials on television. However with virtually only two channels on TV in this country, there were very few game shows, and audiences were still able to watch plays by good writers – William Trevor, Arnold Wesker, David Mercer, Harold Pinter, David Exton, John Hopkins and many others.

In the seventies there was much less violence. It was still possible to leave your front door and your car door unlocked. The Cold War still lingered dangerously in the air, but day-to-day life was safer, and equality of race and sex were at last beginning to become accepted.

Meanwhile our young family was finding its wings. Rosemary and I felt that all the children had been bruised and shocked by the trauma of the fire. We were determined they should have happy, normal young lives. Ravenswood, with its vast space and lovely garden, helped to achieve this. But it was Rosemary, in spite of her disability, who was the quiet strength behind us all. She gently controlled our world, helping with the children's homework and running the home.

I was fortunate to be working non-stop in the theatre and television. It took me over thirty minutes to drive into Soho and the West

End – for rehearsals, voice-overs and performances. I would usually make the return trip three times a day in order to spend time with all the family. When I was acting in the theatre, I never got home before eleven, and then Rosemary and I would have a quiet meal together before bed – which we rarely reached before 2 a.m. Rosemary was always up early getting the children off to school so there was little time to continue with her diary.

Many actors have families, but I have always felt that I am a family man who happens to be an actor, and with so many members of our family there were bound to be disasters and crises taking place. We sold the rear part of our house, and bought a cottage at Treyarnon Bay in Cornwall from the composer Malcolm Arnold. It was heaven for the young children, with the wild surfing sea a few yards away, livestock to feed and ponies to ride. But in those days the journey to get there took over seven hours, and I had little chance to join them on their holidays, and so Rosemary was left to cope with seven children, alone.

And gradually a tragic problem began to materialise. Much of the time was spent trying to reach and help our son Paul, who, without our knowledge, had been introduced to drugs in the sixties. It was some time before we learnt that, when he was fourteen, he had been given heroin – free – as he came out of school. He went through various forms of hell, and we were unable to reach him. It was the Jekyll and Hyde syndrome – at times a warm-hearted, affectionate, enthusiastic, bright, friendly boy, at others a lost soul without remorse.

Meanwhile, with my return to the theatre and the pace of family life, Rosemary was burning the candle at both ends. She had hardly any time to write – and there were times when writing about our lives was too painful. She makes little reference to the desperation of those years – Paul leaving Highgate School and then running off to Morocco at the age of fifteen where he was robbed and somehow managed to return without a passport; of our frantic attempts to get him off drugs – sending him to various rehabilitation centres – and then, in a desperate effort to get him away from drugs, arranging for him to be arrested – only to have to get him off, when we discovered how easy it was to get drugs in prison.

Eventually, as a last resort, we let him go to Australia to work in the theatre for Googie Withers and John McCallum, who were going to meet him at the airport. But, as luck would have it, Googie was the subject of *This Is Your Life*, and they had both been flown to London. So Paul hitchhiked from Sydney to Cairns, in Northern Australia, and there he discovered magic mushrooms. Back at Ravenswood – in the middle of one night – our phone rang. Paul was stranded in the desert. He was suffering from withdrawal symptoms, and was very low. The operator interrupted the call, and said, 'I can hear this is an emergency, so I am not charging for the call. Take your time.' In the diary all Rosemary writes is:

MY HAPPIEST DAY TODAY. Paul is safe and well.

We had to get hold of a private plane, which took five days to find him. Then there was more rehabilitation when we took him off to our cottage in Cornwall.

One reason we had bought Primrose Cottage was to keep Paul away from drugs when he was by the sea in the open countryside. But we soon discovered that drugs were rampant in our area, and we even had to resort to removing wires from our telephone so that he would not be tempted to contact his old drug friends. But it was all to no avail, and in a very short time he had found a partner, Sue, and returned with her to the mushrooms in northern Australia. It was there that Kandy, our first grandchild, was born. After a period of chaos and floods, when Kandy nearly drowned, they returned to England. Later, when they were back in England, we received a call from Bolton that Paul was there – he was unconscious in hospital. He had had an overdose, and was unlikely to recover. Rosemary and I collected Toni from school, then the three of us raced off to Bolton, and Rosemary stayed with him in hospital. Two days later he woke, leapt out of bed – and fled. It was several days before we got him back home to Primrose Cottage to recuperate.

Rosemary mentions none of this – it was too painful. She does not say how many times she wrote to members of Parliament without success, with the government always avoiding the issue. She never mentions that she formed new organisations for people who, like ourselves, were desperate, with no one to turn to.

Meanwhile Paul struggled to conquer his demons, and made a great effort to get back on an even keel. There were positive times when he was able and willing to grasp a helping hand. There were times when he became a sheep farmer in Yorkshire, and when he acted in a play in the theatre. He found a new partner, Irene, a stabilising influence, and his second child, Ben, was born. Eventually, with the help of two members of a Christian organisation, John Harris and Nigel Goodwin, he went to the philosopher Francis Schaeffer's community at L'Bri in Switzerland, where he found religion, and broke free from drugs. He returned to being his warm-hearted, lovable self. So much damage had been done, but gradually he overcame his craving. None of this is in the diary – only occasional snatches of despair. It was not stoicism that prevented her writing – it was trauma.

But, when the family was back in London, I discovered that she did manage occasionally to put pen to paper and I include the few comments she made on daily events in the seventies. They show how our lives had changed, even though Rosemary seemed totally unphased that they had, and how it was possible for her to mix the simple and the sophisticated, and still keep both feet on the ground without losing balance.

Children to school – busy morning – clean sheets – washing, etc, – then prepared a lunch party. Ed Sherrin, Ingrid Bergman, Irwin Kershner, Don Siegel, Denholm Elliot and Sue, John Mortimer and Penny came – John Hopkins and Shirley Knight dropped in later – Paul phoned from Hull and wants us to bring Sue and Kandy home.

We first met Ingrid Bergman when I played opposite her in *Captain Brassbound's Conversion*. On Sundays when we had free days, she would go cycling in the park with our children, and then join us for lunch.

We took the train to Cornwall, and arrived at Primrose Cottage in time for a cream tea. Sheets and blankets all damp. The children are in heaven. Toni and Kirsty went riding. I spent until midnight airing everything.

Penny and Sammy went to Dignon in France. I drove them to Heathrow. Melanie got engaged to Billy [actor Alister Cameron]. Paul flew to Geneva, and then to L'Bri to kill his drug dependence forever – fingers crossed.

Melanie is getting married today. Reception at home. Beautiful day – but it rained non-stop. [Simply by chance, she and Alister were married in Denham, in the church in which she was married, when playing my daughter for a scene in the film, *S-P-Y-S*.] We drove to Grantham, and saw Paul married to Sue. [Unlike Melanie's wedding – this was very much a hippy wedding with flowers and without alcohol.]

Joss read Coleridge to an audience in Coleridge's brother's house. His brother kept him locked up there, when he was on drugs and writing *Kubla Khan*.

The two of us flew to Venice. I'm now in heaven. Joss and I are *one*. Dinner at Harry's Bar. Love all afternoon, and dinner at the Venetian Athlete's Restaurant.

Champagne for breakfast on flight to Munich, with the *Royal Flash* movie charter flight – then a car to Howeschangau. Beautiful views.

Joss, Toby and I took a horse and cart to Neuschwanstein Castle, and we got locked in! Toby had to crawl under an iron trellis to get help.

Back in Covent Garden.

Joss offered the musical *A Little Night Music*. Sammy fainted at school. Toby ill. Sammy ill. Penny – wonderful exam results.

We drove to see Paul, Sue and Kandy. They are all very well. They seem happy, but it looks as though they need help.

I went to see a rehearsal of *A Little Night Music*. It was very slow and lacked life.

Kirsty and I went up north to see Paul for the day – scrubbed their floors – Kirsty cleaned bath and windows. I took Sue shopping, and taught her to cook a stew. We all had a happy evening together. Drove home in a snowstorm..

Melanie, Sammy and I visited Dad and Jane [my father and his partner] and then Melanie, Toby, Kirsty, Penny and I saw *Night Music*, and enjoyed it very much. Joss is very upset though. He's nervous, and doesn't want me at the first night.

I went to *A Little Night Music*. A lovely evening.

Claire Bloom, David Kernan, Anna Massey and Denholm Elliot and family, all came to lunch. Melanie started labour at midnight! Her baby was born nearly three hours later. Both are gorgeous and well. Hurrah. Polly is beautiful.

Jean Simmons is ill – so the understudy was on. I went to see the show. It was dull and dreary, and missed Jean.

Joss did a broadcast re: the referendum, and then we had a lovely, peaceful day, on our own, in the garden. Beautiful relaxation and no visitors.

Toby's birthday. We had the *Night Music* company at home. With help from the family, I cooked for eighty-four people. We had a very exhausting fun day from noon to 1.30 a.m.

Took Paul, Sue and Kandy to the station, and saw them off. Then we went to lobby members of Parliament. [This was when we were trying to wake up the government, who seemed to be unable to understand or deal with the new drug obsession of the young.] Kirsty rang from Spain. She is homesick, and wants to come home.

Hot day. All on the beach. [We were in Cornwall, and decided to sell Primrose Cottage.] Toby was bitten by an adder. We rushed him off at breakneck speed to Truro City Hospital, and stayed in hospital with him for the night.

Toni, Sammy and I left with the car bulging with blankets and presents for Paul, Kandy and Sue. They looked very well. It's snowing, freezing and icy cold. Toni, Sammy and I had an uncomfortable night on the floor. I took the family to Scarborough for lunch.

Joss and I flew to Rio – a dreadful flight through storms.

I was about to play Juan Perón in *Evita*, the musical by Andrew Lloyd Webber and Tim Rice. As no one else had been cast in the show, Rosemary and I went to Argentina to do research, and learn what we could about Juan and Eva. En route we stopped off in Brazil.

Lunched at Copacabana. Saw the carnival rehearsing in the streets. Danced at nightclub till 4 a.m.

Drove to the Campo de Flamingo Ball. Very exciting. Saw the dawn rise – bed at 5.30 a.m.

Walked over Museum Republic. Lunch at Antonio's – lovely. Whatever was in the food made us very high! Danced till 3 a.m. at Big Al's.

We flew to the Iguasso Falls. Quite breathtaking. Walked around the Falls, and took a canoe to the top. Later joined a carnival party by the pool.

We were up at 5.15 and walked around the Falls at dawn. We swam and then flew to Buenos Aeries. Cold!

We hired a car and a young interpreter, Alicia, and then drove to Lobos – Perón's birthplace. We spent the day seeing Perón contacts.

This was not easy because I had to conceal the fact that I was going to play the man. Whenever his name was mentioned, most people made an excuse and fled. The only way Rosemary and I managed to see details and photos of Perón and Evita in their early years was by our being locked up in a basement, with someone on the lookout. We visited Lobos, to see the house where Perón was born. It was now a kindergarten, with no reference to his ever having existed, and he had run the country longer than any man had run any country this century, apart from Franco in Spain. Back in Buenos Aeries, our interpreter – 'gentle, sweet-natured Alicia' – pointed to a statue of a general, and said, 'This was a wonderful man – he worked his way up from the bottom of Argentina to the very top – and he killed off all the blacks.' Throughout all this Rosemary remained as cool as ever, and does not even mention that, at that time, if it was discovered that I was about to play Juan Perón our situation could be very tricky.

We danced at Mau-Mau till 3.30 a.m. – a beautiful evening.

We left Buenos Airies to go back to Rio. A wonderful day – saw the carnival competition, danced at Oba Oba, dined at On the Rocks and on to Big Al's till 3.30.

School opens. Today we lay on a hot beach, and then took the plane to Gatwick.

This evening we saw *Jesus Christ Superstar*. We didn't want to go, but Andrew persisted, so we promised we would. I'm so tired, but we went, and it was very boring – it was not our scene at all. When we got there, we had to pay for the tickets that Andrew had 'reserved for us'!!! Tony Bowles, the conductor, came to dinner with us at the Garrick.

Parents' day at Putney School. I started double packing. Toni is very upset, and Melanie says she is leaving Alister.

It was all the children's holidays and I was about to film in Singapore, and so – in spite of the political unrest – Rosemary took the young ones to have a break in Israel.

Drove to Neviot – very disappointing – overcrowded, and no dinner.

Got up at 4.30, and took the bus to Eilat. We got stopped on the way by soldiers, and people were taken off the bus. Shots were fired, and we were not allowed to get off the bus, which drove on!!!

The security at Eilat went on for three hours. Arrived home, tired and frozen.

Eilat is a dump. A fierce sandstorm all afternoon, and our hut is covered in sand.

After the day on Sea Fox, we returned by bus to Neviot

This afternoon we all rode on camels into the desert. It was great fun. I'm so happy as Joss [filming in Singapore] phoned, and said he missed me. Wonderful.

Back in London.

Visited Joss's dad, and then spent the day with Melanie. She and Alister are in a miserable state. Joss arrived. I collected him – wonderful to have him back.

School opens. Joss's opening night of *Evita*. FABULOUS. Fairy-tale night. Melanie, Toni, Penny, Joss and I party with the company on a boat on the Thames.

At the Garrick Joss joined other actors [John Gielgud, John Clements, Anna Neagle, Donald Sinden and Kenneth Williams] to lunch with Dennis and Mrs Thatcher. [This was just before she became Prime Minister.] I stayed in the drawing room! Joss said that when Mrs Thatcher said to Gielgud that she had been to see his play *Half Life* on the previous evening, she had received an important message and had to leave in the interval. 'Oh really,' he said. 'More of a quarter life – wasn't it?'

Beautiful, tranquil, sunny day – just Joss, Sammy and me. Happiness. I took Joss's dad by ambulance to *Evita*.

I phoned Kirsty – she is very unhappy – went to visit Toby, and then went to Eastleigh and brought Paul home. Sammy, Joss and I went to see Dizzy Gillespie at Scott's.

Paul's son, Ben, born at 6 a.m. Paul is back on drugs. I feel weak, tired and very depressed. I went into the theatre to join Joss. Dinner with Cybill Shepherd. Sammy flew to Athens. Paul came in at 12.30 – drugged. [Paul's marriage to Sue did not last long. By now he had joined Irene, the mother of young Ben.]

Half term. Joss is signing at Liberty's – doing Ogden Nash at the King's Head – and then two shows of *Evita*. Cocktails with Argentine Ambassador and Margot Fonteyn.

We gave a Christmas dinner – fifty people came – great fun, and a great success.

I went into the theatre with Joss, as a new girl was playing *Evita*. The management were auditioning her before a paying audience! Joss was furious – seven people off every night, and now this – so he walked out and didn't play the evening show. Gary Bond had been off with a chest infection, but now he was back, and played the matinee. He asked Joss where he was going, and Joss quoted various cast members. 'If anyone wants to know, my aunt is ill – I've got the curse – and I'm doing a broadcast.' So Gary's chest got bad again, and he left as well! All three principals were off tonight! Joss tried to phone Hal, Tim and Andrew, but without success. Then he got through to Bob Swash very late, who was quite unconcerned; until he heard that a *News of the World* reporter was interviewing Gary when Joss walked out.

The next day the *Daily Express* phoned, and the *Daily Mail* photographer arrived in the garden, because of an item on the front page of the *News of the World* – 'Joss's aunt is ill'! Sammy decided to return to Putney.

My birthday. After the show, Joss and I had a super party together, by the fire. We had pressed caviar, lobster claws, prawns and champagne and a wonderful evening. Bed at 5 a.m.

Penny is learning the part of Nurse Sweet in *National Health*. I rehearsed with her all morning, and then I drove her into town, and saw her at the King's College New Theatre. She was very good.

This evening Joss, Sammy, Kirsty, Toby and I went to see Danny La Rue – fantastic show, and a very gay dinner with him afterwards at Le Baaca. [In the seventies gay meant happy!] Visited Ingrid [Bergman] in her new flat. So sad – she has cancer of the breast.

Joss and I visited Dad. He is so sad and lonely. Dinner with Ingrid.

In the afternoon I went to see the headmaster of Kings. He has promised to take Toby! Hip, Hip, Hooray. Yippee!

Joss contacted the House of Commons to help allow persecuted refugees to find refuge here.

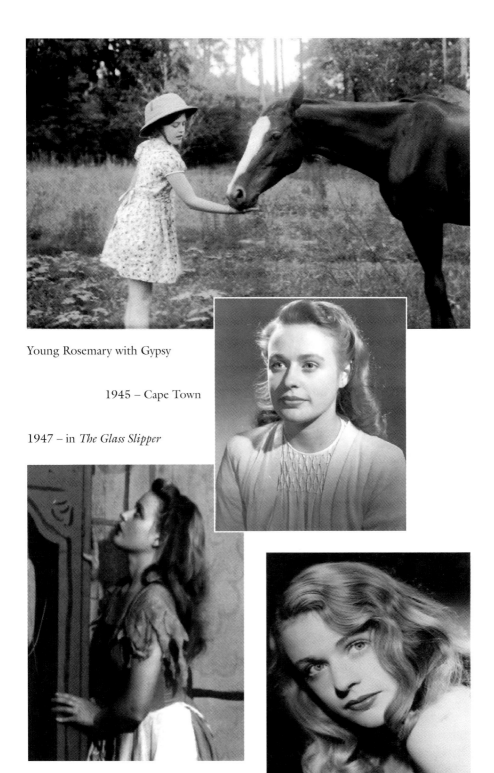

Young Rosemary with Gypsy

1945 – Cape Town

1947 – in *The Glass Slipper*

1949 – London

1951

Arriving in Pitlochry

Mary Rose and Simon

Leaving Pitlochry

Arriving in London

1954

Nachilonga Bungalow, Likanga

Melanie, Paul
and Rosemary with
Scamp at Nachilonga

The family and Friday

1955–1957

With Melanie and
Paul in Cape Town

The two of us in *The Diary of Anne Frank*

Toni is born in Cape Town

1958–1961

Back in England at our first house

The Old Vic group: Judi Dench, Maggie Smith, Moyra Fraser,
Alec McCowan, Rosemary, John Moffatt

THE SIXTIES

The day before the fire

Penny, Paul, Melanie, Sammy and Toni

The morning after

Back home
with Kirsty

First
Christmas
together
after the fire

Back from hospital once more   Number seven – Toby arrives

On the way to Toby's Christening

THEATRICAL WIVES AND LOVERS

Mai Zetterling in
Darling

Maggie Smith in
The Merry Wives of Windsor

Judi Dench in
Twelfth Night

Jean Simmons
in *A Little
Night Music*

Claire Bloom
in *The Cherry
Orchard*

Glynis Johns
in *Come as
you Are*

Lauren Bacall
in *The Visit*

Ingrid
Bergman in
*Captain
Brassbound's
Conversion*

Dorothy Tutin in *The Gin Game*

Dad taken ill. Joss, Samantha and I spent an hour with him. He cannot talk or communicate. Dad died at 6.30 p.m.

Joss is very quiet – we are both very sad. Then this afternoon Joss and I had fantastic togetherness. Love divine. Dinner with Ingrid.

Kirsty and I went to see *Tinker, Tailor, Soldier, Spy.* We enjoyed the series. Alec Guinness was superb. Joss was a bit too reddened up.

Kirsty went to the American Embassy for visas. Penny and I took the chicken to the vet. And then drove to Victoria, to meet Kirsty and Toby, with passports. On the spur of the moment, we decided to fly with one of Laker's cheap flights to New York – only £10 a head. We rushed home, packed lunch, left for Gatwick, and were in New York at 11 p.m.

Took Kirsty by ferry to the Statue of Liberty. Went on to lunch at the Seafare of the Aegean. Then to see *Sweeney Todd* – super.

Got up and packed. Ken arrived, and drove Kirsty, Joss and I to Tappan. Had a lovely time and lunch with Zena and Ken. [Zena had been married to my brother Paddy, who was killed just after D-Day. After the war she took their baby son to America and married Ken.] During lunch Steve Sondheim phoned, and asked what Joss thought of *Sweeney Todd.* We have no idea how he found out we were here in Tappan. Ken took us back to the hotel, and we checked out. We returned on a lovely empty plane, had a long lie-down and slept.

Back in London.

Went to see Paul, but he was out. When we got home we heard that Melanie has had a boy. A very hard time – nineteen hours' labour. We went to High Wycombe to see her.

I took Toby shopping to buy his jersey and satchel. Joss lunched with David Cornwell [John Le Carré] and Fred Zinnerman to see about filming *The Honourable Schoolboy*. When he returned, we watched Lord Mountbatten's funeral on TV. It was very moving, and magnificently staged.

Lovely cuddly day – to begin with! Joss and I had a sit-in-the sun with a glass of champagne and lovely togetherness. Samantha home for steak lunch – then Toby came home happily. There was an argument – Joss started shouting – Toby upset – Samantha foolish. It ended in a dreadful row. In a temper, I threw an avocado out of the kitchen window, and broke the window. It's hell.

Did laundry, and then Joss and I caught a plane to Berlin. So excited.

We got up at 5 a.m., and went to the studios and then went out to the woods for filming. Back in Berlin, Joss and I had a super evening at the Big Window restaurant.

Joss and I took a bus to Checkpoint Charlie. So very stark – a real shock, but in view of what went on at the end of the war, with fascism still prevalent – probably very necessary then. Flight home. No food – and the children unwelcoming – except for Toby, who met us.

MIGRAINE! Joss and I went by Thai airline to Bangkok.

Rosemary could not be with me when I had filmed in the East and I needed us to be together to share the experience.

Woke up at 5 a.m. and we went for a walk in the gardens, then on a tour of the village, and walked round a disgusting market full of frogs and snakes in bags of water. Lovely evening, dancing at the Pink Panther, and overlooking Hong Kong harbour.

Bus to Chang Chow. So interesting, seeing Chinese village and island life. MIGRAINE KILLING so we went up rickety stairs in a crumbling house for me to get acupuncture from a fantastic man – he put about a hundred needles in me. Migraine cleared, so Joss and I went to a luscious lunch at the Repulse Bay Hotel.

Took a plane to Jakarta, and then across the equator to Bali. The air is fantastic – woody – gorgeous. The Tan Jung Sari is a heavenly hotel. Delicious Balinese buffet supper, and then a delicious, exquisite hut to sleep in, and an Iguana to wake us in the morning.

After lunch we went to a fantastic ceremony, where people entered the temple, went into a trance, came out – still in a trance – and stabbed themselves. Very exciting.

A fabulous day. We drove to an ancient Balinese village, and saw a Sanskrit writer, and also a horrific bat cave temple, where sacrifices of water buffalo and pigs were made. Tonight a suckling pig for dinner.

Left the Tan Jung Sari at seven, and drove to mass at the Trante Gallery, and then on to Obud to see paintings, and to the Sacred Monkey Forest and Temple. Joss had a bag of peanuts – so three monkeys mugged him, while the horrid leader bit his hand and grabbed the nuts. After seeing the doctor at Bali Beach – we learnt there was no rabies in Bali, thank God – Joss and I watched a cremation. It was horrendous.

We left Bali two days earlier than planned. Rosemary insisted. I asked her, 'Why? We are having a great time.' 'I don't know,' she said, 'I just feel we should go.' So we went. The next day Bali experienced a bad earthquake, with many victims.

We took a plane to Jakarta, and then another to Singapore and stayed at the Goodwood Park Hotel. We went out for a super Japanese dinner, then to Boogie Street, and its stunningly beautiful 'ladies' [men in drag]. I feel wonderful – without a headache.

After breakfast of pawpaw and yoghurt, we drove to Raffles Hotel, a fabulous place. We had a Singapore Sling, before the most delicious curry Tiffin.

Arrived in Bangkok. The Oriental is a magical hotel, and we have a lovely suite. So happy.

A very smooth flight back to London. Lovely to see the children. Suddenly so much to do.

But with Rosemary there was always so much to do.

THE EIGHTIES

The eighties were quite different. Most of the children were now young adults, and living away from home – either married or with partners. When once more I worked with Claire Bloom, I was playing C.S. Lewis in the little TV movie *Shadowlands*. This was a great success – winning the BAFTA award and also the International Emmy, and had a great influence on our future lives. Despite the fact that I played leading roles in theatre and on TV, in movies I had always played supporting roles. And the movie world is very conservative – it doesn't take risks. When the producer of *Lady Jane* heard that I was going to play Don Masino in *The Sicilian*, he was very confused, and said to me, 'That's strange – that's not your category!' The rule is once a supporting actor in movies, always a supporting actor in movies. There are few exceptions. Humphrey Bogart, Lee Marvin and Anthony Quinn made the transition, but in every case luck played a part. It certainly did with me. The role of Don Masino, the Godfather in *The Sicilian*, was originally intended for Marlon Brando, and it was only after it didn't come to pass that the director Michael Cimino happened to see *Shadowlands*, that I was offered the role. Cimino was staying with Gore Vidal (who was writing the script), when Claire showed it to them. So once again our lives changed. Over the next decade Rosemary and I averaged twenty-three flights a year – mostly transatlantic. With her walking disability, Rosemary was unable to act, but our being together meant that every role I played – we played together. It was always a collaboration. Yet Rosemary would never come on the set with me. She didn't have to – she was there.

After *Shadowlands* luck fell our way. This led to the part of Godfather, Don Masino in *The Sicilian*, followed by Jock Delves Broughton in *White Mischief*, and Arjen Rudd in *Lethal Weapon 2* in Hollywood. I was now a member of the international set, and I started to work worldwide. Rosemary and I could always go together – which we did. For us the eighties turned out to be a decade of travel. Apart from all the movies abroad, we sought to see a great deal of the world, and Kirsty and Toby, who were living with us at Ravenswood, came with us. We took them off to a dude ranch in Arizona for Christmas, which unfortunately proved very dull, and they missed home. Then on to Southern California for the New Year. But by this time Kirsty was thoroughly miserable and suffered some intense teenage-itus.

Before starting work on a play in 1981, Rosemary and I took Toby to the Himalayas in India, where we stayed on a houseboat. At last we had time to ourselves, and Rosemary was able to write in some detail about our adventures.

We left our houseboat and drove to Phalgam, and met our Sherpas and our ponies. We rode to Aru, a fabulous mountain plain. After our tents were set up we went for a walk. This is heaven. After a cuddle we bathed in the river, in the moonlight.

We were up at 6 a.m., packed up, and on the track by 7.30. It was a fascinating – very precarious ride over ravines, rivers and mountain precipices. We rode over rocks and broken bridges, and arrived at Lidderwat. After a packed lunch we had to take a long walk to find a place to pee. This is heaven. After a cuddle, I bathed in the river, in the moonlight.

We rode from Lidderwat to Aru. Toby was thrown from his horse. We had a super day in camp. The Sherpas cooked us great meals.

After a horrid, sleepless night in the tent – only relieved by the unforgettable full moon shining on the trees and the mountains, we pony-trekked to Pahalgam, and I said goodbye to my pony.

We left the houseboat for Kargul in a 'taxi', driven by the 'Ladakhi cowboy' – as Bashau calls himself. The drive over the Himalayas was exciting, thrilling, hair-raising, adventurous and magnificent. We stayed the night halfway up at D'zojiola, in a sweet old-fashioned 'hotel' in the rocks – with no lighting and no heating. Up at five, and left for Leh. It was a hot tiring drive, but with superb mountain scenery. I rode a pony down the hill to see a Gumpa. At 5 p.m. we arrived at our camp outside Leh, 14,000 feet up – the highest point of civilisation in the world.

Toby is very ill and upset. He has altitude dehydration from running up the mountain. Joss is also breathless. This afternoon we walked around Leh, and Toby stayed in bed. On our return his temperature was 103. We sent a runner to fetch a doctor, who said his sinus was very badly infected.

Toby sweated out his fever. Joss and I changed his pyjamas at midnight. By 6 a.m. he was normal, but very weak. Last night the monsoon hit the camp. It was hilarious. The dining room leaked, and all the dinner was soaked. We drank chang with a very pleasant Swiss French couple.

The 'airport' is filthy. We queued to get window seats, and waited for three hours in a crowded, windowless room – and then the flight was cancelled. So we took the taxi to stay the night at the Oberoi Shambha-La.

We left at 8 a.m. for the airport. After another two-hour wait, once again the plane was cancelled.

It was then that we learnt that there had been no plane for six weeks. The only pilot able to do the very tricky take-off between two mountains, said that as the wind was not right, it was too dangerous. The Ladakhi cowboy had refused to take us back by car, because the bridge across the river was down, but we tried him again and eventually he agreed.

Our taxi man drove us to Kargil. We slept once more at D'zojiola. We learn that there have been landslides, and two bridges have been washed away.

Rosemary does not mention that we had to drive through the landslides, and when we reached the river, there was an empty car floating downstream.

We were up at 5 a.m. Bashau drove us to Drass – then a long wait while blasting took place. Toby and Bashau walked and stood on the glacier. There was no way that we could drive across, and so eventually – after logs were placed across the river by many helping hands – we scrambled aboard a bus, which drove over the rocky rushing river, with water halfway up the side of the windows.

Eventually we arrive exhausted at Srinegar, and on to the boat-house Ibrahim.

Took the plane to Delhi. We had to crash land at Amritsar in the Punjab, as a small bird had damaged our plane! [It hit a propeller.]

A relief plane from Delhi collected us. Thank God we were only delayed five hours, and not days, as we had been told. We had a great welcome home, and in time for Joss to start rehearsing *The Dresser*.

By the early eighties we never had time to wonder whether we were on top of life or not – we were too busy. But looking back now it seems we at last had security, and our children were all doing well – or so we thought. At first we had been too occupied to become mixed up with the drug scene, and at that time, like many others of our age, we had known little about it, so when the young were tempted, they became easy prey. Rosemary and I thought that drugs were temptations of another century and belonged to a different world – the world of decadent poets and opium dens. By the time our eyes were opened Paul was addicted, and that's when the hard fight to break away from drugs started. It was a fight that went on for over a decade, and eventually after his hard, long struggle to clean up he seemed to have won the battle. He remained clear for many months, but then, in one weak moment of depression while staying at my father's flat in Maida Vale, he accepted heroin. He paid five pounds for it, and because he had been clear of drugs for so long the battle was lost.

By this time I was playing Falstaff in *Henry IV,* parts 1 and 2, which was the RSC's first production, at the Barbican Theatre. After some months, I also took on Barrett in *The Barretts of Wimpole Street* for television. As I was in *Henry IV* the next day, my scenes were filmed first, and as I left Television Centre that night I wondered if I should visit Paul who lived only a few minutes away. But I didn't – I thought I should reserve my energy, and travelled back home to Kingston. The following morning the doorbell rang, my daughter Penny answered it and as I was running downstairs, a policewoman calmly called out, 'Your son is dead – he died last night.'

Rosemary was doing a course in English at Kingston. I drove there to break the news. She was paralysed with shock, and it was only after we saw Paul in the crypt that she could accept the tragic truth.

During the next few days this is all that was written in Rosemary's diary.

Paul died in the early hours – overdose mistake. Melanie and children arrived. Sammy and Paolo arrived. Kirsty came over. [She was studying at the Sorbonne in Paris, and Paolo was Sammy's boyfriend.]

So dreadfully sad.

So sad.

So sad.

So sad.

Irene arrived with Ben. Dreadful sadness and pains of sorrow.

Sorrowful pains.

Sadness – Distress – Tears – All.

Paul's cremation at Putney Vale – very moving.

When Joss returned, we collected Paul's ashes and drove to Cornwall.

A few days earlier Ingrid Bergman had died, and the day before she died she phoned me to say she was returning the movie *The Little Prince*. I promised her that I would read from the book at her Memorial Service, which I did before leaving for the West Country.

This morning we met the councillor regarding making a bench for Paul. Many of his Cornish friends met us at Clontarf Church. We all had a drink at Paul's pub, and then took the ashes to the Gantry, stood on the bridge, said a prayer, Joss threw a pint of ale in the river, while we threw the flowers and then the ashes, and watched them float out to sea.

After Paul's death it was some time before Rosemary continued with her diary. We decided to leave Ravenswood and make a fresh start. Ravenswood House had too many memories. We moved directly opposite the stage door of the Royal Opera House in Floral Street, Covent Garden, in the very heart of London. Even though Melanie, Toni, Penny and Samantha had all flown the nest, we were still a very close family, and only Kirsty and Toby still stayed with us at the flat. I continued as Falstaff in *Henry IV* and then as Captain Hook in *Peter Pan* at the Barbican.

The following year was unsettled confusion for us all, and Rosemary and I went through the year in a quiet daze. Drugs were rampant, and we were so besieged by the press that I gave only one interview – to the editors of the *Observer* and the *Guardian* who visited me together. I refused to see anyone from the *Sun* 'newspaper' but this did not stop them making up a fictitious two-page 'interview' with me. I was still too much in shock to react, but Roy Hattersley wrote an article in protest for *Punch* magazine. Soon Rosemary started a link line for families affected by drugs. She started a helpline and created a point of contact between people who were confused and unable to cope – people who needed help and advice – people like us.

There is one item in Rosemary's diary which states little – but says much.

Paul's birthday. I woke up this morning feeling frightened – missing him! A dreadful day. I was so depressed that I couldn't stop crying – I feel so confused. If he'd lived he would be thirty years old today. I miss him so much, and wish I could have helped him more. Claire Bloom, Philip Roth and Anna Steiger came to dinner. Joss and I had forgotten – so we all went out.

After Paul died life took on a different tempo. The lights faded and the skies were no longer clear. Everything had less clarity, and the rhythm of life was slower. We had lived through very tough times together as we tried to help Paul in his battle with drugs, but with our oldest son gone, Rosemary and I felt lost. I concentrated on the work machine and, whatever the medium, I went straight from one job to another. After my stint at the Barbican I rushed back and forth from movie to television to TV movies, while Rosemary battled on as she helped to fight the government's inertia. We dare not stop or our strength would go – but we had each other.

And thank God we did have each other; because it was not long before Rosemary had to face another hurdle. She had her second major accident in 1988. We were in Paris where I was playing Hermann Goering in a mini-series, and one evening Rosemary and I were crossing the Avenue Kleber as we returned to the Raphael Hotel. Just before we mounted the pavement as we crossed over the avenue, some teenagers in a car drove through the red lights and knocked us down. I was unhurt but Rosemary suffered a broken femur. When the 'ambulance' (a small truck) finally arrived, Rosemary was put on its floor for twenty minutes, while the police and the youngsters sat and laughed together in front of the truck. Then we were driven to the General Hospital, and the nightmare continued. Rosemary was not given any painkillers, and when a doctor eventually arrived with a yellow duster on his head and two balloons on his chest, he said angrily, 'We are having a wonderful party – I hope you are not going to spoil it for me!' It was in the afternoon of the next day before I was able to get Rosemary to another hospital, where she was given painkillers for the first time. At four o'clock they operated, and inserted a large metal plate and three screws in her side. We later discovered that it should have been a small plastic plate.

Hell. Hell. Hell. The pain in my right leg is unbearable. I get moved from one hospital to another, and I am thankfully operated on at 4 p.m. I wake up blissfully free of pain, but I have to vomit. I can't sit up. I can't turn on my side, and the nurse has stuffed a cloth under my chin.

Kirsty, Toni and David have come over. Joss is suffering from shock, and they are all very supportive. I am still flat on my back, and it's beginning to ache. I stop all painkilling drugs, so that I know what is going on. It is one long wakeful night.

Toni came to see me before flying back. The surgeon told her I would be in bed for three months. I cried and cried. They raised my mattress, so I sat up a little. It's a good angle for me. I'm trying to communicate in French, and managing surprisingly well. My head aches, my shoulders and back are aching, and I'm desperate. Why do I have such pain?

Surprisingly last night I had my first good sleep. I feel cheered today. My physio was pleased with my muscle tone. They took my tubes out today, as I'd been draining blood. They say I'm short of red corpuscles. I need a transfusion, and Joss wanted to give me his blood. Production won't allow him to, as he is fully committed to filming this week. Kirsty is a sweet darling, and stayed nine hours with me.

Hell, Hell, Hell. I cannot take another night like last night. All night my back burnt, and ached terribly. Oh God, why hast thou forsaken me? I feel soothed after the nurse, Regina, massaged me. Roy Conelli came, and I asked him if I could stand on one leg three times a day, to relieve my back. We're going to try it. Pat, Toni's friend, came round – exhausting – she stayed two and a quarter hours!!! I managed to stand and pee. I have a urine infection. I stood this morning as well, and am now sitting on a water mattress. Toby arrived looking wonderful – lovely to see him.

I had tried to persuade the producers to allow me to have two hours off at lunchtime to give blood to Rosemary, but they thought it too risky, and refused permission. It had to be the same blood, and the hospital insisted on the transfusion being given by a member of our family. So Toby was flown over from Newcastle.

Sheer hell. I tossed and turned. The sharp, intermittent pain tearing through my left foot, and the searing heat in my shoulders, kept me awake all night. I feel drenched with pain, and exhausted with frustration. Toby and Kirsty arrived, and Toby gave three bags of blood. He stayed all day with me, and fainted twice – poor boy [Maybe the producers were right], and then took the 7.30 plane home. Kirsty helps me magnificently. She also stayed all day, and is such a treasure. Toby arrived back in Newcastle at 11.30 p.m.

I had a much better night, because I didn't lie down. I sat up, and dropped off to sleep for an hour or two. I lifted my leg up high – wonderful – and sat in a chair. I had a transfusion with Toby's blood – and then I went to the loo – some day!! Kirsty stayed with me again all day, and helped me. Sammy phoned. I slept about four hours, sitting up. I am very stiff, and there are no staff! Chaos! I had a urine test, and then a blood test. The surgeon came – but no nurses. Joss arrived at 11.30, and stayed until 7.30. Kirsty arrived with Samantha, Luca and Romeo. I sat in a chair for three hours, and feel very tired.

I slept for five hours – as usual when I woke there were no staff. Joss, Samantha, Luca, Romeo and Kirsty arrived at midday. Then Sammy and Kirsty left – Sammy for Rome – Kirsty for London. I'm excited about leaving tomorrow.

Maddening night nurse wouldn't answer my bell. Magnificent Joss arrived at 6.40 a.m. – wonderful. He helped me pee, wash and get ready. The ambulance was late, and when it did come, it was a horrific painful drive to Charles de Gaulle airport. Then long waits, while they searched me on my stretcher. They were suspicious of the new metal plate, and the three screws in my side. Eventually I was put on the plane to Heathrow. A wonderful, comfortable, friendly ambulance took me from Heathrow to Stoke Mandeville. I wept when Dr Frankel told me it was a three months' job. Joss and Melanie brought a picnic to the ward. Penny and Kirsty came.

I slept very deeply last night. Woke stiff with a headache. I am in isolation as they want to clear me of importing a virus. They have cleared me, and said I was very healthy. I'm longing to get out of bed – I am so uncomfortable.

I'm still laying here – my lip bleeding badly. All the doctors arrived. Most thought I should be up. Mr Poole, the orthopaedic surgeon, suggests I use crutches and a wheelchair. Joss came back from France at two and helped me go to the loo. He stayed with me all evening, and I did accounts and letters.

I slept for nine hours! Joss arrived. Wonderful. The nurses helped me to dress, and I went in my wheelchair to physio. Joss went back to Paris, and Toby phoned. He'd hit his head badly on the garage door.

Meanwhile I had to finish the movie in France, and so I flew back and forth whenever I had free days.

Painful spasms. Good to get out of bed, and have a shower. I'm bored waiting for Joss to get back from France, so I did his fan mail, and other mail. Joss arrived at 10.15 – how lovely. He stayed and put me to bed.

Slept well. Nurse gave me a basin to wash in – and disappeared for ever. So in frustration I got into my wheelchair, moved all the furniture, picked up my suitcase and dressed myself. Joss arrived at

10 a.m. – very uptight. Toby arrived, and Joss went to France. Toby put me to bed, and did wonders with my swollen foot.

My room is like a florist shop. Melanie arrived, and helped me pack up. She was very weepy. Joss collected me. It was difficult getting into Floral Street, but champagne and smoked salmon soon cheered me up.

The police called for Joss to move our car because Princess Margaret is going to the opera tonight. We left with all my luggage, and arrived at Toni's at 4.30. Toni has turned her sitting room into a bedroom for me, and is very kind. Joss went to Paris at five.

I slept for eight hours, thanks to Toni's massage. Melanie, Polly, Sam and Adam came for the day. I did a lot of exercises on my bed. Joss phoned three times – love him.

Joss and I had breakfast together. It's great to have him home. Penny took Joss's car to the garage and, when she got home, found she'd been robbed, poor darling. Toni and family returned. Joss worked on my feet for an hour. He's worried about my big toe. It is bent in half.

Cristina [our home help and friend] came to give me a hand. After a quick lunch, Joss and I drove to Toni's. The physio arrived, and taught me to walk with sticks.

Joss and I drove to Folkestone, and took the ferry to Boulogne, and then the motor rail through France to Milan. The painful twists of my muscles gave me a horrendous wakeful night.

We arrived at Milan at 6.30 a.m. Four people, in the adjoining compartments of our carriage, were robbed while they slept

The politician Geoffrey Howe and his wife were among them. The only reason that we were left alone was because Rosemary was having such a restless night and our door was locked, and our light was on. As we walked to the rear of the train to collect our car, we were counting ourselves lucky, when –

We found that our car had been ransacked and all the cameras, camera bag and my black suitcase were stolen. Then we drove off to Orvieto and our lovely little place by the lake. A huge rat invaded our lives tonight. Eventually Joss locked it away, but broke a lamp trying to corner it.

I stayed in all day as I'm very tired, but walked with two sticks to the end of the road. Tonight Joss took me to a wonderful restaurant, and we had white truffles, pigeon and black truffles, caviar, fruit in aspic, lovely wine and a great time.

We found two baby rats in the shower. We couldn't kill them, so Joss drove them to the next village. A very disturbed night, but I had a lovely day with Joss in Perugia. My leg is much better today, and I walked up and downstairs a lot.

Joss drove to Bracciano to collect Sammy, Luca and Romeo. Poor Sammy is so sad. Paolo has let her down again, and crashed her car. We sat out, and she told me about him. She loves him, and hates herself for it. She is exhausted.

Arrived for late lunch with John and Penny Mortimer in Tuscany, and the children swam. Penny popped off to meet someone at the station, and said she bumped into twelve different English people on the way. No wonder it is called Chianti-shire. I am so glad we stay in Umbria.

Watched the dawn come up, and then drove leisurely across Switzerland, and through the Gottard tunnel up the Autostrada to Stuttgart, and then to Metz. Difficult finding a hotel. I'm extremely tired.

Back in Covent Garden

It's our thirty-seventh wedding anniversary. I miss Joss who is in New York. It's after midnight here, but he's phoned to say he's just off to the theatre with Milton Goldman and Douglas Fairbanks, who had forgotten to do up the flies of his trousers. I do so want to walk without pain, and without sticks. I feel so fucking depressed about my left leg. I felt better after speaking to Joss. He was wonderfully uplifting.

When I returned, we drove back to Italy.

We braved a heavy snowstorm from Lyons to Geneva, to the Mont Blanc tunnel, and our car had to follow the tracks of other cars, as fog, snow and freezing conditions made it difficult. The other side of the tunnel was completely free of snow, and dry.

A lovely drive to Podere Antico – BUT! – We arrived to a hurricane wind, and freezing cold.

Sammy, Paolo, Gian Luca and Romeo arrived at noon, and we all went for lunch in Orvieto. Then we collected Toby from the station. Supper at Podere – a big family!

CHRISTMAS DAY: Luca, Romeo, Polly and Toby were up at 6.30, and opened stockings. I cooked a side of lamb with basil and rosemary, capon with herbs and pork, cauliflower and fennel for lunch and Christmas pud.

Very bad fog. The house is in sunshine, but the valley below us is under cloud, and there is fog all the way to Orvieto. Joss had a crisis – he suddenly didn't like getting old. We called at the station twice for Kirsty. She eventually arrived – looking tired and very thin. Sammy and family packed up.

After much delay Joss and I got into the car, and waved good-bye to Kirsty and Polly. Here is thick fog and it is difficult driving. I only drove for two hours. We arrived at Torino at six – Joss collapsing ill and being sick. Hell! I wish he'd flown, as we'd suggested.

1989

This year better be better than last! When we arrived at Los Angeles, Joss left his passport on the plane!

Joss's first day of filming *Lethal Weapon 2*. He arrived home at 11.45 – high after enjoyable filming.

Joss and I drove to Santa Barbara. In the evening we saw *Into the Woods*. Cleo Laine a marvellous witch – such a wonderful show.

Filming cancelled again today. Joss and I had a restful time, and a wonderful dinner at Matsuhisa. There was an earth tremor tonight. Scary!

Joss called twice from the film set. Vincent Price collected me, and took me to his beautiful home for dinner. Coral Browne looks fantastic. Joss arrived. Vincent gave me an orchid. Came home – and found heaven.

Joss had a day off filming, so we slept till 10.30. I went to the loo! Success – hooray! Then we went to Santa Monica. We had a delicious lunch at 72 Market Street with Tony Bill, who played Joss's son in Gore Vidal's play. Then, after a long walk by the Pacific, we came home. We had a lovely day – and a wonderful evening.

Filming cancelled, because unit directors, cameramen all have the flu. Joss and I had a nasty hassle with car hire, because yesterday valet parking crashed our car. Warner Brothers sorted it out – replaced the car, which they worked on, and made it like new. Joss and I drove to Chinatown, and Joss bought me nine pairs of flat, wonderful shoes for my difficult, paralysed feet, and a lovely silk jacket. Exquisite pheasant and duck supper at Chinois on Main.

Toby phoned, worried about his workshop and assignments. He doesn't feel he can continue. Joss phoned him back regarding film school. Then we had lunch at Four Oaks with Stefanie Powers.

Joss has done three big scenes today. He was whacked, so we went to the Russian Tea Room at Bel Age, and had a great meal – pancake with caviar, rabbit, venison, borsch and vodka. Toby phoned very worried about pressures.

We went to Warner Studios to see Joss's *Lethal Weapon* producer, Joel Silver. He wants to put Joss into another film in May [to play, as Joel put it, 'the worst goddamned bad guy, to end all goddamned bad guys'!].

We drove to Palm Springs, and hated the wealth and opulence of the place – all glitter and blue rinse. We stayed at Rancho Las Palmas – which was not as yuck as the Marriot, but too expensive. We decided to leave in the morning. My headache has gone.

We couldn't wait to get out of Palm Springs, so we drove off to the desert. Wonderful scenery and drive over snow-covered mountains, and arrived at La Casa del Zorro. Joss is very tired, and we drove back to Anza Borrego.

Joss has got a part in *The Hunt for Red October*. It sounds interesting. He can do it while he films *Lethal Weapon*. We drove to

Burbank to see Joel Silver, who gave Joss the completed script for the projected film in May, and then went to Santa Monica, had lunch at Market Street, and bought presents for the children. We met Michael and Pat Yorke at Morton's for dinner. Joss came home at 5.30 a.m. – the end of the movie – so he was very high. In the evening we walked up to Spago's, had dinner and walked home. It was a crowded, vulgar, chi-chi restaurant and not worth the expense.

Joss had photos taken by Helmut Newton. Greta Scacchi phoned – came to lunch with us at Bel Age. Then a cuddly day. Hayley Mills dropped in, and had wine with us till midnight.

We're off to Washington for Joss to do his last day filming for *Red October*. We had coffee on Sunset Boulevard, and then a long limousine with a table set with coffee, croissants, fruit, yoghurt, orange juice, champagne, lighted mirrors, phones, radio in back and front, video, games, etc etc etc – picked us up, and took us a few miles to the airport!!! A silly woman met us, and took us to the first-class lounge, and then we flew off to Washington, with James Earl Jones and his wife, and stayed at a huge flat at Wyndham, Bristol Hotel. We met producers, who told us that filming is cancelled tomorrow. Joss is not allowed to walk down the steps of the White House in the movie, because the US government doesn't want to take the risk of upsetting the Russians!! [Perestroika had been announced just as we left Los Angeles.]

Arrived at Heathrow. Joss and I spent a quiet day. A lovely quiet evening together – beautiful.

After lunch a wonderful time. Then Bill Nicholson and Brian Eastman came to tea – they want Joss to do *Shadowlands* in the West

End. Tonight we went to the BAFTA awards. Joss was nominated for *White Mischief*, but Michael Palin got it for *A Fish called Wanda*.

I saw *Don Carlo* at the Opera House from 10.30 – 3.30. Joss was so angry that I was out all day – but I don't care, as I enjoyed it!

Took taxi to Heathrow. Economy seats, as Joss has swapped his first class for us to be together.

I was about to play another godfather, in *The Palermo Connection*, an Italian/American co-production, which was to be shot in New York and then Sicily.

Arrived at John Kennedy airport. Took a taxi to the Algonquin – small, stuffy room on the eleventh floor. Had dinner at the Russian Tea Room. Changed apartment.

Car picked Joss and me up, and took Joss for his medical, then downtown, to the unit location. Franco Rosi, the director, was charming, and the Italian crew very friendly. Dinner tonight with Claire Bloom, Philip Roth and Jerry Epstein, a writer/director.

Joss collected for filming at 7.30. A lovely sunny day. I walked around New York. After he finished filming, Joss and I had dinner with Hal Prince at Un Deux Trois.

Arrived in Los Angeles. Taxi to Le Dufy, where they'd booked us a fabulous suite – and a huge arrangement of flowers from Glynis Johns.

Joss woke me up, beautifully, at ten o'clock. Walked up to Sunset, and hired a car. After lunch we went to Warner's and Joss had a talk with Joel Silver about the prospective film. Brian Eastman phoned twice today about *Shadowlands*.

Great decisions to be made. Joss phoned Francesca Annis at 2 a.m. regarding her doing *Shadowlands*.

Drove to Santa Monica, and had tea at Jean Simmons' house. Lots of helpers.

Jean's ex-husband Richard Brooks was there. Jean's hair is grey now.

After flying to Sicily.

We arrived at Palermo. All the roads were flooded on the way to Mondello. Wonderful dinner at Chamade.

We drove to Castellamare, and met Vito, Nino and Francesca at the bar. They had seen *The Sicilian*, and we were doubtful what their reaction would be, because no one here ever uses the word 'mafia'. However the wives had brocaded cushions for me, as presents, and we were given a great welcome. Leonardo said that Joss was very good as Don Diego, because he ate spaghetti like his grandfather. We had lunch with them, and then went off to see Diego.

Woke early, and saw the sun come up over the sea. Joss phoned Michael Anderson regarding *Shadowlands*. He has decided not to do the play. We walked to the village, and had fish for lunch. Back at Mondello Palace we had a siesta. I had a powerful dream about Paul. It upset me. All night filming for Joss.

Happy day. Joss woke up laughing at his dream. We had supper at Chamade. They had three first Communion dinner parties. Mimi Rogers, and her young husband, Tom Cruise, and men from Paramount were there.

Mimi Rogers and James Belushi were the two American leads in our movie – the three character men were Vittorio Gassman from Italy, Philippe Noiret from France and me from England. When the movie opened, one French critic said it was like watching two different movies.

The plane to Rome. The flight okay – but the French youth next to me was horrid – he kept feeling me, and I was so shaken.

Back to Podere. Lovely cuddles. I feel very happy – on cloud nine. Joss and I are having wonderful second honeymoon – only better.

Back in Sicily we have a huge room in this amazing old monastery at St Marie di Bosco – very overwhelming. A huge double bed. Joss and I had lovely supper in the garden at Bisaquino, and I walked there without a stick!

Leg troublesome all night. Joss is filming his big scene here. It seems to be going well. We all had dinner together, with Baron Inglese and his wife Margarita.

Lovely peaceful sleep. The Baron brought us coffee. I spent the day reading Graham Greene's *Means of Escape*. Joss finished filming at eight. There was a nasty racist scene in the car. Baron Inglese would not allow two men from Ghana to sit in the back of the car with Joss. Very embarrassing. At dinner Joss talked about Don Diego Plia – the family said the mafia were very strong and draining – especially at Corleone.

Lovely to arrive at Podere, but I had ghastly pains in stomach all night. 5 a.m. – success. We collected Greta Scacchi to spend the day with us. She was lovely, and much help. Joss had a shocking phone call from Michael – Ray McNally died. How dreadful. They want

Joss to take over his part in a TV film. We are so sorry about Ray – his poor wife.

The script for *First and Last* didn't arrive – so the BBC sent over a messenger with the script – he never got here, and eventually Michael Frayn, the writer, and Alan Dosser, the director, came over, and are staying with us. Joss picked them up in Orvieto, and once they arrived he relaxed.

Joss has agreed to do the piece. Alan took Michael, Joss and I to Orso's for lunch, and they left for London. Joss and I picked Irene and Ben up from the pool, and we had dinner here. I did ironing, then packed and sorted out.

Back in Covent Garden, we found that while we were away, Paolo and his friends had used our flat, and left blood over our bed and the blankets. I've no idea I was so hurt. Samantha is thirty-six weeks pregnant, and in a depressed state. Joss is overreacting.

First and Last was the story of a simple man who, despite illness, is determined to walk the length of Britain, from Land's End to John O'Groats. Ray McNally had started filming the walk at Land's End, but by the time he reached the West Country, he suffered a recurring heart problem and collapsed and died. After their working with Ray I thought it would be difficult for the crew to go through the early filming again, and so I suggested we continued onward, and then work our way up to John O'Groats. This we did, and then flew back to Land's End, and re-shot the first scenes. But Rosemary's diary continues before that when we were halfway up the country.

Travel to Burnley. The unit car took us in pouring rain on top of the moors. Had lunch in Joss's Winnebago – it's too wet to film. Joss has very bad cough and lungs.

Joss is feeling better, and started filming in a remote farmhouse at 3.30 p.m. He was drenched, and fell in a bog, until 3.30 a.m.

I woke at ten, but lay still till midday, so that Joss could sleep. Joss went filming. Dinner with Michael Frayn and Claire Tomalin.

Walked around Penzance. Joss collected me and took me off to the set. It was great fun. Joss had to do a scene on a public telephone in the square, but a brass band was playing outside – so they used it in the movie. Sammy is getting a few pains. I hope she's okay, so I shall return to London tomorrow.

Sammy had one-hour labour. We are all so happy for her. Maria Paola arrived at 5.30 a.m. She is eight pounds with black hair. This evening Toby rang. Thank God he did wonderfully well. He is now qualified as a pilot – has a badge – and he is so happy. Joss finishes *First and Last* on Sunday. I miss him.

MIGRAINE woke me at 4 a.m. Tim Dalton came to meet Kirsty. Poor Toby phoned to say he'd fallen down concealed steps, and cut his head, and had stitches. Penny and I flew to Frankfurt to be with him.

Penny washed blood out of Toby's hair, and examined his spine. We had lunch in Heidelberg. We then heard that Cath [Rosemary's sister] has skin cancer.

Kirsty came, and had some supper. She said Samantha has had a bad car crash, but was not hurt – thank heaven.

We were invited to the first night of *Shadowlands*. Nigel Hawthorne started well, but couldn't sustain it, and Jane Lapotaire way over the top. Francesca Annis, Patrick Wiseman, Michael Frayn, Claire Tomalin and Kirsty, who were all at the theatre, came to dinner. Great fun. Bed 4.30.

We spent the morning at Podere Antico. The sun kissed the yellow vines, made them gold, and we entered heaven.

Hurrah. Toby rang to say he's got his job in Boston. I'm walking well, without stick or limp! Private press showing of *First and Last*, at BAFTA. It is wonderful. Then a lovely day alone with Joss.

News of Romania – shocking! [This must refer to riots in Romania as the country had achieved independence after the collapse of the Soviet Union.] Kirsty, Joss and I went to Weekend TV. Joss presented prize for best actress. It was a boring evening, but great when we got home.

CHRISTMAS DAY: Kirsty came into our room with cups of tea, and her stocking – then Penny and Daniel with theirs. We had breakfast and then Sammy, Paolo, Luca, Romeo, Maria Paola, Melanie, Polly, Sam, Adam, Toni, David, Tom, Emily and Izzie all arrived, and we did presents. We had lunch, and all went well. Joss and I washed up for four hours. A very happy day.

THE NINETIES

The nineties were very full – packed with non-stop action and activity. Here are just a few excerpts from the diary.

I feel fragile. We went to Michael Frayn and Claire Tomalin, for a New Year drink – but only had a sip of champagne. Oh, it's migraine, all right – I'm so cross, as I never had a drink. It must be stress, or after a late night.

Toby phoned to wish me a happy birthday. Sammy and Romeo came, and then Penny, Kirsty, Melanie and Toni. A lovely day. I feel much loved. Toby phoned again this evening – a hurricane has blown off his garage roof.

Woke up with my pillow and sheet covered in blood. My lip is bleeding badly. Dr Lee sent me to UCH. After waiting three and a half hours the surgeon gave me a local anaesthetic, and froze my lip. Very painful – the lip has swollen up badly, and it is impossible to eat or drink. I eventually had some ice cream, and gave Joss a steak. Did washes, and washed out the blood. Had a cuddle with Joss until 9 p.m. – then I had mashed banana and cream, and managed some water through a straw.

I woke up with a big, black blood blister on my lip. During the day it opened, and left a raw patch, the size of a halfpenny. It smarted and burned, and my lip keeps weeping pinkish water. Couldn't eat anything but mashed banana and ice cream, and it's impossible to drink. Heard Joss's lines for Darrow. [I was about to play Clarence Darrow in the stage play *Never the Sinner*.] Then we had a cuddle.

Joss took me to UCH. Doctor said my lip was healing, but will take about two weeks. I managed two glasses of champagne, lobster and coffee ice cream. Joss worked hard on lines, and I helped. A hundred miles per hour wind today – many people killed.

NELSON MANDELA FREED TODAY after twenty-seven years in prison. Wonderful

Woke up with bad MIGRAINE. Car collected us, and we went to Grosvenor House for the BAFTA awards. It was a long, tiresome evening. John Thaw got the best actor! But he was in a series – this was for a play!! Others nominated – Joss, John Gielgud and Alfred Molina. All rubbish.

Saw *Never the Sinner*. Joss's performance as Clarence Darrow has changed?! Worrying.

Penny and I went to see *Never the Sinner*. Joss's performance was too emotional. [She was right of course, the audience will sense emotion if the actor conceals it.]

Joss slept till 11.30. I gave him breakfast in bed. It's his first night of *Never the Sinner*. I did not go to the performance because I felt I was a jinx – but I joined him in the dressing room. Melanie, Michael Radford, Jennie and Malcolm Cook came to dinner with us at Joe Allen's.

MIGRAINE. What started off as a quiet protest against the poll tax turned ugly when the Black Flag brigade started looting, setting fire to cars, breaking windows and then violence taking over – from Trafalgar Square to Long Acre.

I went to see Joss in *Never the Sinner* tonight. His performance is much better. Back to champagne and a cuddly evening.

A limousine took us to the theatre, Joss put on his Clarence Darrow costume, and we were escorted by police cars to the Royal Premiere of *The Hunt for Red October*, just in time for Joss to join Sean Connery and John McTiernan [the director] in the line up, and at the precise moment that Charles and Diana arrived. As everyone was in full evening dress and tails, shabby Clarence Darrow looked slightly out of place. After the line up, we all went in to see the film and Joss was whizzed back to the theatre again escorted by police cars. The curtain-up was held until he arrived. After the show he put on evening dress, and joined me at the Paramount party at the war museum. It was a lovely day.

Had a horrid dream, and woke up in terror at 4 a.m. I dreamt that Joss had been wrapped in a suitcase, and was going to be thrown into the sea. I sent a man to stop them – he ran as quickly as he could – and then I woke up. A journalist came to interview us. She was clueless, and Joss told her to go away and do her research!

Michael Frayn, Claire Tomalin, Penny and John Mortimer, Pauline and John Alderton, Robert Bolt, Sarah Miles and Kirsty, all came to dinner. They left at 3 a.m. A very good party.

Last performances of *Never the Sinner*. Started packing for Africa.

I was about to film in *The Sheltering Desert*, and so Rosemary and I flew to Namibia in southern Africa, and the Skeleton Coast.

Last night I had vivid dreams of the fire – horrid. I woke with a very bad MIGRAINE. Arrived at Windhoek – changed airport, and took a fourteen-seater plane to Swakopmund. The director and line producer met us, and we came to the Hansa Hotel. After lunch we had a rest and then dinner with the boys Joss has to chase in the movie – Jason Connery and Rupert Graves.

I woke up with a bad headache. We drove to Walvis Bay – a real dorp! Had a chop lunch, and then drove towards Karibib. After thirty kilometres there was a sign with the word 'tree' written on it, and about two hundred metres further, there was indeed a small tree, beneath an umbrella, placed there to protect it. Forty kilometres later we turned around and came back. Such long distances between any forms of habitation in this desolate desert. We stopped at an oasis for water. An exceedingly hot day.

Lovely dinner at Eric's restaurant with Jason and Rupert. Huge, lovely oysters – Joss had eleven! Joss phoned Toby at Podere. Hooray. All's well.

After breakfast I walked around this totally deserted town. There are very few shops here, but one shop sells nothing but Nazi uniforms – apparently on Hitler's birthday it is emptied!!

We went on a safari trip into the desert. We drove on the sand through the dunes to Goancontis, and on to see a fantastic vista 'moon landscape'. We drove down between the canyons, saw the lava and came upon an oasis right down in the middle of the ancient volcano.

Joss came back for lunch in his butch uniform and boots. When the manager saw him he was apoplectic with excitement, and screamed, 'That is the way it should be – that is the way!!!' Joss and I stared in amazement. Later we discovered that during the war he was in charge of propaganda for Joseph Goebbels.

We left Swakopmund at 1.30, and Robert drove us to Windhoek. We are staying in the Kalahari Sands Hotel – very posh!!

We left by Namibia Airways to Johannesburg. Because of apartheid, we chose to wait in Transit for our tickets, and put our luggage into lockers, and waited in the Capricorn Club for our flight to Malawi. The Air Malawi plane is the pits, and we were glad to arrive safely in Lilongwe. We hired a car, and drove to the Capitol Hotel. We had a great welcome. My Chinyanga is coming back.

Breakfast of pawpaw, toast and jam. Then we drove to the 'town'. On the way Joss took photographs of schoolchildren being taught under the trees. The children gave him a tumultuous reception. They are always so welcoming and giving. Back at the hotel Joss ordered fix and insema, and hated it. We read. Slept well.

It's a hot day. Packed up and off we went. Stopped for chicken curry at the Kudya Discovery Hotel, and watched the hippos snorting away. We drove in intense heat to Club Makalola, and have been given a wonderful rondavel, with a double bed, overlooking the lake. We unpacked, changed, had a drink and delicious grilled chambo. We are now under a large, generous mosquito net.

Joss and I drove to Cape Maclear. It was a fabulous drive, over an impossible road, through dense jungle. Baboons kept racing in front of the car. We called in at a completely changed and dismal Monkey Bay – so sad. Even the sand and the palm trees are gone.

After breakfast we set off for Blantyre. There is no public transport, so on the way we gave two women, a man and a baby a lift, and then took a sick man to Zomba Hospital, and a lady to Limbe – which is quite unrecognisable – such a mess. We checked into Ryall's, and have suite number eight, because of the double bed. Joss drove me up Sunnyside. I couldn't find my old house, or even recognise the roads. We had dinner in Ryall's Grillroom. Then sat on our balcony, and felt *so* glad we were leaving for Zomba tomorrow

We drove to Zomba plateau, and have a lovely room in Kuchawe Inn. At Zomba township we picked up a husband, wife and sick child, and gave them a lift to Malamula Hospital. Back in Blantyre we went to Frank Johnson's bookshop, and were delighted to see he has a copy of my grandmother's book. [Rosemary's grandmother had written a small book about her early days in Africa.] I agreed to sponsor five thousand kwachas [local money] to polio, and publicise the book. Then we drove to Mlanje, and saw our old Nachilonga bungalow. Very sad – all the trees have been cut down. No more tea fields – it's now a coffee plantation.

Hooray we've made it to Johannesburg – in transit again at the Capricorn Club.

Very comfortable flight back on British Airways – we arrived at 6.30 a.m. I'm so pleased to be home. I phoned Penny at Toni's. She'd had her baby on the fourteenth, all by herself, in the hall of her house. When her contractions started she was alone, so she called the ambulance, and waited – but the ambulance didn't arrive, so she started down the stairs, but her waters broke, and she didn't have time to get to the phone. She had the baby on the floor – a boy, seven pounds. She managed to open the front door a little, but couldn't move, and the ambulance didn't arrive for another half hour. One ambulance man had to squeeze through the door, and pull Penny back by the legs, so that the second man could get in to help, and get her to the hospital. After lunch, Joss and I had an hour's sleep, and then Melanie brought Penny and Daniel, and baby Inigo, back to stay. All the family came. It was lovely to see them.

Another chunk of the diary is missing. After recording *Never the Sinner* for television, I joined Rosemary and Kirsty in Italy for two or three weeks, and when we returned, Rosemary and I went to visit Toby in Boston, before flying to Los Angeles. We were still there, staying at Le Dufy, when the diary continues.

We went to lunch with Susan Smith [my new Los Angeles agent], and then to Chinatown to buy flat shoes – because my stupid feet are paralysed – the only ones I can wear. A possum was in the hotel when we got back. Joss chased it along the corridors, but was careful not to upset it, because he thought it was a skunk.

Worrying news about Baghdad – could be trouble.

Arrived at Gatwick at 2.15 p.m. Quick lunch, a half-hour kip and then found an invitation from Steve Sondheim, to see the London opening of *Into the Woods* this evening!! In spite of jet lag we really enjoyed the production. A horrid set but the lyrics and music wonderful. We have now seen three versions.

I heard Joss's *Murder of Quality* script right through. Irwin Kershner and Judy came in before they went to the theatre. My left leg keeps going into spasm, and is sore. Anthony Hopkins has dropped out of *Murder of Quality*. They asked Paul Scofield, but he doesn't feel it is right for him, so now they've got Denholm to do it.

Mrs Thatcher was made to resign this morning. Kirsty, Joss and I had drinks with David Cornwall and Jane. Then we came home and I cooked mushrooms on toast. Kandy arrived. Penny, Daniel, Inigo, Sammy, Paolo, Luca, Romeo, Maria Paola and Kirsty to supper of roast beef.

1991

English and American soldiers are waiting in the desert to kill the Iraqis that have invaded Kuwait. Will Saddam Hussein retreat, or will war start at midnight today, as threatened? Bed 1.30. Still no war.

Toby arrived. War had begun, and was two hours old. American, English and Saudi planes had bombed Baghdad military bases in Iraq.

Kirsty came. She was very hyped up about the war. Joss and I watched the depressing news, and went to bed.

Woke up bright at 5 a.m. Got up and watched the Gulf War report on TV. Joss came up, and brought me down to bed, and we cuddled, and slept till 8.30. We went to Mr Catterall, and I had two X-rays. He said my bone is healthy – but causing chaos with my muscles. It depends on my pain, whether I should have the metal removed or not. [This was the large metal plate which was put in after she was knocked down in France.]

Met Ron and we got to the hospital at two. Poor Barb looks so ill. She has cancer of the sacrum, and is having radiotherapy. We stayed till half past four. In the Gulf oil is seeping into the sea, and the sea is polluted. Poor cormorants killed by the oil. The Gulf War is looking bad. We drove to Anna Ford's home for dinner with Anna, Michael Palin and Bamber Gasgoine.

Joss was on the phone *all* day worried about buying a house for the family.

We drove to Stowford Grange. Wonderful position, but derelict, and would cost half a million to re-do. Then I slipped on the ice, and fell and hurt my right knee and left shin – I feel shaken. *Murder of Quality* is over. We've seen so many houses, and we return to London tomorrow, and we only have time to see one more before we leave – either the one very near here by Sherborne, or the one miles and miles away, in Clovelly in North Devon. So of course Joss and I drove across the moors, through rain, fog and sleet, to see the one in Devon. Lovely house, position and grounds, with great possibilities. Back to London.

Joss took me to oral dental hospital about my lip. The consultant wouldn't touch it, and is going to get a Chinese doctor to do it.

After breakfast Joss helped me to Macklin Street – the roads and pavements were so slippery I couldn't balance. Then I met with Jon Snow and Peter Canter regarding the homeless.

We woke up this morning worrying about whether Melanie would be lonely out in North Devon. We thought it would be silly to get a house. The family would only occasionally be able to join her. Joss had a cardiac test. Melanie phoned and put our mind at rest, as she is desperate to move. The nightingales sang through the night.

Saddam Hussein has till 5 p.m. to stop the war and get out of Kuwait. Melanie gave in notice to her school, ready to move west to Clovelly. Joss took Ben and Luca to *Into the Woods*, before he flies off to Los Angeles tomorrow. The nightingales are singing again tonight.

MIGRAINE. Joss phoned from Los Angeles. He had been to see Ron Howard – who he had seen before in Ireland. This time Tom Cruise and Nicole Kidman joined them, and Joss is going to play Tom Cruise's father in *The Irish Story* [later filmed as *Far and Away*]. They are shooting in Ireland and Montana, so Joss will have to change his shooting dates in *Ashenden* in Budapest. PEACE in the Gulf. I listened to the radio all night, and slept only for two hours.

I woke up every half hour – so excited about seeing Joss today. I'm trembling with anticipation. Joss arrived. We celebrated with a bottle of champagne.

Joss heard the bad news today that he had not got the part in *The Irish Story*. Of course, none of the US production team had the nerve to contact him with an explanation, even after all the rearranging of schedules. They are such wimps – and so pathetic. Because of this he has to go to Budapest at weekends as his shooting dates for *Ashenden* have been fixed to help him out. We are all very sorry for him. Film business is so cruel, and Hollywood so vulgar and phoney.

Sammy had a baby son. I visited her. She looks lovely, and the baby is gorgeous. Joss phoned. Graham Greene died today in Switzerland – eighty-seven years old.

Joss did charity voice-over for the poor Kurds, who are being killed by Saddam Hussein.

As the Royals are coming to the Opera House, the police came and wanted to borrow our balconies for security. Kirsty called on her way to France to do some work with Anthony Baring. [Kirsty was working for Peters, Fraser and Dunlop, the theatrical and literary agents, and Anthony Baring also worked there.] Hope it goes well for her.

Joss went to the BBC to record a TV spot with Neil Kinnock. He got back at half past ten. I had opened a bottle of champagne, as I was fed up waiting. Joss came in much hyped up. We are very short of money now, and both of us are worried.

We thought that Kirsty and Anthony were in France, but they arrived back and told us they got married in Gibraltar yesterday. Joss opened champagne for them, and then Toni came round, with flowers and chocolate, and more champagne. Joss and I are thrilled – Kirsty and Ant are so sweet together. I pray they have happiness.

Bad news – Joss believes he has lost the part of Onassis, because the studio executives think he is too tall. Police marksmen were on our balconies for three hours because John Major and Gorbachef were at the opera.

I'm so worried for Joss, regarding his playing Onassis. The director and the producer want him, but the TV company don't. Please God, let him get the part.

In the middle of the night Susan Smith phoned to say Joss was fixed for Onassis. Thank you, God.

Sammy came over very upset. Paolo was on ice and crack and heroin, and she is desperate. I had a talk with Paolo – I want him to go to Broadreach. It is terribly sad.

I had a sleep on the plane – woke up feeling nauseous, and with a bad head. Many people were very ill – something wrong with the air-conditioning when it was turned on. I was sick every twenty minutes until we landed. We took a small plane from Washington to Richmond, Virginia, and were met by the director Larry Peerce and the producer Lester Persky.

As usual a 5 a.m. call. After shooting the last day at sea on the yacht Joss gave me my anniversary present – a fabulous pair of emerald and diamond earrings. They are exquisite, but had been set upside down. We rushed to Main Street, and the Greek jeweller reset the earrings, and took Larry and Madeleine [Larry's wife], and Joss and me, out to a Greek meal. Then we went to the Edgewater for drinks, and came home at night by dinghy. Fun evening.

Succinct and laid-back as always, this is what Rosemary simply tosses aside as a 'fun evening'. After our Greek meal we suddenly remembered that Larry, Madeleine, Rosemary and I had promised the multi-millionaire owner's 'girlfriend' (the owner was abroad) that we would go back to the Edgewater for a farewell drink. The Edgewater was Onassis's yacht in the movie. It was huge and luxurious – much bigger than the original, which was still moored of the Greek coast. So back we went. We were all still wearing tatty jeans and T-shirts, and when we arrived at the vessel, we were greeted at the gang plank by the girlfriend – and her girlfriend – both dressed in gold lamé, and the crew in immaculate white uniforms. The four of us were piped on board, and offered lashings of champagne, caviar, truffles and smoked salmon, and we had only just had a large Greek meal. However as we were the only guests, we did our best, and waited for Roma Downie, who played Jackie, and Lester Persky, the producer. When they finally arrived, we thought that after a few minutes we would make our farewells, and slip away. So we relaxed and had another drink. Then – we suddenly realised to our horror – we had weighed anchor, and were out at sea. I was filming at dawn and there was no way that we could return for several hours. Eventually I persuaded one of the crew to help, so I whispered to Larry, 'Let's go'. He thought I had gone mad.

'What do you mean, let's go? We're in the middle of the fucking ocean!!' However they followed. The crew member had attached a small rubber dinghy to the yacht in the water below. Rosemary jumped. Madeleine jumped. Larry landed on top of Rosemary, I followed and, crouching together in the little dinghy, we spent the next half hour in a flood of laughter as we were guided back to the mainland. As Rosemary says it was – a 'fun evening'.

Joss woke me beautifully at 6 a.m. Our fortieth anniversary. Toby has arranged a wonderful surprise. At 8.30 a.m. a huge tray arrived with magnificent orchids, flowers, plates of pawpaw, melons, fruit, coffee and croissants. We are very touched. Plane to Washington was re-routed, because Hurricane Bob is on the way tonight at Virginia, Norfolk. So a lovely room at the Ritz Carlton.

We watched TV. Russia in trouble – a coup in Moscow. Hurricane Bob is headed for Boston. We are flying off tomorrow.

Melanie met us at Tiverton. Robert [Rosemary's brother] died in Sydney at 6 p.m. God Bless him.

A mucky day. I couldn't concentrate on anything. I heard Joss's lines. I went to the post office to post parcels. The man was horrid, and told me to hurry up and move quicker. If he had any idea! I did poetry with Joss all evening.

Kirsty called, looking beautiful. She'd been out with John McCarthy – the man who had been jailed for five years by Iraq.

We caught the plane to Nice – arriving at the Negresco Hotel at midday. It is a magnificent place. We had a sleep. Wonderful. Then Toby phoned. He has had big disappointments in Boston – he broke up with Nanette, and has lost his wallet. Then we went downstairs and had tea with Anouk Aimée, who plays Joss's wife. She seems very pleasant.

Joss is filming here in Nice. I've had very horrid dreams during the last few nights. It is nine years ago today that Paul died. I wish he were here. I miss him so – so, so very, very much. Joss came in and cheered me up. We had a glass of champagne, and then walked to lovely Marianne, and had a wonderful meal of grilled sardines and mesclun (a great salad), and loads of rosé. A wonderful evening.

MIGRAINE. Back of head – agony and stiff. I feel I have a metal weight pressing on my forehead. We watched the shocking hearing from Washington, on CNN. How despicable is Anita Hill, smearing Clarence Thomas like that. We tore off to a demonstration outside the theatre. Joss got a huge round of applause for turning up. [I can't remember what the demonstration was about.]

We caught the train to Menton. In 1952 we had planned a trip here. It was a dream of ours to have a holiday abroad. We were so poor then – it would have cost nine pounds return from London. In those days it was always proved too much for us to even consider! At last we've made it. We went to the Chanticleer and had a most exquisite meal. It was fantastic. A wonderful, happy, romantic day.

It is lovely to be back home in London. A very busy day. Sammy called, and we had coffee and a chat. Sammy came with Romeo, Paola and Nico. Kirsty and Ant came for tea and cake. Joss rang British Airways. Cheap flights stop tomorrow, so we decided to fly to Italy.

We went to Montecchio and bought some food – had lunch in the Grotto – then back to Podere, and Joss made a fire. It is so romantic, Joss and I being in the little house on the hill. We are so happy, and so much in love.

Back in England.

Samantha phoned and said Paolo had come home, and she was getting guidance for him – good girl. Ron has just phoned to say Barb [my sister] is dying. Joss is very upset.

Sammy arrived. She is having guidance about access for Paolo to see Luca and the children. Joss and I took a taxi to Westminster for Peggy Ashcroft's memorial. It was a huge, pompous affair. Peter Hall gave a very good talk.

Ron rang to say Joss's sister was slipping away. I'm so very sorry for them all, and for Joss. Ron [Barbara's husband] rang at five to say Barb had died. It is so sad for the poor family.

Sammy and the four kids arrived. Paolo in trouble with drugs again. Kirsty and Ant arrived. Kirsty is pregnant – goodie.

Melanie has gone to London with Polly. Adam had breakfast with us. We spent the morning in Bideford. I cooked kidneys and bacon. And then – on the floor in front of the fire – Joss and I reached Illyria. Got up and had a cup of tea. Then Joss did carpentry. Adam stayed the night with his friend. Toby phoned. He is off to Manchester to get a plane abroad.

Toby phoned. He had got to the airport, and decided not to go!

I am very depressed today. Toby has a hangover, and I'm worried about him. He now says he is off to the Lake District. He cannot make up his mind what to do next. I fear for him.

Melanie and I went to Holy Communion at Clovelly church –

only Mary Rous, Melanie and I were there. It was very spiritual. Toby sounds much happier today – I prayed for him, and Joss, and Paul, and everyone. Joss is in London, and had to read a story for the BBC, and turn on the lights in Covent Garden.

I spent all afternoon ironing the children's clothes and sheets. In the evening Melanie and Polly went carol singing. Joss phoned from London in a panic. He had caught the 3.40 train to Birmingham, but because of major bomb threats, the train didn't arrive till 10 p.m.! He'd missed the concert – and his poetry readings were half the show. So Simon Rattle and the Birmingham Symphony Orchestra had to fill in the other half as well.

CHRISTMAS DAY: Joss and I got up at 8.30, and had breakfast with 101 two-year-olds!! Did presents in the basement, which is transformed into a wonderful studio. All the children very excited. Delicious lunch. Presents all afternoon. Joss and I had a kip.

Irene and Ben, Toni and David, Tom, Emily, Abbi and baby Izzie all arrived. Cooked two legs of lamb. Polly and I washed up, and Joss and I went to bed at 3 a.m.

Joss drove to Tiverton, and picked up Anne, Billy, Ron, Michael, Ann-Marie, Brendan, Robert, Daniel, Sean and Rebecca. [My sister Barbara's family.] I cooked ten pounds of roast beef. We had lunch until about 4 p.m., and tea in the basement, and then all played bowls.

1992

This was a year of non-stop activity so I have only included a few typical examples, to show how Rosemary spent her days.

The day started wonderfully. It was exquisite. We had a cuddly day. Joss off to do an interview with Michael Parkinson, and then one with Terry Wogan. We had Dulcie Grey, Michael Denison and David Kernan to dinner.

Joss left for Prague. Mary Treaty phoned about those working for New Horizon – some becoming too political, and losing touch with actually helping the homeless.

Last night my head was so bad, I was scared to go to bed. I walked to the Strand and got the bus to Barnes. Diane Lasselle [the faith healer] was wonderful, and so helpful. She gave me a spiritual healing, which made me breathless, and as I walked out of her house, the sun was shining, and I felt thirty years younger. Toby rang – he'd been mugged.

Joss arrived. I bought flowers for his homecoming. We had lovely caviar for supper, and then a kip, and a beautiful wake up. Joss's back is bad, but we've had a great day together.

It's New Horizon day. The sixth meeting with Jon Snow at the flat – gave the sack to eight people! Joss and I had another lovely evening together.

We flew over Greenland to Minneapolis.

When Joss returned, from *The Mighty Ducks* set, he went to the office. They want him to go to LA. We packed, had lunch at Yvette's and caught the 6.15 plane. A long limousine fetched us from the airport, and brought us to Le Dufy.

Had lunch with Stefanie Powers, and then went to see *Once Upon a Crime*, and walked out of it – it is dreadful. We didn't even wait for Joss to appear.

Another huge black-windowed limo collected us and drove us to airport. We arrived back at Minneapolis. Dinner at Goodfellows.

Joss collected at 6 a.m. Then I listened to the news. SOUTH AFRICA VOTED TO END APARTHEID AND GIVE BLACKS THE VOTE. Fantastic. De Klerk said, 'Today is the real birthday of South Africa'. However in America Bush is winning again!!

Back in England.

We had just arrived home when Sammy came round, and she told us she had decided to take the children out of school, and go to Italy. Joss pleaded with her – oh – with Paolo too!!! It's a dreadful, stressful period. Joss is desperate.

We woke up to discover that the Conservatives are still in. Neil Kinnock lost, and John Major is now Prime Minister! Big Bombings in London – many injured: IRA.

Off to Italy.

Arrived in Rome. We got the train to Orvieto. I walked down the hill and couldn't get up. I had to crawl.

Very peaceful day. Joss and I drove to Todi, and then had a lovely lunch in Torgiano at Tre Vassilli. I lit three candles in the little church for Joss, Toby and Kirsty. Came back and packed, and wrote off and arranged kwachas for Baxton and Frank in Malawi. There are riots in LA. Four police officers beat up a black motorist, and the jury let them off!!

Ray Taylor and Sue, and their children Clare and Peter, arrived here, in Clovelly, from Kingston.

Ray, or 'Mr Sparkle', as he was known, cleaned our windows for sixteen years when we lived in Kingston on Thames at Ravenswood House. When we moved to Covent Garden, in the heart of London, we contacted Ray, and he agreed to come for a day and do our windows there. So over another sixteen years, he would always come on a Sunday, while his wife Sue had fun shopping on the piazza. Then when we moved hundreds of miles away we thought 'Why not?', and Ray and Sue thought, 'why not?' So they did. They would arrive with Ray's ladder on top of their white van, and stay here a few days.

Ray cleaned our windows this afternoon, and we all drove to Hartland this evening.

Ray cleaned the inside of the windows, and then Joss took eleven of us to the Coach and Horses. We went over Joss's lines, had fun, and after he'd finished doing the garden, Charlie [Charley Littlejohn – our gardener] had tea with us on the lawn.

We flew to California where I was playing the 'bad guy' in *Nowhere to Run* with Jean Claude Van Damme and Rosanna Arquette.

MIGRAINE. It was a long flight to San Francisco. Jackie met us, and drove us to Columbia Pictures. We've been up twenty-four hours.

Walked to the *Nowhere to Run* office, and met Robert Harmon, the director.

Toby phoned with his university results. I'm so pleased he's passed. He now has a BA Honours 2. What a relief. Joss and I had a lovely day.

We drove to Sonoma, to Marcia and Tommy Smothers' lovely home in Tommy's vineyard. We drank their wine, and we had a delicious supper of corn and chilli fish.

We left at 9.15 a.m., as Tommy had a show with his brother in Reno. We drove up to Mendocino, through the redwoods, and by the sea. We found a fabulous barn flat at the Stanford Inn, by the sea.

We drove to Mendocino, which was crowded, because there was a very American, very colourful, very enthusiastic 'parade'. Came home to the Stanford, had lunch, a Jacuzzi, and had a walk through the deer and the llamas. I heard Joss's lines, and then Joss did my feet.

Got up at 5.30, and had a lovely drive along the coast to San Francisco, and then got the plane to LA.

Flew to London. Kirsty arrived looking wonderful. Her baby

is due in six weeks. Sammy phoned three times. She is leaving Bracciano.

Joss didn't sleep, and I had horrid dreams of snakes. We arrived at the Rectory.

Kirsty had a baby girl last night. A difficult forceps birth. She went home but was re-admitted at 8 p.m. We visited Kirsty in hospital. I collapsed with migraine this evening, but then a lovely, lovely night, together with Joss.

There was a big accident at Covent Garden tube station – a body under the train. Messy day altogether – a bomb scare in the piazza. I bought ballet shoes for evenings. I am so limited with what I can wear – stupid, paralysed feet.

We caught the train to Tiverton, and found our car window had been smashed in – and the police there. Melanie, Polly and I went to midnight mass.

1993

Once more Rosemary and I were about to leave our home, and we would be away for several months. Little did we know that Rosemary would have to cope with yet another crisis. I was about to play a priest with a wooden leg in *Georgino*, a movie with a young French producer/director and his girlfriend, a young French pop star, playing the leading role. Although we did not know it at the time, they had just split up and the movie was his farewell gift to her. The film would take several months to make. Eventually it would have its premiere in Paris, and close two days later.

Up early for the flight to Prague.

After lunch and a walk, we took another plane to Bratislava, and on to Poprad. Met by the film crew, and then to the Satel Hotel where we had dinner with the director.

We were driven out to the Tatras, to location. Very snowy up in the mountains, but the sun was shining. Joss's wooden leg was fitted this evening.

Bad night in our most uncomfortable bed. Glad to get up, but

I have migraine through my right eye. Joss hired a car, and we drove to Strbske Pieso, and we stayed at the Patria Hotel, with a wonderful view overlooking icy frozen, lake. We tried to walk to a restaurant this evening, but it was solid, frozen ice, and we slipped – so we returned to the hotel and had champagne.

We drove to Poland, crossed the border through the Tetras, at Lysa Polana, and on to Zakopne. Fascinating town. Back in Poprad, all the snow is melting – and the film crew all depressed. We had a disgusting meal at the bistro.

Joss and I watched 2,000 people walk into the church opposite, and many, many more waited outside, and listened to the service on loudspeakers. Joss and I walked for one and a half hours around Poprad, and then Louise Fletcher and Joss worked on the script.

Joss is not filming today. We had a long political talk at the travel office. There is great unrest in Czechoslovakia. Splitting the country will leave Slovakia with nothing.

Joss went to the office to sort out dates. They said he has to be here a week longer – so he loses his next film, *Six Degrees of Separation*.

Melanie has been worrying Toby all week. He is getting fed up. It seems to me that you can't lead your life for your children – if you do, they can't live life for themselves. If things are right for you, there is a better chance things will be right for them.

Making this film is some kind of hell. For the third day we are stuck indoors. Poor Joss is so tired – so in pain. I feel stuffy and fed up. I can't walk outside because I slip.

No filming all week. Joss is very irritable today. He did my feet, as they were sore, and I heard his lines.

However the very next day –

Shit. Shit. Shit. I can't believe this is happening to me!! At breakfast I went to get the milk for the coffee, and a huge twenty-ton, clumsy technician – French, of course – stepped backwards, and fell on top of me. I went up to the room to have a shower, but the skin over my metal plate burst open, blood spurted out, and the shower looked like *Psycho*. Joss got me to the hospital by ambulance – the metal plate had burst out of my leg. I'd lost three pints of blood – I had stitches, and another X-ray. Now I'm back in bed in the hotel, bored, cross and fed up. Flowers from Joss and from the hotel management.

MIGRAINE. I went to hospital to have another stitch in my leg, and spent the rest of the day vomiting, and in pain. Poor Frances Barber – her brother was killed today in a car crash.

Thank God – the pain has gone. I took off my bandage, had a wash, cleaned the wound with Dettol and bandaged it up. The hospital had to fix my leg again, because it started to bleed. Joss is so worried about me, and so I packed and decided to go back to England.

Joss saw me off in the production car at 6.15 a.m. I was taken to Poprad airport then on a very bumpy flight to Bratislava. I stayed in the plane, and after half an hour, flew off to Prague, where I was put in a wheelchair for three hours. The Europe insurance people wheeled me to the plane. Arrived in London, where I was wheeled through the luggage collection, and brought home. The insurance people were excellent. Cristina had made the bed, and put flowers in. She unpacked for me. Kirsty and Daisy came. Sammy had brought me milk, bread, salmon, satsumas and potatoes. Penny is very pregnant. These children are such a comfort, and such darlings. I'm lucky to have them. Joss in an unreasonable panic, as our phone is out of order. He phoned Toni, Sammy, Penny, Kirsty, the insurance, and Bertorelli's [the restaurant beneath our flat], because he was trying to contact me. He'd also given me his wrong phone number.

Joss is still filming in Poprad. I spent the morning tidying up. I saw Mr Catterall and, suddenly, here I am in the London Clinic, waiting to have an anaesthetic. I've had a bath, blood test, etc, and am very comfortable. Kirsty came, and brought me a nightdress, and some things. I've just phoned Joss.

When Mr Catterall examined Rosemary, he realised that an immediate operation was vital because the poison was almost touching the plate, and once infection took hold, it could prove fatal. And then during the operation it was discovered that some cotton wool had been left inside when Rosemary had been stitched up in Poprad. Thus Rosemary was given no advance warning, and after seeing Mr Catterall, the operation took place in the Clinic, only a few minutes later.

I have a bad headache. I had an operation to take out a haematoma, and drain the poison away from the plate. I'm very tired – slept most of the day.

Good night – I feel much brighter. Kirsty and Daisy stayed for two and a half hours. Penny had a good, long talk with me. I phoned Joss. He is grumpy.

Mr Catterall arrived and said I could get up. I walked around the room.

Sammy was going to pick me up, but she shut the baby in the car and lost the key, so I took a taxi, and had a weep when I got home. Sammy turned up, and we had lunch. I did a bit of washing, wrote letters and then rested in bed. Joss phoned tonight. I love him so.

I spent the day organising plane bucket tickets for Malawi. Sammy came to lunch. Poor girl is tearful because Paolo is still on drugs, and there is no hope.

Dressed at 5.30. Penny had a baby girl. I bought presents, and visited Penny and baby Ella – red-haired and beautiful.

Luke, the first assistant on the film, rang to say Joss is arriving home tomorrow. Sammy and I bought lovely food to welcome him. Luke phoned again. Joss is not coming till Tuesday! I got very bad-tempered, as no one at the hotel ever answers the phone, and I cannot get through to Joss.

Joss returned from Prague, with thirteen bags. We have such happiness together, with deep, exciting physicality – such bliss.

After a few days Rosemary and I fly to Malawi.

Arrived Lusaka. I took a bus to the Pamodsa Hotel – very comfortable – arrived with migraine. I felt lousy this evening, but at midnight Joss changed all that. I am ecstatic.

At Lilongwe we were happily met by Alison Mathews, with some kwachas and a car. We had a magnificent drive down the escarpment on the lakeside road – but had a bad skid on the corrugated surface. A five-hour drive. Wonderful chambo dinner at Nicopola Lodge.

We had more chambo for lunch, by the pool. Yippee! Toby was circling above, in an aeroplane, and it landed at the Nicopola Club. Toby, Joss and I spent a quiet afternoon in the garden. It is such a joy that Toby has arrived safely and is with us here in Malawi.

Pleasant evening with David and Gay. Blantyre was as awful for me as always, but it was good that Toby should experience it all, and take in the atmosphere. [Rosemary had never described Blantyre to me as 'awful' before – each time we returned to her birthplace it seemed to release a hidden repression.]

MIGRAINE. Woke up with a dreadful head. Toby, Joss and I went to the Shire River, to see a hippo, and then drove to Nicopola Lodge. There was a barbecue this evening on the beach. African dancers performed for us. It was a fun evening. I've had a migraine hanging on all week. I'm so in love with Joss, and Toby is so thoughtful and understanding.

No headache – wonderful. Joss is enjoying his books by David Livingstone that he bought in Blantyre. Joss and I went to the cashew nut factory, and saw Baxton, Rose and Abigail, and they came back to the hotel with us.

Baxton and his pretty wife Rose and their little daughter, Abigail, were a family Rosemary tried to help. She kept in constant touch with them, sending them essentials, but sadly, it was not long before both Rose and Abigail died, most probably from Aids.

Tomorrow we get a plane to Lusaka, and then another back home to London.

Back in England.

We waited in all evening for Judy to ring from LA about *Sister Act*. It has been offered to Alec Guinness, so it looks as if it is a no go. Anyway, maybe something better will turn up.

I'm lost in Pepys' diary. Amazing – in 1665 his aunt had a breast cut off, tobacco was thought poisonous and the plague began.

Up at 5 a.m. Joss and I fed Jelly, and drove to Stoke Mandeville. It took four hours. Then a very exhausting day, having X-rays and blood tests. The lousy doctor slipped, and the needle was pulled out of my arm, and blood shot everywhere. He tried to push it back in again, and got hot air inside. What a mess! Got back to Floral Street, and then Joss and I saw *Attila* at the opera house. During the interval, Joss and I crossed the road, and came back home and had a glass of champagne. Very romantic.

Sammy came round early. She is so upset about Paolo, who is in Brixton Prison. Joss left for Rome and comes back tomorrow.

Rosemary and I fly to America.

The hot air hits us, as we stepped of the plane at Houston – ninety-two degrees. The Lancaster Hotel was like walking into a fridge – lovely.

Slept for nine hours. Heard Joss's lines at 3 a.m. Then we slept from 4.30–5.30. Later we got into our Chrysler, and looked for grocery shops. Very sparse, spread-out town, with car parks, open areas and big banks. Not encouraging – it doesn't seem to have a heart. Tomorrow is the first day of filming *Occhio Pinocchio*.

I woke up so happy after a beautiful night, without a headache, and feeling very loved. The *Daily Mail* rang [obviously because of Paul] after a beautiful night to ask our reaction regarding the two young British girls imprisoned in Thailand for drugs. They had been released. The government and Church made a deal with the king of Thailand. Joss collected for filming and returned at 3.30 a.m. I waited up for him.

Well, here we are packing to go to Los Angeles. Despite the town and the red-neck attitudes, I've really enjoyed my twenty-three days here. Joss is very happy filming with the Italian company. I am worried about Toby's depressions. I must try and get someone to help him. The heat here is horrendous.

Joss and I had a lovely day. We called Susan, who has got Joss a visual commercial for $150,000. He always said he wouldn't do one – but $150,000 does help!! We celebrated by Joss buying me an exquisite leather coat, and dinner at Le Chamarde.

I woke up with a splitting head. Had a desperate, horrid dream of Toby – found with a string around his neck.

The Gold Mountain Manor at Big Bear has to be seen to be believed! It is so twee! The host is so depressed that he's unable to talk – and his wife Connie is potty. Our room is so cluttered with toy dogs, teddy bears, holiday books and old knick-knacks that we had nowhere to unpack. The streets here are all called after Peter Pan characters, and the main street that encircles them all is named Nana. Yoicks!!!

I read Pepys while Joss left for the studio to try out his costume and rehearse. He returned very excited. He is filming with a four and a half foot iguana sitting on his lap.

We drove to Frank Oz's home to party in his garden in Malibu. Enjoyable afternoon. Joss played netball with the group.

Here I am in Chateau Marmont's sitting room. We have a charming flat in the garden. Chris Walken came and had coffee with us this morning. He is weird, but very nice.

We fly to New Orleans.

This is New Orleans. Joss and I are having such fun. It is a very vibrant, exciting port. We have taken a streetcar down St Charles to Washington, and had a most delicious lunch at Commander's Palace. A jazz band was playing and we have a window seat, over-looking trees. This is sheer heaven. Our first impression of this hotel was so awful, but today we see the charm of the place, and love it. I guess we were overtired. The courtyard here is so beautiful, with all the magnolia trees and foliage. We had a good espresso, sitting out under the canopy at midnight.

A two-hour drive to St Francis Ville. We have the bridal suite in a plantation house, the Myrtles – which is supposed to be the 'most haunted house in America'. We did have a very disturbed, suddenly ice-cold, wakeful night between one and four this morning, and then heard that all the other guests were awake during those hours.

We moved to a cottage on the swamp – more peaceful – but stiflingly hot.

Joss is bad-tempered, as he feels I pressurise him because I'm more enthusiastic about going to movies than he is. He doesn't understand that for years I've had to stay in – first with babies, and then in hospitals. Eventually we went to River Oaks, and saw the documentary film *Popha*. A very raw film – I cried very much. At 7.30 we saw the Swedish film, *House of Angels*. Great fun. Better evening.

We fly to Italy.

Flight to Milan, and a car met us and took us to Brescia. I finished Pepys – lovely, lovely book. We had dinner with Francesco Nuti, who is directing and acting in the movie. Came back and made passionate love.

Joss was collected for filming at 3.45. The director was late again, and arrived at 6.30.

We arrived on set at 11 a.m., only to be told that Nuti was not feeling well, and it's a beautiful, bright day – just right for the shots! Nuti finally arrived at 1 p.m.!!

Took boat bus to Torcello. After a delicious lunch we went to the Basilica, knelt down, prayed and lit candles.

We had a fun lunch in Mezzeria. A mafia-type gave Joss his New York card. 'If Joss wanted a favour sometime?' and another customer, who had seen *The Sicilian*, told us he was shot by Jock Delves Broughton's son!! It was a crazy lunch. It is now after midnight, and I'm sitting in Joss's winnebago in the pouring rain.

Lynn rang to say that the film was suspended, and wants us to go to either Umbria or London. Chaos!!

Back to England.

It is wonderful to be back in Clovelly. Penny arrived with her family, and then Sammy with hers. Kirsty had her baby tonight, quite naturally. Hurrah.

We visited Kirsty in hospital, with darling little Florence, then back to Clovelly.

Tony and David were wonderful when *Hello* magazine came to shoot us. They really took the initiative, and fed all the children. There were twenty-seven of us for lunch and supper.

NEW YEAR'S EVE: I had a bad night, and feel lousy, with a bad cough, and pain in leg and back. We took all the children out to Barnstaple, to give their parents time to themselves. We all had champagne and crackers. Bed 3 a.m.

1994

Sammy came round in a sad state, because of Paolo, and we gave her the telephone number of Broadreach. She seemed to pick up and have a glimmer of hope. This evening Joss played some old records, which revived wonderful, sentimental feelings about our days in Cape Town. We danced in the kitchen to those old times. We go to Clovelly tomorrow. No time to finish this tonight, as Joss wants to lower the lights.

Today Sammy took Paolo to Broadreach – at least I hope so – I'm waiting to hear how it went. LATER – Sammy delivered Paolo to Broadreach, and no one is allowed to contact him for four days.

Bloody Broadreach has sent Paolo back to London – the idiots – stupid, fucking place. Poor, dear Sammy is so desperate. I made her bed up. I phoned Broadreach, Scoda, Coke House Trust and others. No help anywhere. It is such a hopeless situation. We are so worried. The drug helpline is no better than when Paul died.

Sammy phoned at 1 a.m. Paolo had arrived at her house at eleven looking fine. She has decided to go to the hospital tomorrow, to talk to the psychiatrist, and then bring Paolo down here. Joss has been on the phone all day to Broadreach. They won't accept Paolo. So I rang Barley Mow, and they are taking him tonight. We've had an exhausting time phoning. I hope it works out this time, and Paolo settles there.

It is snowing back here in London, and looks so pretty on our balcony. Sammy came to Floral Street to have dinner with us. She was very talkative, worried about Paolo's psychotic behaviour. She had been so upset visiting him, because he threw things at her. Joss dropped her off at the hospital at 1 a.m.

This evening we cuddled, and watched TV. The Russians have quietly, and admirably, marched into Bosnia, to help them against the Serbs. The UN has been dithering for weeks, and the bloodshed has been disgraceful. The Croats have been madly violent and difficult – even bombing the Red Cross. Such ghastly trouble in what was Yugoslavia.

Joss's non-birthday. [I was born on 29 February, so we celebrated my 'non-birthday' on the twelfth stroke.] Toby phoned as midnight struck. I had a glass of champagne ready, which Joss and I shared, to catch the tick of the birthday, as it flashed by and Toby shared the moment on the phone, as we toasted Joss. Wow!!! I am so in love with Joss, and so happy with him.

SHIT! MIGRAINE! I woke up in agony – and nauseous. After lunch I had one-hour kip with Joss, and then he left for Golders Green to rehearse *Let Them Eat Cake* for the BBC. He has been so patient and thoughtful with me today.

When we got back to Clovelly, we drove to Hartland, and took in breaths of sea air. The most beautiful sight there – through the black rocks – was a shaft of golden light on the water. Back at the

Rectory, the pheasants were all chasing each other – round and round – and mating on the back lawn. The rabbits were also mating and – so sweet – washing themselves afterwards. I'm so in love, and we are so happy down here in Clovelly – together.

We are so happy in Clovelly – so we fly back to Africa together for me to film *Jacob* for the American Bible series, directed by Peter Hall, with Matthew Modine as Jacob, Sean Bean as his brother and Irene Papas and me as Mum and Dad.

We flew to Casablanca. We were driven twenty-seven kilometres to the Regency Hyatt – and a fabulous room. Sean Bean and Sue, and Joss and I, had a beer in Rick's Bar, with pictures of Ingrid and Humphrey Bogart all over the restaurant, and we were served by a waiter dressed like Bogart.

We woke up with the sun pouring over the bed. After breakfast I heard Joss's part, and then visited the new, amazingly ornate mosque. Later we were driven to Mohammed V airport, and took a tiny charter plane, with about sixty of the film company, over the snow-covered Atlas Mountains, to Quarzazate.

Joss rehearsed with Peter Hall. Peter is here with his young wife Nicky, their baby, Emma, and Stephanie – Emma's nanny. The production lot have organised a plane for Samantha to come and join us. I called her, and asked her to go into Floral Street to collect Joss's wig and books, and my hat and swimming costume. [Sammy's recent life had been very hectic and traumatic in her efforts to help Paolo – and when the doctors told her there was nothing more she could do, she felt lost and emotionally exhausted. She needed to escape and breathe again, and so we arranged for her to join us.]

At 4.30 the Muslim prayer call woke us up – very spiritual and mystic. Sean Bean and Matthew Modine joined us for lunch – palm hearts and pepper seeds, and then couscous. Sammy should be in Casablanca tonight. Hope she is okay. Dinner with Nicky and Peter. We had just got into the apartment, when Sammy phoned from Casablanca. Good.

Irene Papas joined us for breakfast, and talked philosophically about religion and acting. At three we went to our room, and put a 'Don't Disturb' sign on the door, and then slept. The driver brought Samantha in. She was so happy, and had a lovely journey.

After breakfast Joss, Sammy and I took a car to the set – twenty-seven kilometres into the desert. The drive was sheer madness – the Italian girl drove over rocks and bumps so fast we bounced up to the roof. At last we reached thousands of goats, a dozen donkeys and ten camels on the location, at a very pretty oasis. The black tents looked wonderful on the hillside. We had lunch in an exquisite Arab tent, and then went up the hill to shoot. Very hot, with interminable long waits. We were driven back to the hotel, had a cup of tea, and I heard Joss through his script twice. A pleasant surprise awaited us in the rooms – a magnum of Dom Perignon champagne, and olives and almonds, from Gerry, the American producer. Sammy, Joss and I shared the whole bottle, and had a little party.

At 4 a.m. the moon shone brightly over the bed, and the Islamic call for prayer broke the silent night. Joss left at 4.30. I went back to bed, and slept deeply. Sammy and I sat by the pool. A wretched fly flew up my nose, and then bit my arm. Little devil! We walked to the town. Sammy is looking wonderful – we must help her change her life. Peter, Nicky, Sammy, Joss and I ate at Chez Nabil. Peter and Nicky don't eat meat. The entire restaurant was taken over by jolly Italians, who cooked their own pasta, and sang cheerful songs. It was a great evening.

Slept well. Joss was off bright and early. He was so sweet – he came back to the hotel at 9.15 to pick me up – he came in his make-up and long grey beard. The reception looked shell-shocked!!! I didn't go as I wasn't organised. I'd left washing soaking, and I couldn't find my hat or dark glasses, so he arranged for me to be picked up at noon. The filming was interesting – Joss and Irene Papas working well together.

We had a three-hour drive to Marrakech, through the Atlas Mountains. Delicious Moroccan dinner at the Mamounia.

We return to England.

Back in London – poor Toni is ill, eleven weeks pregnant with twins. Penny is fine – her baby is due in nine and a half weeks. My New Horizon meeting was cancelled, because Jon Snow has to go to Africa to cover the voting for Channel Four.

Dreadful news about massacres in Rwanda – between two tribes, the Tutsi and the Hutu. We must go in and stop it. Now I'm packing this book, because we are catching the plane to Chicago in the morning.

Back to the United States.

Well, here we are – at the Four Seasons Hotel, on the forty-fourth floor, in a king-sized bed, overlooking Lake Michigan. The lake is like the sea. It is a massive 354 miles long. Tomorrow Joss starts on *Miracle on 34th Street*.

Yesterday in Pretoria, President Nelson Rolihlahla Mandela vowed to create a 'rainbow nation'. He is sworn in as president. WONDERFUL.

Back in England – en route to Chichester.

John Smith, the leader of the opposition, died last week. He died so suddenly that it shocked the nation. He was such a good man. We hadn't heard because we were in Chicago, and with the time difference, we left before the news reached the USA.

We've arrived here at Gillian Lynne's cottage, and Gillian and Peter helped us move in. Joss's first day of rehearsal for *The Visit*, playing opposite Lauren Bacall, with Terry Hands directing. I went into the theatre with Joss this morning. Duncan Weldon met Joss at the stage door, and asked me if I would be going in. 'Not likely!!'

Joss rehearsed the second act all day, and I walked around Chichester. I looked north, south-east and west for a first-night present for Joss. It started to rain, so I went into the Cathedral, and prayed for Joss, Rwanda, the family and Toby and Angie and their new embryo. I then found the most beautiful art figure, which I know he'll love – as I do.

Lovely long sleep – Joss very pleased to have the day off. We went through act three before lunch, then a wee kip, and then we heard the play right through. We heard on the news about a

Nigerian girl who is to be deported, because her Nigerian employ-
ers had been taken to court, and deported for mistreating her.
Appalling! Joss rang up Channel Four to say we would give her a
home. Jon Snow was going to sort it out.

I wrote to Baxton in Malawi. His eldest child has died. Joss
picked me up, and I watched the technical rehearsal. It was exhausting, and boring.

A lovely sunny day, with Toni, David, Georgia, Lettie, Emily,
Tom and Luca. We collected the Sunday papers, and we all sat in
the garden and read them. Better reviews for the play – excellent for
Joss, and, thank heavens, at last some okay for Lauren.

Joss got hold of Richard Branson for Toby. I do hope Toby
manages to get a job, now that he has an opening. Lauren
Bacall and David Bowden are coming to dinner, so I cooked
asparagus, and undressed prawns. We had a good evening together,
and Joss and I finally got to bed at three o'clock.

Last day of *The Visit*. Waited backstage for the show to end. Joss
got a magnificent reception – whistles and 'bravo's. We arrived back
at the cottage – had some berries, and got to bed at 5 a.m.

Woke up to heaven. Always such bliss. Joss learnt lines for
Matisse, and then we watched Princess Diana being stupid in an
interview on *Panorama*.

Back to Africa to film *Deadly Voyage* – a true story.

We got the plane to Ghana – such a good flight – and arrived at
Accra at 5.30. The *Deadly Voyage* company collected us, and took us
to the Golden Tulip Hotel.

This evening we joined Danny Glover and his wife [Danny produced this film] and the Scottish director, John Mackenzie.

Heaven help us!! Joss has learnt that the captain he is portraying has been found guilty in the courts in France – so Joss is re-working *Deadly Voyage*. I heard him through *Firelight* [my next movie] this morning, which he now knows. Joss woke me up at 1.30, and we reached heaven. We cuddled until 8.30 a.m.

Joss came in, hot and sweaty – but happy – at 8 p.m. We went down to dinner, and John Mackenzie and David Suchet joined us. It was a fun evening. Tomorrow we leave Ghana for Joss to finish shooting the film in England.

Christmas Eve back in England.

Joss didn't finish filming at the studios until past midnight, and then he had to be driven all the way back here to Clovelly. At last the movie is finished. He had had to do extra scenes, because he had to wait till the trial in France was completed, and the captain's fate was determined. Most of the film crew had left for Christmas, and he was the last actor there. The first assistant laughed, and said to Joss, 'If no one is here for the last shot, just press the red button, and say your lines!!' So late supper and bed.

CHRISTMAS DAY: At 6 a.m. we heard the little patter of Daisy's feet, dragging her stocking into her mother's room!!! Such excitement. The children were all very happy. Joss said it's the happiest Christmas he can remember.

1995

Joss drove us all to Bedford. We saw round Toby's romantic little flat, and then walked around the little town, while Joss reminisced over the war years, when he was evacuated here. He wanted to show us the school he went to – but it had gone – and was replaced by shops. After lunch we drove to Cranfield, where Toby is training to be a pilot, and looked over Toby's new workplace and airfields.

We went to estate agents in Marlow, looking for houses for Penny, and Kirsty. Then we dropped in on Melanie, and had tea with her. Sam and Adam are very handsome young men. Nico has grown a foot in a month, and Paola and Romeo are so clean, tidy and happy. Melanie has done a remarkable job on them.

The immigration minister – a real prick – is sending a Nigerian couple, and their three children, back to Nigeria when they've lived in Britain, legally, for thirteen years, and their children only speak English. This really incenses me. I despair of this idiot government. Sammy left for Rome. I heard Joss's lines till 1.45 a.m.

The car collected Joss for the first read through of *Daisies in December*. I wrote to two MPs about the Nigerians. I heard Joss and

Jean [Simmons] through their lines – at first a bit sloppy and inaccurate – we made good progress though. Mark Haber, the director, came to dinner.

Woke at 4 a.m. with a dreadful nightmare of Paul, at his worst stage. I woke in a cold sweat. Joss was ill too.

Jean, Joss and I got the car to Sennen Cove. I had a wonderful walk across the fields, and over four stiles (not bad, eh?), to the Success Inn. Joss and Jean are filming on the beach. Hope the tide stays out!!! They were on the beach till 3.30, and then they went for shots in a car. The air was perfect and the view wonderful, so I went for another walk, and then re-read *A Suitable Boy*.

Joss and I watched rushes. They are so exciting – Joss and Jean are superb together.

At eight we left to have dinner at Russet's with Robert Halmi, the executive producer and head of Hallmark – who left Los Angeles yesterday afternoon. He flew to New York – got Concorde to Heathrow – a private plane to Penzance – where he picked up a hired car – and arrived just in time for dinner. After the meal Robert left in the car, and returned the same way, and he will be back in LA tomorrow afternoon!! He must be so exhausted – well, that's movies! As Joss said, 'It was a long way to travel for an ordinary meal.'

Joss came in. He'd finished the film. As always, after a show ends, he was a little depressed and tired. He rang Jean to come and have dinner with us. We ate at The Pig and Fish, and then Peter drove us to the wrap party. Joss made a little speech of thanks – and it was a good, positive finish.

We fly to Italy.

Samantha picked us up in Rome, in blinding rain. Joss drove to Orvieto, and we had a good lunch at the Crypt Grotto.

DISASTER DAY – First we left Podere with the car packed. We had only got as far as Vassani's restaurant, and – crash – the boot opened, and twelve bottles and the demi-john of oil fell into the road. Only the demi-john broke. We collected all the bottles, swept up the glass, and cleaned the oil from the road. Luckily a police car passed by, and was able to alert drivers about the road, and the danger of skidding. We dropped Samantha for a thyroid check-up at the Perugia Hospital, and waited for her for three hours. Then we drove off, and as we were driving down the hill, a car coming up took the corner too wide, and crashed into us, taking the wing off our car. We took details while Sammy and the driver deliberated, but couldn't do much, because the occupants were desperate to get to the hospital, which was obviously the reason they were rushing. So we sent them on their way.

Spent all morning chasing doctors for Sammy. Eventually, in frustration, Joss phoned the London Clinic, and the doctor spoke to Samantha. He was very understanding, and Samantha had a scan, and will go into hospital on Monday. Toby and Kirsty went on the shuttle to Paris.

Joss dropped Sammy at the London Clinic, where she is having her thyroid operation this afternoon. She went into surgery at 3.30, and came out at six. She is being kept in recovery ward all night. I'm longing to speak to the surgeon tomorrow to hear what they found.

Off to Los Angeles.

At nine we collected Samantha from hospital, and drove her to Dean Street. Joss bought her some food and fruit, and we left for the airport. I feel sick – with a dreadful migraine. A wheelchair met me, and we were taken through Los Angeles customs. No one met us, so we took a taxi to the Chateau Marmont.

Joss changed into a suit, and left for CBS – to present an award to Tom Cruise!! He returned, and we went to Pavilions supermarket at 1 a.m, and met Billy Connolly, who was in great form, chatting for ages, over his trolley.

Alan Parker and David Wimbury came to the Marmont, and we all had champagne, and chatted about *Evita*, which Alan is going to direct.

After lunch at Bel Air, we drove to Adelaide Drive, to see Jean. We got there at 4 p.m., and she was in bed, so we got her up. We went for a long walk to the beach, returned and had tea together, and a car drove us to the airport.

Back in Devon.

TOBY AND ANGIE'S WEDDING AT CLOVELLY: It is pouring with rain. So we moved the trestle tables out of the marquee to the house, and started setting up lunch in the basement. Toby is in a nervous state. The church bells rang, and we all went across the road. Angeline and her mother and bridesmaids arrived. A pleasing service and everyone came back to the Rectory. About 120 people came – all the food was enjoyed – and they all drank so much. Irene and David decorated Toby's car, and the couple left with tins clanking and balloons. Toby and Angie look so happy. They drove to

Minehead. Their friends stayed all evening – and went to bed here at 5 a.m. We were exhausted. Joss and I went to bed at 2.30.

We left the house at 7.20, drove to Clovelly beach, got on a small boat and went to Lundy. The tide was out, so Joss and I had to transfer to a dinghy, to go ashore. A truck took us up to the village!! There was a bar, which was closed – they wouldn't even give us a cup of tea – and we were the only visitors that day! We discovered later that even the big boat cancelled, because rough seas were on their way. Then we walked, in a horrendous strong wind, over the bleak landscape of ACKLAND'S moor – but too windy – so we stopped walking, and sat and read. It is a miserable, desolate place. The boat trip back was hell. The boat rolled from side to side, unable to move, while great waves splashed over it, covering it, as it almost tipped on its side. At last we reached Clovelly – shaking – thank God to be home. Apart from the ashen-faced man at the wheel, there was only one other visitor on the boat, and as we stepped ashore, she was threatening to sue the man. A glass of champagne, and then bed – exhausted.

Joss and I watched the fiftieth memorial anniversary of D-Day on TV. It was most impressive, and some of it really stunning. Choirboys were singing a hymn at Portsmouth Harbour. Millions of names were printed there – Joss's brother was one of them. Then a fleet of small boats passed by, bearing a poster with the words, 'Thank you for our freedom'. There were thousands of ships in the channel, and aeroplanes above; and the Queen, the Queen Mother, Margaret, Diana and the heads of all the states were there – all except Mitterand. Sixty-seven-year-old veterans parachuted into France. Joss and I cleared up, and drove to London.

It is very hot. I walked with difficulty – I'm very wobbly – to the post office. People are walking carelessly, and knocking into me, so I came home as soon as I could.

The Rwanda massacre continues – the violence is heartbreaking. David Russell, in Malawi, phoned. He is planning our itinery, and arranging accommodation for us. So we are all set to go out on 3 August. How exciting. Melanie arrived to discuss the children, so that Samantha can have freedom to start a new life.

Rwanda is still in a bloody mess. At last the French have gone in to see what help they can be! I went to New Horizon – it was so hectic.

We spent hours trying to get Kandy her place on the flight to Malawi. When we reached her, she was so excited and was over the moon with excitement. Joss is thrilled with her enthusiasm.

Joss has dreadful worries, trying to juggle dates for *A Kid in King Arthur's Court*, *Occhio Pinocchio* and Africa.

All day I sorted out drug letters, and re-filed them. It is heartbreaking reading some of them – so very sad – and it is backbreaking answering them. Then just as I was hearing Joss's lines, Penny and Robin had to rush the baby to Barnstaple Hospital. The baby had a lumber puncture and a drip. Her temperature was 102 degrees. Poor Penny was in tears. [Even though the baby was so ill, I heard Robin mutter to himself, 'Why do these things always happen to me?' and that was the moment I knew their partnership would not last.] Robin returned, and Penny stayed with her nameless baby.

Samantha, Luca, Romeo, Paola and Nico arrived. I'm so happy to see them. Robin came in, and irritated me with his moaning. He sounds like John Major on a bad day.

Penny phoned to say she was able to leave hospital this afternoon, so Joss and I drove in to pick her up. The poor wee nameless one looks very frail.

Joss went off, and did a charity appeal for Rwanda. Penny phoned. She'd had her laser treatment on her eye, and was having a row with Robin.

We were met at Budapest, and dropped at the Hotel Aquincum.

I was about to play Arthur in a Disney film for kids, *A Kid at the Court of King Arthur* – which was hardly a memorable experience – but could have been fun.

Joss and I were married forty-three years ago today. I had dreadful dreams all night, of Arabs chasing me for my purse. Massaged Joss's back, and then we had breakfast.

I was thinking of writing about Paul, and how living with a drug-taker changes the natural reactions that one should have. I can't get rid of the guilt I feel, of the time I wouldn't let him in the house because he'd taken drugs, even though it was raining hard. How could I have been so cruel? How we lack understanding, when under pressure, and when one is desperate. One puts up with the theft, rudeness and violence – but where and when should one draw the line? I massaged Joss's poor back, and then we had breakfast.

Back in Italy to go on with the movie *Occhio Pinnocchio*. The green light is back on after a more than two-year break.

Now that Cecci Gori has given it the go ahead, tomorrow is the first day of the continued filming of *Occhio Pinocchio*. We are keeping fingers crossed, and hope Francesco Nuti has pulled himself together. Samantha came back after her horse ride looking fabulous. Francesco arrived, and called out, asking for Samantha's hand in marriage!! Joss and I went for a walk, and saw a most astonishing sight in the street – a man tightrope-walking up to a roof – and then a ten-year-old kid on a motorcycle, flying over a ramp, and over three children – madness.

It is 10 a.m. on a very hot day, everyone and everything is ready and Franceso Nuti has not arrived yet. It is now 2.30. No filming has been done. What a waste of day, and time and money. It was 4 p.m. before Joss was called for his first shot. At six he returned to the trailer, very stressed. Nuti had left the set, and Joss refused to go back until the director was there. There was a state of tension. Filming stopped at 7.20. Everyone is frustrated.

Joss went down to find a call sheet, and – HORROR – bumped into Paolo, who arrived out of nowhere. Samantha was in the dining room with the crew, and couldn't believe her eyes. Joss had words with him – so did Samantha. John Mortimer called – so did Melanie and Toby. Sammy came in at midnight. She'd sent Paolo off. She seems okay.

Joss went off to film. I sat out in the front to read, but boiled inside as time ticked by. Francesco was still asleep, and his assistant sat near me drinking coffee. No one was moving – so I picked up the telephone, woke Francesco and said, 'It's a lovely afternoon – you've missed the morning's filming. Everyone is waiting on the set for you – up you get!' 'Who is this speaking?' 'Your conscience,' I replied.

Francesco thought he was dreaming. The manager came down – the assistant was called up – no one spoke to me. Nuti left at 1 p.m. – came back, and didn't leave again till 2 p.m. I have a headache today, and am unable to read because of pain. I've never been in a noisier place. Motorbikes, screeching lorries, squeaking swings, loud radios, bangs, bells, cars, revving, hooters, children screaming, boys shouting, Italians arguing. Toby phoned. He has got a seat for Luca. I'm so pleased. Sammy will love to have him in Africa. Joss returned, utterly fed up. Nuti's shots were ridiculous. Joss's back in real agony – made worse by the tension.

Paul Lyon Maris phoned early, and Joss told him he wanted to do *Voyage Round My Father*, and also the Scottish script he was offered. Paul doesn't know how to fit both in. Joss refused to go on the set before Nuti, so he and I read the *Herald Tribune* till Nuti appeared.

Joss has just phoned – he's done no filming today. Francesco still can't get up in the morning. He didn't leave the hotel until 1.30, and so the helicopter was unable to negotiate the afternoon wind. Problems!! Joss and the crew returned, depressed.

We rose at 6 a.m., drove to Amalfi and arrived at Gore Vidal and Howard Austen's home. Joss, Gore and Howard had a swim, and then we were shown around Gore's house, which is fabulous – wonderful pictures, and patios, and acres of vines and olives – very Romanesque and over the top. Hillary Clinton had been staying a few days previously, Tim Robbins and Susan Sarandon and their kids had only just left and Gore was quite shattered. We all had a very happy, jokey lunch. Arrived at Podere, but there was no heating and no lights. We lit candles, and got to bed at 3 a.m. – exhausted. However we had a wonderful night. So romantic.

Back to *The Court of King Arthur*. We arrived at Rome airport. I had a bad migraine so I went to the loo to put cold water on my face. The plane left at nine. Kate was a bit overpowering, telling me what a fabulous film she'd made in New Zealand, and how everyone had kissed her, and said, 'Bravo, Kate'. I had to move, as I felt too ill to enthuse. She's very young. [Kate Winslet had just returned from Los Angeles after seeing her breakthrough movie *Heavenly Creatures* for the first time. Kate played my daughter and young Daniel Craig was her boyfriend.] Good flight to Budapest. Back to the Oquincum Hotel.

Joss was up at 6 a.m. for filming. I repacked all the cases – some to leave at the Marriott for the next film – he is going to play Bondachuk in *Citizen X* here – and some for Italy.

Joss couldn't sleep this morning. When I reminded him it was the twelfth anniversary of Paul's death, he remembered that last 7 October he was also wakeful. We got up at 5.45, had a coffee and packed the car.

Oh dear, I've missed several days. We've been so busy. Joss finished *Citizen X*, and we returned from beautiful Budapest. We flew to Dublin with Jason Connery to see *The Sheltering Desert*, which the Irish production company are trying to resuscitate, and went to hospital see Joss's old friend Chloe Gibson, who is ninety-seven. She was lying in bed and said, 'I am alive – and that's all.' It upset me dreadfully. It makes me angry about old age, and what it entails. Later Joss and David Putnam were on *The Late, Late Show* with Gay Byrne.

Back in London Toby helped us get loads of stuff out of the car, and as the lift was not working, he ran, in a flash, up the stairs with everything. Oh, to be young, and not paralysed! I went up to New Horizon, to their new opening. Jon Snow came up to me to chat, and was very kind. Lord Longford, who is eighty-nine, gave a very funny, clever speech. They all said they were very sorry I was leaving.

Back to Africa for Christmas.

Sammy, Kandy, Luca, Joss and I caught the plane to Johannesburg, and then flew to Lilongwe.

We drove to Nkopola. Our room here is a dream – with a lovely double bed, mosquito net and a balcony. We all had chambo for lunch. While we were eating, several monkeys got into Kandy's room, and stole all her cashew nuts! She was furious – especially as we had warned her about covering everything up. This evening a full moon shone over the lake. A local group danced ritual village dances to a local band. There was a wonderful atmosphere. It was most enjoyable, and under our mosquito net Joss and I found Illyria.

We woke at 4.30, and Joss took a photograph of the dawn, and after breakfast we read. I've started *Birdsong* by Sebastian Faulks. It's a wonderful book. We had tea on the patio, and the monkeys drove us off. Hilda and Bashir Sacranie arrived, and brought loads of exercise books and pencils that we had ordered to distribute among the village children.

CHRISTMAS DAY: Luca phoned at 6 a.m. and woke us – it was great – we leapt up, ordered tea and rang Kandy. We all gathered on the khondi and exchanged presents. Joss has got food poisoning, and feels weak, so I have kept him on pawpaw only; and he has slept, on and off, all day. This morning we went to see Baxton and Rose for half an hour, and gave Baxton a coat and T-shirt, and Rosa, a brooch, T-shirt, coat and two bras. Sammy and Kandy tried to hand out books and pencils to the local children, but it all got out of hand with the grabbing – the children are so desperate to learn, read and write. None of us wanted the Christmas lunch of turkey! The temperature must be 120 degrees. Luca played football with the villagers, and then joined Kandy and Sammy to eat at pirate's night.

Joss is much better today. We got up at 4.50, and took in the golden dawn. We sat under the flame trees, and Sammy lay on a huge surfboard, and floated across the lake, followed by a dozen kids. Luca went out on a boat, and it overturned – great drama because of crocs and hippos. We drove back to the hotel, distributing clothes to delighted villagers.

1996

We return to London – very busy, so very little written.

Back in Floral Street – the flat is lovely and clean, but it is very crowded here in Covent Garden, and the young girls are very pushy, and kept walking into me. [These are the first signs that walking and keeping upright were both difficult.]

On our way back from the Laurence Olivier awards at Grosvenor House, a bomb went off in a bus, where we had just driven three minutes earlier. Coincidentally, Penny had just dropped Joel off, and was immediately behind the bus, when she saw it explode. She was very shaken.

It is 29 February so it is Joss's seventeenth leap year birthday. [Rosemary was sixty-seven – I was a year older.] We had a party, with Frank Hauser, Johnny Dennis, Pauline and John Alderton, Annie Skinner, Eddie Kulukundis, Georgina and Jessica Andrews, Michael Frayn, Michael Anderson, Sarah Miles, Duncan Weldon, Melanie, Polly and Adam, Samantha, Kirsty and Ant, Kandy and Tony, Toni and David – a very lovely evening.

We fly to Italy.

We went to Orvieto. I had a bad fall in the piazza, and hurt my arm and right hand. Yesterday I cut my right leg on the iron rail outside the house.

Samantha picked us up. I drove back in her car, so that I could have a long talk with her. She does really want to stay in Italy with her children, and today the sun is shining, and things look more positive. She talks about Tracy, an American who lives in Italy – they met up when he was modelling in Rome.

Sammy rang to say that she and Tracy were getting married. Lovely day.

We return to London.

At 6.30 I took a taxi to the Princess Grace Hospital. Joss had his right knee operated on. The operation was two hours long, and he recovered very well. We returned home and I packed for Devon.

Joss managed to dress himself today, and he was able to drive. One of my happiest days. I was at the sink washing, and he came in, and put his arms around me, squeezed me – and we went upstairs – to heaven.

Later, back to Italy.

Sammy met us at Rome airport, looking wonderful. She is twelve weeks pregnant.

When we reached Podere, Toby rang. He'd passed his flying exam – I'm so happy.

We all got up at 6 a.m. – took the train to Rome, and then to Sammy and Tracy's civil wedding. It was beautifully done. Jake, the American priest, joined us for lunch.

Toby, Angie, Joss and I went to Orvieto market, and bought loads of strawberries, salads and cheeses for the wedding. David, Toni, Emily and the twins arrived.

MIGRAINE very bad. I stayed in today, and prepared strawberries, salads, prawns, asparagus and cooked peppers, etc, with Melanie, who was a magnificent help. Joss brought in five trays of pasta, a wild boar and masses of food. Dozens of chickens and plenty of porchetta were being cooked in the ovens in Montecchio, and crates of wine were collected from Barberani at the bottom of the hill.

Samantha's wedding day. Glorious sunshine. Joss led Sammy, looking radiant in her wedding gown, down through the woods, and Father Jake wed the couple under the trees. It has been an extraordinary and really beautiful day. Graziella, Santino, Melanie, Toni, David, Toby and Kirsty all helped. At four o'clock a huge wedding cake, made of ice cream, arrived up the hill, on a truck, at the perfect time at the end of the meal. A hundred beautiful people danced through the trees and around the patio until 2 a.m.

Exhausted. We had coffee in Montecchio and then Tracy's family, his mother and father, Carol and Roger, and his sister and brother, Kate and Forest, descended for lunch. They left as Jonathan James-Moore and family arrived for dinner.

At 6 a.m. we got up and flew to London. There was a bomb at the Olympic Games in Atlanta – Dreadful.

Joss rehearsed *The King and I* with Barbara Cook, and tonight I cooked dinner for Barbara, Wally Harper, Warner Brown and us. It was a very good evening.

Joss and I were picked up, and taken to Golders Green Theatre, and I watched Joss and Barbara rehearse with the BBC2 orchestra, and big choir and children. Audience and show tonight. Penny, Melanie, Toni, David, Izzie and Abbi all came.

After a late night, packed up the car, and left for Clovelly. The rhododendrons are magnificent – the Rectory is lovely – and the garden lush. Kandy phoned – she's pregnant with our first great-grandchild, so we made romantic love.

When he started on the movie [*Amy Foster*] we were staying in Padstow, but we are almost as close to the location here, so Joss is now picked up for filming from the Old Rectory. The gale last night brought down two of our highest oaks, and cars cannot get in or out of the driveway.

Back to Italy.

We had a pleasant flight to Rome. Tracy met us, and drove us to Podere. Samantha had made green noodles for the family, and peppers for me. She looks tired, and ripe for giving birth.

A fine, sunny crisp day. Samantha, Tracy, Kandy and the children picked olives. Then Kandy, Joss and I drove into Orvieto. Sammy's waters broke, and Tracy drove her to hospital. I gave the children supper and cooked pasta for us.

Last night Sammy brought baby Tommi home. Joss drove Kandy and me to Todi. We had lunch at the Umbria, and then went on to Assisi, which was magical. This evening we all went up to Civitella, to see the olives pressed.

Back to London.

Tonight we went to the film premiere of *Evita*, and on to dinner with Alan Parker and co. The film was noisy, but it was a starry evening, which I enjoyed.

Joss and I drove on the M3 to Devon. It is such bliss to be in our own home again. Joss was very upset talking to Toby. He is depressed again.

We stayed at home in Clovelly all day, and sorted out letters. At 11 p.m. we noticed smoke coming through the floorboards – the basement ceiling was on fire. Three engines, with blue lights flashing, came and sorted us out. Joss and I had a brandy, went upstairs, and reached heaven.

CHRISTMAS DAY: Joss and I went to midnight service in the candlelit church. The moon was full, and it looked so beautiful, making patterns through the trees. We had champagne, opened presents and then had lunch and Christmas pudding.

SHIT day. It was such a lovely, happy beginning. Had a glass of champagne, and when I cooked Italian rice and prawns, Joss suddenly shouted at me, and said I was drunk. He made me cry, and I walked out – I feel so desolate and confused.

With hindsight, I am now convinced that her slurring of words, when I stupidly accused Rosemary of being 'pissed' was in fact the early stage of motor neurone disease. I believe that Rosemary was subconsciously; aware that something was wrong, and also subconsciously, so was I. But I was afraid to accept that there might be a problem, and went on making stupid accusations, helping the molehill to become a mountain – which later it it certainly did – but not as either of us anticipated.

Made up last night! All's well. This evening we took Penny, Daniel, Inigo, Ella and Nancy to Barnstaple, to see the panto *Aladdin* with Anita Harris. We all enjoyed it.

NEW YEAR'S EVE: Kandy and her boyfriend, Carey, arrived. This evening Joss and I went to have dinner with the Rouses – a good ambience as we welcomed in the New Year. At 12.15 we came home to Kandy and Carey, looking cosy in front of a big fire, with cracker hats, and glasses of champagne. We joined them and then came to bed at 3 a.m. It is a very windy night with a bright new moon.

1997

At 3 a.m. we came to bed – so blissful – and a wonderful birthday present. Then poor Toby rang to tell us that Angeline had left him, and taken Arthur to South Africa. He is shattered and distraught, and was going to come down today, but bad fog and ice stopped him. Joss and I recorded poems for Toby's project at Lantern Radio.

We drove to Covent Garden. Toby brought loads of boxes to pack. He is very unhappy.

We had moved from our lovely flat opposite the stage door of the opera house, to a smaller one, also in Floral Street, because the vast restoration to the opera house had driven us out.

Gosh – am I tired and exhausted. Packing and bending, stretching and pushing and lifting all day. So is Joss, who has packed all the books. This evening Helen and Tony Bill came for champagne, and then we all went to the Ivy and had a delicious supper. Angie phoned Toby today, and wants to come back.

Polly rang to tell us that Kandy had gone into hospital and had a little girl. We were very excited – our first great-grandchild. Paul would have been so happy. We opened a bottle of champagne to celebrate.

This morning we drove to see Holly – Kandy's baby. Such a good little thing. The contract was signed today, so at last we are solvent! But now things have to be paid. Ben came round to see us. He is a lovely boy. He went to see Kandy's baby – his niece.

It's Joss's non-birthday, so we had delicious dinner at the Ivy. The paparazzi were out in force – we had to force our way in. I had crispy duck salad and then white fish fillet on tasty lentils. Joss had won ton prawns, and then sausages and mash, and we shared a scrumptious pear tartine. Liam Neeson was at the next table. Joss laughed because I thought he was an undertaker. It was a lovely evening. I am so happy, and am totally in exciting, wonderful love.

Two agents arrived at the Old Rectory from London to discuss the script for the Labour Party TV ad for the upcoming election. I cooked pasta for them. They were very nice chaps, but Joss thought the script was not positive, and was moaning too much about the Tories, without saying what New Labour had in mind, or what changes their government would make. Toby flew to Cape Town this afternoon – to see his wife and Arthur. I wonder if their marriage is saved.

We sat ready to watch the Grand National, and suddenly it was cancelled, because of a bomb scare. The IRA has put coded bomb alerts all over London, which has come to a standstill. Joss is learning *Misalliance* for Chichester, and finding it hard.

Went to matins. It was a lovely service. It rained last night, so it's nice and fresh, and the plants are saying 'thank you'. We opened the paper and saw that Pete Postlethwaite is doing the TV for New Labour that Joss was going to do. When the New Labour lot had phoned after their visit, Joss said, 'I can't do this script – I'm a socialist!' So for the first time in his life he was fired – and fired from something that he was doing for free!!!

The air ticket for Czechoslovakia arrived – but it was just for Joss. So he had to ring up, and arrange one for me. Mike Radford, Ouida and Jennie Cook came to dinner. Mike has just got his divorce, and Jennie's was coming through. It was a very good evening.

We went to visit Rosemary's sister Catherine in Shrewsbury. She had just had a cancer operation, and the prospects were bleak. Once again we moved to a flat in Chichester, and I started work, as John Tarleton in *Misalliance*.

Lovely sleep, and then Penny rang to say Princess Di and Dido Fayed had been killed in a car crash in Paris. The world is in shock. We watched conflicting world reports.

Slept till 10 a.m. – then I watched TV. It was Diana's funeral service. Millions of people lined London streets. The gun carriage with six horses carried her coffin. It was very moving. The coffin's royal cloth blew in the wind, and a bouquet of white lilies and snowdrops were on top of the coffin. All we heard was the sound of the wheels of the gun carrier, and the horses' hooves. Thousands of people were totally silent.

Kirsty and Ant had a wee boy. They are calling him Ned Milo Patrick. I phoned Catherine. She wants to leave hospital, as she is not happy there. I read the script *Under the Sun* that Joss has been offered – shooting in Zimbabwe. Toby phoned, and hurrah! Angie is pregnant again.

We flew to Zimbabwe.

We arrived at Harare. Everyone is very friendly. The producer and the director, Paul Seed, joined Joss at 7.30, and worked on the script for two and a half hours.

I massaged Joss and helped him dress. His back was fine, but he went in a car without suspension, and it's buggered it up. [I have had back problems ever since 1960 when I jumped through a rostrum on the Old Vic stage in *The Oresteia* and slipped a disc.] He came in and we went to have an African meal of beans and roasted caterpillar, sweet potato and flying ants.

I took a taxi to the Dominican convent in Harare, and saw Sister Octavia, my old Latin teacher. I haven't seen her for fifty years, and she recognised me! I said a prayer in the chapel, but it is all changed and rebuilt – except for the garden that Sister Josephine designed. I am totally bemused, and very moved.

Carol has just phoned to say my sister Catherine died this morning. Melanie phoned, and Toby phoned.

Darling sister Catherine is having her funeral today. Melanie – I hope – is with Carol and Lorraine. I've just heard that Toni and Kirsty are going too. I'm sorry I'm not there. God bless her, and care for her soul. There is no electricity, and the lights are off. At 3 p.m. Joss and I came upstairs for a kip. We slept deeply, and woke at 5.45. The lights came on five minutes later. Fancy dreaming in the afternoon. Horrid. I don't feel very secure back in this country.

We fly to Malawi.

MIGRAINE. David Russell met us at Chileka. He drove to Mount Soche Hotel, and booked us in. We have a fabulous two-roomed suite, with two bathrooms!!! We had lunch at Ryall's – it was weird being back there.

My head is almost gone – I'm so grateful. David picked us up, and drove us to Chileka. After an hour and a half, filling in forms, and paying tax with American dollars! American dollars – in the middle of Africa!! A tremendous relief to leave Malawi – I'm always treated like a queen, and feel shoulder loads of worry.

We got up at 4.45, and flew to Victoria Falls – it is sad I never came here as a child. The Victoria Falls Hotel was packed with tourists, and our room was not ready. We had a glass of mango juice, and walked all along the Falls. There were the most beautiful rainbows over the water, with the early morning sun. It is stunning, and the spray bathed our faces, and we were happy to see such beauty in the world. We returned hot and sweating – it is 140 degrees – had a shower, and changed. We went to dinner – old-time 1940s song and dance, but rotten food.

Back at Harare.

Joss's alarm didn't go off, and his driver woke him!! Mad rush. He came back in a dreadful temper – the script had come back worse than before. He yelled at me to get a vodka, to find the soap, to do receipts, to do his cuffs – expects me to be fucking Mary Poppins – I'm fed up with him. Now his back is very painful, so I massaged his bum.

Slept well. Got up at 5.20 and Joss left for filming. I took a cab to the Anglican Cathedral, where I was confirmed in 1945. It was just the same service, which I knew by heart, and I took Communion over the same rail, as I did over fifty years ago. When I got back to the hotel I read – I'm going back to the William Trevor – I feel Doris Lessing's writing is so boring. I sat by the pool, and watched little weaverbirds feeding their young, high up in their nests in the date palms. Joss came in very sunburnt. He had two vodkas. Most of the cast left on British Airways. We came to bed – hot and stuffy.

We had tea with Paul Seed and Geoffrey Bayldon, and then drove to the airport, and checked in, with all our heavy statues and things.

Back in London.

We left for the Albert Hall. It was Barbara Cook's birthday concert, and she was in great form. She was seventy on 25 October. Elaine Stritch also sang. We met Duncan Wheldon and David Bowness, and they told us they had been sacked from Chichester. We were shocked. Tomorrow we're off to Italy.

Back in Devon from Italy.

Lovely to be back in Devon, Paul and Liz Seed came to dinner. Paul was Joss's director in Zimbabwe, and they live at Fairy Cross, only eight miles away. Small world, eh? We had a lovely evening. We had smoked salmon, fish pie and treacle tart. Bed at 3 a.m.

We had pasta and truffles, and got ready for midnight mass. Polly, Melanie, Sam and Adam arrived. Polly and I went to church – Joss followed, and we all had Communion together, and sang carols.

CHRISTMAS DAY: Joss left for Lantern Radio, where he acted as Father Christmas. He was a bit fuddy-duddy and waffled. He returned, and at 11.30 we had champagne, and did presents.

Joss and I recycled the bottles and papers, and what an amazing recycling hut! – on a cliff, and overlooking the sea. Toni, David, Emily, Luca, Abbi, Izzie, Georgia and Lettie arrived. I cooked curry, chicken and couscous.

1998

Today there was a 102-degree force wind, and hail. It was a hurricane, and two trees came down in our garden, and two outside the church in the avenue. Joss very sweetly drove me to church, and collected me. This afternoon we worked in the office. I cooked black pasta and prawns for supper. When Joss was making coffee, I went in to tell him something, and he said, 'You're pissed'. After such a lovely day, and delicious meal together, why did he so insult me, when it wasn't even true? I overreacted, and was very hurt. We had a gigantic row, and neither of us could sleep. At 3.30 we got up and had a cup of tea. Then we didn't sleep till about six.

We didn't wake up till noon. It is very windy and wet and freezing cold. It was so exciting. I went to wash, came back into the bedroom, Joss was sitting on the edge of the bed half-dressed, and when I said, 'Good morning, darling', and bent to kiss him, he wrapped me in his arms, kissed me ferociously and pulled me down on top of him on the bed. When we got up we had great coffee and breakfast. I cleaned the Aga, and then we went to the recycling overlooking the sea, and were nearly blown away.

Joss went to Blake's to change his jacket, and he called me down from the flat to help him choose an alternative one. He tricked me, because he had bought me a very warm, winter fur coat – very smart.

Bad world news as America and Britain want to bomb Iraq, because Iraq will not allow them to inspect their depots of nerve gas and anthrax.

Joss and I drove to Hartland Lighthouse, parked our car and went for a lovely long walk. It was really romantic; we crossed two stiles [not easy for Rosemary], and stopped to kiss each time for luck. Came back, had lunch, Joss learnt his script and I ironed. There is much discussion about whether or not to bomb Hussein as he will not let the Americans go with the United Nations to check their arsenal for the 'so-called' weapons of destruction. At 8 p.m. Joss and I had vodka, and we watched a dreadful film, *Liar Liar*, with Jim Carrey – an actor I never want to see again.

It's very hot and stuffy here in London. Joss panicked because he left his razor in Devon, and so I ran!! (Just kidding) over to the Garden Pharmacy, to buy him a wet shave. Came back and we walked to the Aldwych to see *Amy's Way*, an excellent play. Judi Dench was splendid. She opened a bottle of champagne, and Ronald Pickup joined us.

Melanie is fostering a newborn baby. The mother is thirteen and the father is twelve!! What is the world coming to? I went to the post office and collected my pension, but the post office was so crowded I found it difficult keeping my balance, and also it was a problem walking on wet pavement.

Virgin looked after us very well, and we flew to Los Angeles.

We have a beautiful cottage at the Chateau Marmont, surrounded by trees.

We called in at Susan Smith's [my Los Angeles agent]. She was away in Chicago. Gabriella and the other girls played Joss's show reel, and said it was brilliant, and not too long because she said Americans cannot concentrate on anything for longer than six minutes!! They seemed quite proud of this, and were so laid-back, that I was shocked. I hated it all.

We went to Santa Monica, to Jean Simmons' house, but she'd already left for the restaurant. So we jollied down there, and joined Jean and Glynis Johns, who were upset that we were one and a quarter hours late. We had a fun lunch, and Glynis was very chatty, joking with Joss. Then Joss and I drove to the Beverly Centre, and saw *My Giant*. Joss's entire performance, the only serious part of the film, had been cut out, leaving nothing but a mass of Billy Crystal gags – so the balance had gone. It was a very disappointing movie – and sad for George, who was sweet as the giant. It upset me more than Joss. He just laughed, and shrugged it off.

Jean woke us up with an early phone call, and then there was another long call from Glynis. I saw Chaplin's *Gold Rush* again, and then *A World Apart*, the best apartheid movie I've seen – so beautifully played and directed. A perfect example of the South Africa we knew, when we were there. It was very sad.

Joss came in at 1.30 in the afternoon. He had been working all through the night and morning – for eighteen hours – exhausted and overtired. He crept into bed with me, and cuddled drowsily, but couldn't sleep, so at 3 p.m. we got up and had 'breakfast'. We then went back to bed, and slept till seven. Two hours later we left for Pinot Bistro at Ventura, and had a beautiful evening.

Back in England.

I went to the Portland Hospital for another check-up, and Dr Bourne gave me an internal ultrasound. It was quite uncomfortable. We packed up, and took the train to Tiverton. As we got out of the train, the heavens burst on us, and we got drenched to the skin. Oh bliss! It's so lovely to be home.

Off to Spain.

Results of my scan were pleasing – all negative. Thank God. Joss learnt lines for his Italian script in India, and I heard him. A very comfortable flight to Barcelona.

Joss has the day off, so we went to see the port, and walked around some little, weird old streets. We just love this city. We found a great restaurant on the seafront – Salamanca – and had the delicious parrilladas.

We have had a lovely day. We took the train to Stiges, by the sea, and found the most wonderful market. We walked up to the museums, then through the old town and, as the temperature was 36 degrees, we arrived back at the hotel exhausted. We collapsed on the bed for a rest, and woke up an hour later, and made heaven. Then off to El Pescados again. We sat in the yard – it was so pretty under the trees. A tranquil evening. We are so lucky.

But then –

I slipped on the hotel mat, and broke my right wrist. I took a taxi to the clinic, and had it set. It is in plaster, and is very painful, so I slept in my clothes.

Over the next six weeks the writing was written with her left hand.

My arm is not so painful today – but is badly bruised. Joss got back, and we had room service. He got cross with himself, because he couldn't close the suitcase. It is so difficult to pack with one hand.

It is difficult to judge now whether Rosemary losing her balance, falling down so frequently and finding walking so difficult might have been the first signs of motor neurone disease. It would tie up with the start of speech problems, but very difficult to identify as Rosemary was a walking paraplegic. It would be very unusual because the lifespan of MND is very rarely more than two years, and these were early days.

Anyway, despite Rosemary's wrist being badly broken, the next morning we were up at six, and then flying off to Sri Lanka, where I was about to start my next movie for Italian television.

We arrived at Sri Lanka at 3.30 a.m., and took a long, perilous two-hour drive, with oncoming cars passing on either side of us – to a fantastic hotel, Taj Exotica. After a chilli omelette, we slept for six hours, unpacked and then Joss had a costume fitting.

After Joss sponged me down, he bought me two cool Indian outfits, which are both easy to put on with one hand and a lovely silk scarf, as a sling for my wrist. Then he went off to film, and I sat on the balcony and removed my elbow plaster so that the sun and the sea can repair my arm. I watched the Clinton inquiry on CNN. It is disgraceful – and so pathetic.

Back to England and Devon.

It is lovely to be back at the Rectory, and relax. I had my wrist done by Mrs Langdon in Clovelly. Joss was all day on the phone – trying to find a leading lady and a director for *The Gin Game*.

Dorothy Tutin and Frith Banbury came to Floral Street, and read through *The Gin Game*. Dreadful news – this morning two Clovelly fishermen, Mark Gist and Dave McBride, went missing at sea.

Penny phoned about the fishing disaster. Dan the fisherman came for tea, and discussed with Joss what to do down by the beach for David and Mark. Joss is to make an appeal to help the relatives.

Packed up the house and car, and Joss did his appeal, then we drove to London.

The doorbell went, and it was someone delivering a poem for Joss to read in church, at the funeral of Mark Gist. So he rang Jackie, and cancelled the voice-over.

Yesterday America and England bombed Iraq, because they would not allow United Nations to inspect their 'arsenal'!!! I stayed in all day, as I feel ill and tired.

1999

It's very quiet this morning in Floral Street, after all the celebrations last night. I heard Joss through his lines. We had a rest, after a lunch of scrambled egg on toast with white truffles, and lovely red wine. When we woke up, I heard Joss's lines again. He rehearsed all day. After washing up, making the bed and ironing – I went to Holy Eucharist. A lovely service.

Joss came in, and I heard his script through. He said Frith fell asleep during the afternoon run. Well, the poor man is eighty-six years old! I think it amused Joss and Dottie. Joss had strained his back, so he had a hot bath, and I massaged him.

Joss left for rehearsal, and I cleared up, did some washing, and then walked to the church, and had Holy Communion. It was a very moving service, meaningful and comforting.

First preview here in Cambridge. They rehearsed for two hours, but Dot couldn't go on, so we came back to the hotel for a sleep. The show went very well. The house was full, and the audience adored it. Joss and Dot were right on form. There was a little confusion, and a loud prompt from Rick – he should try and be quieter.

Here I am sitting in the circle with Frith. It is the interval, and the show is much better. They are playing with real cards for the first time and – yes – it does give an extra edge to the performances.

Arrived at Malvern Festival Theatre, and moved into the Mount Pleasant Hotel – well named. Joss arrived back from rehearsal, and we switched on BBC2. *Daisies in December* was stunning, and Joss and Jean are superb. I cried and cried.

Then we went to the theatre. The show had the brakes on, and did not work so well. I feel now that the author Don Coburn is here, he is too close to it. He doesn't see it in perspective – so it's not working.

I squeezed four blood oranges for Joss, and he gave a magnificent show. *The Gin Game* was great tonight. Jeremy was thrilled, and so was Don. He is off tomorrow.

Back in Covent Garden we had a lovely cuddly night. My cough is bad. It is a freezing, icy day, and the pavements are slippery, so Joss won't let me go out again. When I was walking up Drury Lane, the wind was so strong that it would have blown me over if two young girls hadn't helped me. They were very sweet. Joss opened in Richmond tonight. He said it was a very good show, and they had cheers at the end.

Joss was on the phone all morning, because Dorothy Tutin was making a fuss about doing the play in town. Frith Banbury, Jeremy Meadows and all were worried, and asked Joss to sort it out. We packed up for Coventry. Had pasta for lunch, a sleep and then drove to Michael Frayn and Claire Tomalin at Gloucester Crescent. We had champagne, and then Peter and Thelma Nichols arrived. Very good dinner in their splendid kitchen. Joss had a 'non-birthday'.

Oh, it is wonderful being back in our own little place. We cuddled all night. It was beautiful, and we got up at 11 a.m. We are having a wonderful day together. I do so adore my very best friend. We watched *Gods and Monsters*, a movie about James Whale, who directed us in *Pagan in the Parlour*. Ian McKellen was not at all like him – didn't get his wicked humour – but Lynn Redgrave was excellent as the maid. We had superb red wine with our duck, and saffron rice and dahl, and then two lovely tarte tatin citrons. A lovely, lovely day.

Joss did coffee, and I left for Stoke Mandeville for my regular scan. I checked into X-ray, and they prepared me for my MRI. It took half an hour, and I had to keep very still. Then I took train and taxi back to Floral Street. Joss had left for Southampton, and left a lovely note for me. He'd made the bed, washed up and bought loads of herbs and sausages.

Bliss to be back home! We slept beautifully. I went into the kitchen, and when I turned round, I had a very nasty fall. I fell for no reason, and landed on my left leg. Joss took me to Dr Cracknell, and he put a dry dressing on it. I feel very shaky and insecure.

We got up at 6 a.m. Joss was in agony with pain with his back and neck, so I massaged him. The car collected him. He talked about *The Gin Game* for *The Big Breakfast* show. He coped well, but the presenters are hopeless. Such stupid, mindless dumbing down – horrid. What a sad age we live in. Joss and I had lunch, a kip and then a nice evening together, because the Savoy is setting up for the rehearsal and preview tomorrow.

Opening night of *The Gin Game* at the Savoy in the Strand, which is just a few yards away. We had a long sleep. Joss left for the theatre, and Adam and I walked down later. Kirsty, Toni and Sam were waiting for us. Kirsty looked radiant in her yellow summer dress – very pregnant. David and Ant turned up, and we all went into the theatre. Polly and Sean, Kandy, Luca and his friend, Penny and Daniel, Toby and Angie were already there. It was an excellent show. Afterwards Michael Frayn, Claire Tomalin, Eddie and Susan Kulakundis, Moyra Fraser, Frith Banbury, Jonathan and Jeremy were all in the dressing room, and also Don Coburn, with his eyes shining. We all had champagne. Our family left for Floral Street, and put all the food out and the music on. The others followed, while Joss popped in to the party at Simpson's for a minute, and then he came here, and we all had supper and wine.

Nicholas de Jongh gave the play a stinker in the *Standard*, but a very good notice for the acting. This was the only review today. Joss and I had a quiet morning. He left to do a matinee, and I left to see Dr Lee. Got back to Floral Street, and forgot my keys, so I had to sit on the stairs, and wait three-quarters of an hour for Joss. We had a kip, and then he left again for the theatre.

There was a brilliant notice for *The Gin Game* in *The Times*, and a very good one in the *Telegraph*. So things are looking up. I have a migraine, and feel sick. Joss didn't have a performance today, as it is Good Friday, so we had a lovely day at home relaxing.

Joss did an excellent interview with Parkinson. When he got home, we went to Cleveland Square, and took Arthur an Easter egg. Angie was very sweet. Joss still loved the flat. It had been cleaned up, and tidied, and looked much better. I'm now very confused.

Joss was collected for an interview with Sheridan Morley. Gore Vidal and Howard are at the show tonight. They came back with

Joss, but Gore has claustrophobia and wouldn't come up in the lift, so the four of us walked to the Ivy. Gore and Howard drank a lot of vodka cocktails. I only had half a glass of wine!

Samantha left Tommi and Natalie with me, because she has such a busy day sorting things out. Joss had a bit of a rest, and then went to do the show. The children were very good, and I do love them, but carrying Natalie was a strain – balancing – and I had to hold on to the back of a chair so that I didn't fall with her. Samantha collected the children and Joss came in. I have a bad headache, and we were both exhausted – so we got to bed early.

Joss left for the matinee. He said the streets are very crowded, and said that I shouldn't go out, as walking would be difficult. The bombing in Kosova is dreadful, and I feel so sorry for the refugees.

Lovely sunny day. Sammy came round. We put on evening dress, and a car picked us up, and took us to the BAFTA awards, where Joss presented a prize. I had a lovely time. Then a car took us to the *Vanity Fair* party. We met Adam there, and Judi Dench's daughter, Finty, was with him, also Isla Blair and family. Headache gone!! Thank God.

Oh, I am so in love. It is wonderful. We got up to a windy, blistering day. Dreadful news. Fascist gunmen in Denver – Nazi sympathizers – shot and killed twenty-five students. They were targeting black athletes. Absolute horror at the high school. It is so foul and sad. Melanie phoned for an hour. She'd been at a meeting with the Social Services, and she has agreed to take a very disturbed thirteen-year-old boy. Good luck to her. Samantha had good health news – no more thyroid problems – her cells are normal.

After breakfast, Joss and I went off in the car to Soho, and Joss bought pasta at Camisa, and fruit, herbs and bread at the market. We had a kip and then Joss went to the theatre. A bomb went off in Soho, at 6.30, at a gay pub, right opposite Camisa – two people killed, seventy injured. There were legs blown off, and streets full of injured, bleeding people. Luca, Adam and Toni are all okay. Melanie phoned five times, and Toni and Sammy rang.

Joss went to do a matinee. I was just going out, when Antonia called. She looks lovely, but was very concerned about Tom's exams – about Emily's teenage rejection – about twin mouth ulcers – and about David. Joss came in, and we had a kip. People came to see the flat, but Joss was in a bad temper, and would not let me show them around because he wanted the estate agent to do it. She was late. So they left. I worry about Joss's rudeness.

Greta Scacchi woke us up. She can't get into her flat, as someone went off with the key. So Joss got her a room at the Savoy. She and Carlo are going to *The Gin Game* tonight, and on to supper here. Paul and Liz Seed are also coming. I massaged Joss's back, and we had breakfast. We all had a lovely evening.

Joss phoned from the Ivy. He is meeting a girl from the *Telegraph* to talk about religion. I went with him to the Savoy, and watched *The Gin Game*. Joss and Dorothy were really wonderful, playing with great depth.

I recorded *One Foot in the Past*, which Joss did about Clovelly, and after the evening show we watched it. Samantha loved it. I had reservations.

Woke up feeling happy and well and in love! It's a beautiful Devon day. Antonia arrived with Abbi, Izzie, Georgia and Lettie. They enjoyed their lunch, and then went down to Clovelly. The children are very excited, jumping downstairs, and yelling. Abigail asked Joss why he didn't work?!!! The children are so funny. Started packing for Italy.

Woke up at Podere to hear Natalie singing. It is so sweet. I'd just got dressed, when Joss came in from the bathroom – and how!! – and so back to bed. Then I got washed, and dressed again! We all drove off to the stables down the hill, to have lunch. It was full of partisan freedom fighters from the Second World War, and was very jolly – and very moving. We had a delicious lunch, with lots of wine, and went on for five hours. It was such fun. Romeo, Paola, Nico, Tommi, Natalie, Tracy, Samantha, Joss and I had a real party.

We flew off to Rome. Boring flight, the air pollution was bad, and when we landed at Heathrow, I felt dizzy. We waited till most people were off the plane, and as I got out of my seat, someone tripped me up, and I fell across a seat, tore the skin off my left arm and strained my left leg. Blood poured all over my clothes. Inside the airport, a girl repaired my arm and first aid put on a bandage. [The falls were now getting more frequent.]

Harry, the man who is buying our flat, came for a drink. He seems very pleasant and honest. We left for Frith Banbury's, and had delicious paella for dinner. Ian Holm and Penelope Wilton joined us. Frith played tape recordings of John Gielgud. Off to Clovelly tomorrow.

Lovely sleep. It rained last night, so it's cooled down a bit. Joss woke me up early – and how! He took me by surprise, and it was so beautifully romantic. I do love him so very, very much. Toby flew to New York – Angie seems okay. Joss and I spent hours cleaning up, answering letters and making phone calls. John Rous came round with two excellent bottles of wine, and a thank you note for Joss's Clovelly programme, and to say how much he'd loved *The Gin Game*. I don't feel at all well today. I think it is bowel problems.

The removal men arrived. We met them at Cleveland Square. They had to take out all Toby's stuff, for storing, and then brought in ours. Joss was on the phone non-stop, and I had to decide where to put things. It was a stressful and demanding time. Bed 3.30 a.m.

Joss and I drove to Dulcie Grey's lovely home for lunch. Dick Lester and Deirdre were there. I feel so sorry for Dulcie. She is very brave now that she has lost Michael, after so many years together. A very hot day, thirty-two degrees.

Joss and I have been married forty-eight years today. How wonderful. I'm so in love. After lunch we had a cuddle, and then I cooked a huge fish pie for fifteen people – Sammy and her family, and Penny and her family. Dottie and Frith arrive tomorrow.

Dottie, Frith and Joss went down to rehearse until 1.45. After they'd gone through the play, I gave them scrambled eggs and smoked salmon. Then we all drove to Hartland and Dottie ran along the sea wall. John and Zeenat Rous came to supper. I cooked monkfish and scallops and mashed potatoes, and Dottie helped me lay the table, and prepare a pudding. Everyone got on well, and was happy. Joss and I got to bed at 1.45. It was sheer heaven, and a moon shone into our bedroom and completed the romance.

Got to Cleveland Square and Joss spoke to Toby. We are worried that Angie might have an abortion. I will never speak to her again if she does.

Car collected Joss to record *Richard II*. I'm so concerned about

Angeline. Joss rang her, and was very comforting. Toby called at midnight. He'd been in tears, talking to Angie for four hours.

Bad news. Toby has been mugged in New York. Early this morning he called from a New York hospital – very traumatised. I don't know what happened, but he had his head kicked in, and was in shock. Joss talked to him before rehearsal, and called him again after rehearsal. Angie stayed in all day to receive calls. Eventually she heard that Toby was getting the flight tonight. There are tornados in New York.

We got up at 4.20, and saw Angie off to the airport to meet Toby. They both arrived back at 6.30. Toby looks stressed, and has a bad headache. Joss left for the theatre to rehearse, and came back with a broken wrist. A cyclist had run him over at thirty miles an hour in Tottenham Court Road. I took him to casualty. He had an X-ray, and his arm was put in plaster. We were in casualty for two hours. Toby is stressed, and has pain in his head, and Angie keeps being sick. Everyone is in such trouble. After a late supper Toby and Angie went to bed. Penny went home, and Joss waited for me to help him undress.

First night of the second tour *The Gin Game*. We took a taxi to the Royal Bath Hospital, and Joss had his heavy plaster removed, and a lighter, stronger plaster put on. Then he and Dottie had a dress rehearsal, which went on and on. I made him a coffee, and then went front of house, and saw the most wonderful performance by them both. It was funny and moving, and the whole audience stood up and cheered. I do so admire Joss managing to deal cards, and act so well, with a broken wrist. After the show we took him to casualty because his fingers had gone black. They X-rayed his wrist, and re-bandaged his plaster, and put a sling on. Joss phoned Toby, when we got back to the hotel. Poor Toby is worried that Angie still wants an abortion. Silly, stupid girl.

A car collected Joss, Dottie and me, for Lincoln. Raining heavily and Joss is in agony. He can hardly move, because of pain in his right breast. Went with him to the hospital, and we were there for over two hours. He had his chest X-rayed, and was given more Tylex. No broken ribs.

Joss had a bad, painful, hot night, and woke up cross. Then he had phone interviews all morning, and was phoning Toby to sort things out with Angie. After breakfast, Dottie and I got a cab to the cathedral and said prayers in the chapel. A taxi picked us all up, and took us to the hospital clinic, where Joss saw a doctor who X-rayed his break once more, and he had a new plaster on. We got back from the hospital, had a sleep and then Joss and Dottie went to the theatre, and came back, elated, at 10 p.m. The show had gone so well, and had a standing ovation. I'm so thrilled.

A devastating train crash this morning, at Paddington. The local train went through two red lights, and ploughed into the Great Western train. It is a shameful, horrific mess, with seventy dead, and many in hospital in intensive care, and burnt. Such dreadful carnage – so utterly sad.

Paul died this day – seventeen years ago. Joss is managing to do much more now with his broken wrist. He made the bed this morning. I cried when I read more horror about the crash – about the poor people trapped and burnt to death on the train.

We arrived at Brighton. Then I walked with Joss to the theatre, and sat in the dressing room, because we only have one key. The play went exceedingly well, and there were cheers and loads of whistles, whoops and claps – a great reception. Joss and I had vodka to celebrate, and then walked to English's and had tiny, young mussels and grilled sea bass. On the way back to our digs I fell on the pavement and hurt my left knee and cut my skin.

When I read the diary now – the frequency of Rosemary's falls is disconcerting, and so much more obvious than at the time – partly because one could assume then that these were paraplegia symptoms, and also because secretly I was hiding the fear of tragedy ahead.

Once home I took my trousers off, as blood was rushing down my leg. Joss helped me clean up, and we put plaster on, put my pants in cold water, made coffee and went to bed.

When we arrived at Chichester, a kind stranger helped us with our luggage, and drove us to the theatre. Then a taxi brought us to this lovely cottage in Orchard Street. Joss was in pain, and bad-tempered. He stood in the bath, while I sponged him down and rinsed him. I got out the painkillers, and fed them to him. Then he left for the theatre. When he returned, we phoned Toby, who seemed settled and happy – thank God. At 2 a.m. I had a nasty turn – I felt sick, went hot and cold, was drained of energy, and felt I was going to faint.

I feel better this morning, even though I fell in the bathroom and hurt my left leg. Joss and I went to the theatre together, and I saw the evening performance. It was an extraordinary experience. It reached pinnacle perfection – in timing, emotion and cross playing, and was sheer joy to watch. Joss and I walked home – both with painful legs! – and both exhausted. Joss had a long phone chat with Toby. Bad news. Angie has lost her baby. I think she had an abortion. Shit. Then Joss and I had a dreadful row, and he accused me of being drunk again – slurring my words – and I'd only had one glass of wine. He knows that it upsets me. Whenever I disagree with him, he accuses me of being drunk. One day he'll go too far. We tried to watch a movie, but it was difficult, so we went to bed.

Once again my ignorance over Rosemary slurring her words created pointless confusion and anger. Was I that blind after speech problems and so many falls? I'm afraid I was.

Back in Devon.

It is lovely to be back at the Rectory. We got home at 2 p.m. and sat down to eat, but I couldn't because *Daisies in December* was on television. It was so beautifully acted and enthralling, I cried and cried. I felt quite exhausted afterwards. We had a kip and then changed and went over to the Rouses for an Indian meal. It was a jolly party – but walking home, the wind was so strong, I couldn't stand up. However at 11.30 we walked back to the church, and went to midnight mass. The priest, Mr Honeybun, gave a stupid talk about Barbie dolls and Christmas trees, which put me off. We went to bed at 4.30 a.m. I had a horrid sleep, dreaming all night of Jean Simmons. She was accused of murdering a man in a bordello, but she didn't do it, and the whole night we were arguing in court.

After a late lunch we were watching a fascinating programme on TV about Rogers and Hart and enjoying a cosy fire, when a stranger arrived in our sitting room. He was a local who lives near us. He had a very red face. He was very pushy, and forcefully vocally tried to get Joss to go on a pub-crawl with him. He kept saying, 'Aren't you human? You're human, the same as me. Come with us.' I'm glad Joss was insistent, and said, 'No.'

THE LAST DAY OF THE CENTURY: Penny arrived, and we all had lunch. All the grandchildren had three helpings each. After washing up, we all went to have a kip, to prepare for tonight's millennium celebrations. Just before midnight Penny woke the children, and we collected crackers and put on the TV. There was a marvellous display of fireworks from Sydney Harbour. As Big Ben struck twelve, Joss and I kissed away 1999 for a whole minute into the next millennium. We had champagne and mince pies, as we watched the celebrations around the world. London had the Dome – but the Wheel didn't work. The river fireworks were okay – but half of them didn't go off. However – let's have a peaceful, healthy and happy New Year.

2000

Clovelly.

I am seventy-one today! Lovely cards and presents from the children and grandchildren. We drove to Paul and Liz Seed's for lunch, with Ian Richardson and his wife. We are very worried about Toby, who is depressed, and given up his work. Angie says he's been shut up in his bedroom for two days. Joss spoke to her for forty minutes this morning.

A car arrived at Cleveland Square to pick Joss up for interviews at the Savoy for his 'Pipe Man of the Year' do. Toby phoned – but he found it difficult to talk to me. The car is to pick me up to take me to the Savoy. How exciting! I arrived, and was taken in to join Joss, who was being interviewed, and then photographed with Greta [Scacchi]. Then we went upstairs, and had champagne, and I met Kirsty there, looking radiant and beautiful. Anthony arrived, and he also looked splendid. I sat next to Jack Rosenthal and the committee convener. We had white wine with smoked salmon, and then red wine with steak and kidney, which I couldn't eat – then fruit salad. Barry Norman gave Joss a splendid introduction speech, and Joss replied well. Joss was presented with a box of Dunhill pipes, loads of tobacco and a model movie camera and clapperboard, which can be smoked. It was a fun day, which we all enjoyed. Bed. Delicious love.

Joss went off to have lunch with Norman Stone and Hugh Whitemore. He came back, and we took a taxi to Harley Street, and Nick Parkhouse operated on my lip. The injections to anaesthetise it were agony. [Rosemary invariably took pain without flinching, but now I could see that she was really suffering. As he worked on the lip, Nick Parkhouse went on asking me questions about our lives, and about the theatre. I wish now that I had left the room. Maybe he would have concentrated harder. Normally this was a very minor operation, but I feel now that in this case there were hidden complications, and a sign of things to come. I have since learnt that David Niven had a similar lip problem before his motor neurone disease was identified.] We came home, and I started to bleed profusely into the basin – then it stopped. Joss got panicky, and drove me back to Harley Street. Nick Parkhouse was still there, and gave me two more injections, took out some stitches and re-stitched. Came home, and felt desperate pain, with swollen lips and deep bruising. I couldn't eat.

I feel better today. We slept with the bedroom window open, and I think the fresh air was beneficial. My chin is reacting to the arnica, and the bruising is subsiding, but my lip is still very swollen and painful. Very worrying news – Austria has voted in the fascists again. How can they forget history? How can we join Europe now? Shit.

Last day of antibiotics, and the stitches are removed tomorrow. Hope I can then drink. My bottom lip is very bulbous and swollen, and the bruising is still dark. I look like a walrus.

Joss drove me to Harley Street, and Nick Parkhouse took my stitches out. He tugged, and it hurt, and he made my lip bleed. I was glad to leave. Joss dropped me at the Hale Clinic for irrigation.

Joss has been in a very funny mood today – accusing me of being in a dwaal [African hypnotic dreamlike state]. He is studying, and getting irritable and tired, and so we had a kip until Garfield Davies phoned, and told me about my swallowing – all healthy and good news. I'm thrilled. Joss is still very uptight. During the night he was very sorry, and we made up.

My lip was very painful all night, and I woke up five times so I cuddled tightly up to Joss, and it eased a bit. I slept with a cloth in my mouth, as it was so painful. Joss worked on *Heartbreak House*. He is flying to Germany tomorrow to film.

Dr Cracknell took out two stitches from my lip, and it feels much better. I heard Joss through act one of *Heartbreak House*. He has nearly got it. The studio car collected us, and drove us to Marlow-on-Thames to film.

I had a lovely day reading and resting. Joss came in exhausted. He'd been doing a scene in a village street, and the locals deliberately drove their cars up and down, again and again, in order to disrupt the filming. The police had to be called. We had a glass of red wine, and had dinner downstairs. After the meal I felt I was going to faint. I staggered upstairs, and brought up all the soup, and then – after a difficult time – I went to the loo, and went to bed feeling ghastly.

Back in Cleveland Square.

It's 29 February – so it is Joss's eighteenth birthday. Spent the morning preparing food. Camisa delivered lovely foodstuff for us. I made tea for us all, and then cut up chickens, and made couscous, peppers, tomato and potato salad, and so on. The first to arrive were Greta Scacchi and Carlo, and soon after the Seeds, then Moyra Fraser and Alec McCowan, John Moffat, Frith Banbury, Anna Ford, Claire Bloom, Ion and Sue Trewin, John and Penny Mortimer, Eddie and Susan Kulukundis, Georgina and Tony Andrews, Zeenat Rous and Toni and David. Penny, Kirsty, Ant and Penny all came at the same time. Eddie gave Joss a 1928 bottle of Lafitte Rothschild. It was a jolly party, and Joss got lovely presents. Mike Radford arrived with a maddening girl, who put everyone's back up! Georgina got on very well with Zeenat. Ouida and a friend arrived. They left in dribs and drabs. I started cleaning up, and gave Penny some food. Joss got very bad back pains, and could hardly move. We got to bed at 3.15.

Joss was in bed all day with stomach pains. Poor, poor darling, I feel so sorry for him. He rang the *Mumbo Jumbo* production lot to alert them, and Dr Baker called, and told me to get kaolin and morphine. Joss got dressed at 5 p.m., and it's so good to see him up, and looking a wee bit better. He had broth, and then three tiny pieces of toast with avocado, and half a pawpaw. MIGRAINE BAD.

Poor Joss is still feeling very weak and insecure. He was really angry with the producer of the film, because he was given a second blood test yesterday – they had forgotten that he'd already had one

– and also because no one working on the film has been paid. I phoned Rosalind Sopel regarding leaving the Rectory to all the children, and then phoned Trevor Nathan to get our wills to Rosalind, and Patrick MacNamee to change our mortgage to our London flat from the Rectory. So it's all go.

Clovelly.

Lovely to wake up in our bedroom, in the fresh country air, and as always, in Joss's arms. I love him so very, very much. We made exquisite love, and both had a shower. The migraine hangs on like a terrier with a sharp tooth, through my right eye. Bloody mice in my bedroom have eaten holes in my bag. But it's a lovely sunny day, and so blissful in the Rectory. A car collected us, and took us to the airport. Our plane was delayed because of fog, and we finally arrived in Glasgow at 6.30. Norman Stone met us, and put us in a taxi to the Malmaison Hotel. We bad a half-hour kip, and then joined Sally [Sally Magnusson – Norman Stone's wife] and Norman and an Australian director, and we had dinner.

Joss left for filming. [I was recording Arnold Wesker's Barabbas soliloquy for television.] I washed, dressed and packed, as we leave this evening, via Bristol, for Devon. Sally drove me to her lovely old farmhouse. She was very busy doing laundry, dropping her daughter at ballet class, and her au pair and son at the bus stop. Her dog jumped up at me, and nearly knocked me over. They have three very fat, tame sheep. After filming we flew in a tiny, very noisy, plane to Bristol. A driver picked us up, and drove back to Clovelly. It's so wonderful to be back there. We slept for two hours, and then came downstairs, and a horrid black cat was terrorising our cats, Gigi and Ton Ton, and they were screaming like babies.

Lovely bright day. We finished packing the car, clearing up and making Gigi and Ton Ton comfortable. We stopped for lunch at a thirteenth-century pub near Bampton. I had venison medallions, and Joss very sweetly cut up the meat for me so I could swallow it. We arrived at Church Norton at 6 p.m. The two boys who own the place helped us unpack the car, and made us comfortable. We got to bed at 3 a.m, and slept well.

Church Norton – Chichester.

A lovely sunny day. Went into Chichester with Joss and set off with my trolley for the first time. It was great! This evening we saw *Tales for Easter* on TV. Joss played Barabbas beautifully – such a good script by Arnold Wesker. It would have been even stronger if the camera had simply concentrated on the mind of the man, and not jiggled about. We went to bed at 1.30, and made exquisite love. Oh, what bliss!

Kirsty and five arrived – such a sweet, exuberant family, good-looking, healthy, happy and full of initiative and energy. Joss arrived with Toby. It was so good to see my son after such a long time. We had a really happy lunchtime. Then we drove down to the beach, but it was very cold, so we came back and had tea, before taking Toby to the station. He was only here four hours – but it was so good to see him.

I woke at 2.30 feeling very ill, and vomited and vomited. Then I had dreadful pains in my tummy – I felt I was dying. Got back to bed and woke up at six feeling better. Got dressed, and a car collected me at 6.30, and dropped me at Chichester station. Train was rattling and so bumpy, it was difficult to read. Got to the Hale Clinic, and Ursula gave me a colonic therapy. After getting a taxi back to Victoria, I had a horrendous time. Because it was late no one knew which platform the train would come into. They thought it was platform nineteen, and then, at the last minute, said it was on platform nine. So I had a very long walk. When I got there the whistle went for the train to leave. I shouted for them to stop, as I had to get on board. They let me on, at the rear of the train, but they said only the first two coaches went to Chichester. So, when the train had a long stop, the guard moved me all the way to the front. When I got to the theatre, Joss said he had an hour off, so he brought me home, and then went back to the theatre. I tidied up a bit and had a kip till half past six, when Joss came home. Both exhausted, and we went to bed early.

We intended to go to see the opening night of *The Recruiting Officer* and so Joss met me in the theatre restaurant. He was tired after rehearsal, and didn't feel like going to the theatre. I also felt tired, so we decided to go home. As I left the restaurant, my coat caught on a chair, and I fell flat on my face, I cut my chin, and got a black eye!!! So I staggered to the car, we drove to Waitrose and the first-aid men came with an ice pack for my face. Joss did some shopping as I sat in the car, and then we came back to the cottage, and disinfected my cuts and we put arnica on my eye and plasters on my chin and hand.

Joss said *Heartbreak House* got cheers at the end of the performance tonight. When he got back we had smoked salmon, and prawns, which I had marinated with oil, garlic, ginger and parsley, avocado and salad. Joss brought in the coffee, spilt a cup on the tablecloth and then blamed me for picking my teeth, and said I was drunk – which no way I was [here we go again – how can I have been so blind?] and he behaved like a bore and a bully. Evening ruined. I went to bed, fed up and miserable. Woke up with a headache at 3 a.m. – then I went back to sleep and prayed.

We drove for a lunch with friends of the theatre. It was a jolly time. We sat at a table outside. Joss brought food for me as I was having a difficult day, balancing and talking. My mouth and spine were wobbly and I feel dreadful, but enjoyed the ambience. On the way home Joss stopped for me to pee at a pub. I overbalanced and hit my face on the floor – also twisted my left hand. I found it difficult to get up. It was a relief to get home and have a rest. Felt much better after a sleep, and my speech was back to normal.

It's quite an overcast day. Joss is busy phoning Mr Catterall about my lip, and to get Samantha booked into North Devon Hospital to have her baby in December. I just feel the lip operation was the straw that broke the camel's back. I'd had too many operations to have such a traumatic one at the age of seventy. It was not worth all the pain, aggravation and effort. Hey ho! We went to bed at 1.30, and found Illyria.

Joss is working on a John Mortimer play *The Summer of a Dormouse* – he is going to do a reading of it later this week at the Minerva as a try-out. We went to bed early at 1.30. We had the most wonderful time and reached a peak of ecstasy – sheer wonder and delight.

We have sold Cleveland, but we have to move out by 10 July.

What a nightmare – such a hurry, and we are here in Chichester, and I have three appointments in London on three different days. Phoned Penny and we can stay there. Phoned Field's to move us on the tenth. At the theatre Nat is getting two chaps to help us, because I can't manage to do it all myself. Joss shouted at me because my speech is sloppy. I wish, I wish, I wish I hadn't had the operation. I feel so frustrated. I do my exercises so many times a day – but by midday my muscles are tired. I don't know what to do.

Joss and Dulcie had fresh orange juice and cereal for breakfast [Dulcie Grey had stayed the night] and we left for the theatre at 10.15 a.m. to see *Summer of a Dormouse*. Joss was superb and brilliantly brought the script to life – he was humorous and exciting, and John Mortimer was in tears with joy.

After the show we drove to Cleveland Square, and got to bed at 1.30. We got up at 7.15 before the removers arrived. They were very nice but kept me on the run as they wanted to know what went where. Joss and I spent the rest of the day sorting out things. This is our last night here.

Removers arrived early, took away the bed and last-minute things, and left me with one chair. The estate agent came to collect the keys, and helped us into the car with our bits. We said goodbye to all. We took ages to get out of London, and arrived back here exhausted. My right ankle is agony with hot and cold waves of pain.

We got up at 6.35 and got to Stoke Mandeville at 10.15. I had a stomach X-ray and a kidney and bladder X-ray – they took three bottles of blood for testing – said I had a small lump on my liver – it didn't worry them.

We left the cottage, and Joss was so helpful and arranged for me to get a wheelchair to the end of the train, and settled me in a first-class compartment. I arrived at Victoria – a long, long walk to the taxi rank, and then a long, long wait. Got to Harley Street and saw Dr Mans Lyon. He was very concerned and gave me a good examination, and then I took a taxi to Richard Stubbs, for my physiotherapy, and he was able to see me at once. Penny phoned, and came to meet me. She was so sweet and took me to Victoria station and saw me on to the platform before she left – but once again the number was wrong. Eventually the loudspeaker said platform nineteen but only the first four carriages were for Chichester, and the train would leave in two minutes. Of course I knew I could not walk there in two minutes, but a young black man gave me his arm and helped me on to the train and the right carriage. He was wonderful and shouted to the guard to hold the train for me. A very bright, entertaining group kept me amused, and all were kind and helpful and fun. Got to Chichester, and waited twenty minutes for a cab. Got to the Festival Theatre at 9 p.m., and what bliss to walk into Joss's dressing room and see his wonderful, welcoming smile. Oh, I adore him and he is so precious to me.

Joss phoned airways and stations trying to get us a flight to Italy. I had a Guinness before lunch. I am still forty-two kilograms in spite of my Guinnesses and high-protein drink. Funny!! Maybe it is because I have a very quick metabolism. Hope so! We had a kip and made exquisite love.

I don't feel well today. I sorted out what to take to Chichester tomorrow, as Joss has a matinee and so many friends are going. Greta Scacchi plus three, and Claire Bloom, Hugh Whitmore, Penny, Daniel and Inigo.

We went to the theatre. Penny took her two children to the matinee and I walked into town with Ella and Nancy, who were very good, and I did some shopping. When we got back to the theatre, Claire and Greta were there, with Greta's brother, and her daughter and step-daughter. We dropped Claire at the station, she loved the matinee, and thought Joss was born to play Lear. Greta and her family and Penny and family came home to supper. Bed at 3 a.m.

I saw Dr Cracknell. He took me on his books, and I had a thyroid blood test. He also arranged for me to see a neurologist at Exeter. Penny kindly drove us to Exeter and saw Dr Honing with us, which was helpful.

Sunny day, so Penny and the children took surfboards to the beach, and they had a great day. I am feeling a lot better now that we are in our own home. Bed at 3 a.m. and we made exquisite love, and there was moonlight on our bed – beautiful.

It is our forty-ninth wedding anniversary, and I love Joss more and more each day. My cup runneth over with love for him, and my happiness in him. Tonight I cooked couscous and chicken curry for the family. Penny's children loved it. We had a glass of champagne to celebrate – and got to bed, after watching a film, at 2.30.

A lovely sunny day. Penny took a picnic to the beach. Joss and I had a celebration lunch of lobster and champagne – delicious. We then had a cuddle and I cooked fish and chips for everyone for supper. Penny got in, Joss was on the loo, and Penny sat down in the kitchen and talked to me about the tests. She said she is preparing me, because the results point to motor neurone disease. She said that there was a lot that can be done for it. It was such a surprise.

I was shocked but too numb to react. I don't want to think about it. I feel so well and happy – I can't be ill, although I do feel weaker each day. I will overcome what I can.

When Rosemary and I were alone she gently told me what Penny had said to her. The life surged out of me as the truth finally surfaced. We held each other close, wept and said, 'To hell with it – we will fight it together.'

Joss left for Ron's eightieth birthday party. I didn't feel well enough to attend, but persuaded Joss to go – I think it's important. I did about three hours' ironing and tidying up. Penny was going to leave at 10 a.m., but her children were naughty and she didn't leave until 1.10. Joss came in at 4 p.m., and we had lunch of fish and chips – a rest, then phone calls and letters. Joss spoke to Trevor Nunn – their long conversation interrupted our dinner!

We left early to go to the Nuffield Hospital in Exeter. Pouring with rain. I had an MRI scan of the brain and face, in a mobile unit. We drove home and stopped at Barnstable on the way. Joss shopped and I waited in the car. Back home we had lunch, and then a kip for two hours. Bed at 2.30 a.m.

It's a lovely hot day. We went to drop off a bottle of red wine and beers to Charlie for his birthday, and then recycled all the newspapers and bottles. What a fabulous recycling place, over-looking the sea. We left for Barnstable to see Dr Honan and get results from Bristol and Exeter. The muscle test at Bristol proves I've got motor neurone trouble, but the scan on my brain shows nothing unusual, so I'm quite cheerful, and feel things are not too bad. The prognosis is two years! We came back and had a glass of champagne, and supper of egg and bacon flan and ham and avocado, blackberries and meringue. Then went to bed early and made exquisite love.

Kirsty and Ant are so kind; they are going to bring our stuff down that we were keeping in London when we were going to share a house with Penny. Of course that is out now. It will be lovely to have something in which to keep our things. When Brenda came, we sorted out the rooms upstairs and made a space for our cupboards and bed. Then Joss and I went to the doctor and collected our medicine. I came home and looked up the steroids and decided not to take them. We went upstairs for a kip and then came down and had the most delicious dinner of lobster, avocado and wonderful white wine. We finished up with berries and ice cream. Bed at 2.50.

Kirsty arrived and then Anthony came with a vanload of our stuff. Cooked pasta – they all enjoyed it, but I couldn't swallow it, so I had fruit and meringue.

Sally Plumb arrived and was very helpful. [Sally was the first of Rosemary's advisors to visit her.] She left us some useful literature, and was very understanding. She stayed two and a half hours. Kirsty was so helpful. She took the children down to Clovelly beach for a walk and back, and then she gave the children sandwiches, grabbed a bit of bread and cheese and left. Joss was on the phone all afternoon, trying to arrange flights to Italy. [Rosemary decided that we should live life together as normally as possible, and she said, 'After all, life was to be lived'.] We had a kip and then got up and had smoked salmon, crab and champagne. We had the most delicious dinner together – and then treacle tart and ice cream with

Rose. Toby was only here four hours – but it was so good to see him. I so enjoyed the evening. We watched TV for a while before going to bed.

Answered all my letters, and sent books to each grandchild that wrote – Georgia, Izzie, Abbi, Romeo, Paola, Nico, Tommi and Natalie. I really need to post them all. As we were finishing lunch Sue Hoisdon, the occupational therapist, came to assess our problems. She suggests we get a stair lift or a proper lift. What a bore. When she left I washed up and cleared the kitchen. I felt depressed about what the future holds for me, and so sorry for poor Joss having this burden of my weakness, and all the expense of adapting the house for my illness. We cuddled for a couple of hours, and then changed and drove to Paul and Liz Seed's for dinner. Their two sons – Jack and Robin – joined us. We had spinach and bacon bits and croutons, and then baked bass and new potatoes and green beans. The croutons helped the fish go down. We came home – had a coffee – left the cats asleep on the sheepskin and went to bed.

I had a shower and breakfast. The therapist came. She was so depressing – she wanted wheelchairs and handrails and lifts. I found her forcefulness oppressive, and I want to escape. Joss and I can muddle on together – it's much better. We left, and I collected my disability and pension money and we collected the laundry and went to the chiropodist. We don't like the new chiropodist, personality-wise. He is insensitive and clumsy – maybe be is just nervous of us. Joss did shopping chores while I had my feet done. We had brill for supper. At the end of the meal I suddenly felt very tearful and could not stop weeping. My speech is getting slower and my right hand weaker. I am so frustrated and desperate. Joss gave me a good

THE SEVENTIES

Penny, Kirsty, Melanie, Joss, Toni, Toby, Sammy and Paul (at Lemnos in Greece)

Games at Ravenswood

Rosemary and Toby
in the Himalayas

Family concert

Working with Samantha …   … and with Toby

Rosemary, Paul
and Sammy

Sammy and
Rosemary at
Primrose Cottage

Melanie, Penny, Rosemary, Joss, Sammy, Toby, Polly, Toni and Kirsty

THE EIGHTIES

Ben with his father

Kandy with her grandfather

Irene, Joss, family and friends carrying Paul's ashes at Clontarf

We leave Covent Garden

Kirsty, Sammy, Toni, Melanie, Joss, Rosemary, Toby and Penny

Leading some of our family up Clovelly

Two thirds of the family at the top

… and quite a few after Kirsty and Ant's wedding

Sisters, brothers and cousins

At home in Covent
Garden

In Toronto, coping
together with Motor
Neurone Disease

Rosemary kept her diary till the end

cuddle. Then we went upstairs and made exquisite love. Life is so wonderful when we make love. Had a good cuddly sleep. Rained heavily all day.

Got up at 8.30, and I went to the loo. Yippee! We had breakfast and as soon as coffee was ready we had phone calls! Simon arrived and started working on the new lavatory, and as luck would have it, the occupational therapist, Rosemary Smith, arrived with a lavatory help stand, and a stool for the shower. An aggressive man, Howard, arrived about lifts, but Joss and Simon couldn't get on with him – he was too bureaucratic – so goodbye. Someone rang for me to see a speech therapist at 2 p.m. today. Shit. I'm so sick of medical people and things. After a snack we went into Bideford Hospital and saw a young Scottish boy, who was very nervous. He relaxed a little eventually, after testing my swallow with his fingers. He gave us a long speech about how food comes back through the nose, if the sphincter muscle is weak. Charming!!

Having determined that life must be lived – off we set for Italy.

The phone rang every five minutes. Packed our cases, and we left at 2.15, and then called in at the surgery for some sort of breathing machine that Joss collected. We then drove off towards the M5 – and got lost. We arrived at Toni's at eight. Lovely to see the children. Toni gave up her bedroom to us, which was so clean and comfortable, and convenient with the bathroom next door. We had a wonderfully comfortable night.

Toni drove us to Stansted. She parked the car and came and

helped us to check in, and then we said goodbye. The security man was overzealous searching Joss, which made him very cross. Then the 'help' man, who was pushing me, left me so that he could push someone else. The flight was called – then the flight 'closing' was called and he hadn't returned. I caught hold of another man who wheeled us off, while he telephoned the man who was supposed to be seeing to us. We were so late and I became stressed. He wheeled me to the plane and I was so angry that adrenaline pushed me out of the chair and up the stairs as fast as I could go. The seats in the plane were very narrow, and Joss was most uncomfortable. I felt so sorry for him. Toni had packed us a lovely lunch, which I enjoyed. When we arrived at Rome we waited until everyone had evacuated the plane, and then a wheelchair was brought up by forklift. I got in, and the attendant took my passport and wheeled me to the baggage, and deposited me there. Joss got a trolley, put the luggage on it and asked for assistance to push me in the wheelchair. No one would help, so Joss got frustrated. He left the luggage at a counter, wheeled me out and then went back and collected all our stuff. Samantha was standing there like an angel – a wonderful smile of welcome, and a big hug. She was looking so pretty and well, and I felt better immediately. We drove to Orvieto, bought a dishwasher for her, and did an exciting food shop. Drove to Podere Antico. The house was so welcoming and very clean. We had a delicious supper and loads of wine before bed.

Windy morning! Joss and I went to Montecchio to get cappuccino. It is a feast day and everyone is dressed up. The sun came out, and the wind dropped so it was a lovely calm day. We had a relaxed evening together.

After breakfast, Joss and Sammy went off shopping. I stayed in because last night I took lactoberyl, and I am insecure. Not any more – success. So I read outside. Joss and Sammy returned. They had bought me two fabulous cushions, and an air bed thing. They also bought lots of lovely food. Simply delicious. Joss and I made wonderful love and slept.

Woke up 7.30 to a hive of activity with Nico and Natalie shouting loudly. Joss has woken up with a headache, for three mornings now. I'll give him an extra painkiller for the pain in his leg. Natalie watched Joss pee in the garden yesterday – and I saw her part her legs and wee, trying to direct the flow like her grandfather!

Joss and I left for Orvieto. When we got home I asked if they would like supper, but Sammy said, 'No, we are having ours later!' Joss made a fantastic tomato salad, which we had on bread, and Joss also had Parma ham and cheese. I felt bad, eating without the family. Sammy said she wouldn't eat with us because I needed to be peaceful. Shit! I feel so awful. I hate being made to feel an invalid or punished because of my eating problem. Why can't people be normal when one is ill? Why treat us as inhuman and special? It's a very warm night – so Joss and I just slept with a sheet on us. The flies are such a nuisance – they are rampant, and settle on our hair, face, eyes and ears, and are really annoying.

I washed up and Joss had a very constructive talk with Romeo, which ended in a cuddle. Good. We all drove to the restaurant Casanova – Sammy and Tracy, six children, Ouida, and Joss and I. It was a wonderful jolly party, and I so enjoyed the food and wine. We got back at 5 p.m, and had a sleep. I was definitely the worse for wear. We watched *The Goldiggers of 1935*. Wonderful film.

Got up at 8.30 and Joss washed my hair and then helped me have a lovely shower. Then the sweet love dried my feet for me. We walked upstairs, got dressed and packed. Samantha drove Joss and me to the airport. It was a pleasant drive, but very windy and cloudy. A helper got us off the plane, took us through security and Toni, looking radiant, met us. She drove us to her house in a Mercedes – a very comfortable car – very high and a good seat for me. Toni made us very welcome and her children were sweet.

Woke at 7 a.m. We washed and dressed, and waited for Toni to call us. Joss and I went with her to the craniologist – a homoeopath. It was very successful. I felt very refreshed after treatment. We got back, and had lunch, and then Toni drove Joss and me to King's College to see the consultant, Professor Leigh. He was most help-ful and Toni was good, asking important questions. They took three bottles of blood for research, and then we went back to Toni's, had a glass of wine and watched *The Sopranos*.

Back in Clovelly.

Simon and the first lift man came. There were great discussions for two hours until we decided that the lift should go outside. We had a kip at 7.30, and woke up at 9 p.m. so we just went to bed and made joy together. I'm so happy.

After lunch we went to the post office and collected new books. Raining gently all day, and Joss and I are so very happy, and in love. It makes life very rich. We had a cuddle for one and a half hours, and then I cooked sausages and mash for supper. I had a difficult time eating them, but I got down three sausages, and Joss's delicious mashed potatoes. Bed 2.30 p.m. I've walked all day without my stick! Good.

Woke up at 8 a.m. and feel as sick as a dog. Horrific accident on a Greek ferry to Pharos – eighty-three people drowned. How dreadful. I have intense stomach pains – had a little Yakult and feel a little better. Cooked salmon fishcakes for lunch, and I had a Guinness. Sue called and spoke about a wheelchair for me. We asked her to get a nurse to give me an enema. Success. I'm very tired tonight.

Got up at 9 a.m. Joss is feeling lousy, with a bad cold. I'm feeling fine, thank God – so far. Went to the loo after breakfast – which was a good surprise!!! After lunch we went into Bideford, I had my feet done, and shopped at the health shop. Found walking very difficult – even with my trolley. I kept tripping. Joss was very supportive. Came home and I made a fish pie for supper.

Simon and his carpenter arrived when Joss and I were still asleep. Joss had to rush down in his dressing gown to let them in. It was difficult sliding off to the loo and bathroom with them there, but I managed to get quickly dressed, and was in the kitchen by ten, when Simon came in. Joss went to Barnstable thinking he had an interview at Lantern Radio, but then Bristol TV arrived to interview Joss at home. When he got back he had his interview.

We spent the entire day in the basement, sorting out files – except for an hour recycling, and Joss trying to get accommodation for the BBC crew who are coming tomorrow for the television arts programme. Anthony phoned – he was full of excitement. He and Kirsty would like to live in Malawi!

We got up and had breakfast. Joss was expecting the artist Ken

Paine, and the director and film crew to arrive at 10 a.m, but they came at 11.00, and brought a beautiful bouquet of flowers. Ken Paine painted a splendid portrait of Joss, while they talked, and were both filmed. Ken and the crew left to have lunch at the Red Lion, while Joss and I had a snack. They were a nice and easy bunch, and finally left at seven. I'm going to get supper as it is 7.15 and I'm hungry!

Joss and I had prawns and avocado for lunch. I had a shock because my fingers had lost their dexterity, and I couldn't peel the prawns – nor could I undo the buttons on my trousers. Shit!! We had a kip, and then I cooked pasta with prawns and mushrooms, and we had stewed apples out of the garden. Another blow – I couldn't peel the apples. Shit. Shit. Shit. Watched two movies, went upstairs and made the most exquisite love.

It is the anniversary of Paul's death. Toni has reached the pinnacle of the Inca trail at dawn – I am sure she will meet Paul's spirit there.

Carpenters finished the built-in wardrobe today – it looks wonderful, and I'm excited to put my clothes inside. We worked in the basement, with Joss sorting out videos and me filing things from Cleveland Square, and looking for presents for the grand-children. It was a very bad evening for me. My saliva formed a clump in my throat, and I choked, and found difficulty in drinking wine, because it went up my nose. It is very depressing because I do enjoy a glass of wine and meals. [You will have gathered by now that good food was a great joy for us – and so was our wine. Rosemary's diaries were full of meals which she described in loving detail – far too many for me to mention.] Oh well! *C'est la vie.* It can't always be good. Joss was so understanding and such a comfort. He is truly wonderful to put up with me. It must be so horrid for him, dealing with my meal times. I look forward to going into Bideford with him tomorrow.

Slept very deeply – I feel exhausted today – too weak to go shopping with Joss. Good gracious me! It is now Saturday. We've had such a busy week; I've not had time to think of my diary. The builders started on the lift on Monday. The noise was ghastly as they cut a deep hole in the ground outside. The wardrobes were finished and painted – so we spent Friday putting clothes in, and then I saw Dr Cracknell. He gave me new bowel medicines. We returned home and cooked cod and chips. Feeling confident, I walked into the sitting room, with a stick in one hand and a plate of cooked cod in the other. Stupidly, I tripped on the mat and fell, and my fish flew into the air and on to the floor. What hell! We ended up sharing the other piece of fish, and opening a tin of sardines.

I had a ghastly day – took Dulcolax on Wednesday and felt ill all Thursday. Joss and I worked in the basement for hours and hours. It was pleasant because we had lovely CDs to listen to, and we got a lot of things sorted out.

The occupational therapist came with another lavatory stand and bath step. She was very helpful. Joss is very tired, but I'm not. However, I enjoy the cuddle.

Daniel, Inigo and Penny helped to carry things downstairs – Joss and I filed things. Then Daniel helped Joss on his iMac for three hours. Liz and Paul Seed got married today and invited us around for dinner. We took Penny, who enjoyed herself. We went to bed at

1.30. Then I woke up vomiting and with excruciating pains in my stomach. I was awake all night, shivering, vomiting and in pain – shit. Shit.

Last night Britain came to a standstill, with ferocious winds and heavy rain flooding many places. No trains ran. Simon came to start the lift. We packed the car and left at noon. It was a lovely day. We drove to London, in perfect spring sunshine, with rainbows every few miles, and then arrived at the Hale Clinic. We stayed the night with Moyra [Fraser], at Harrington Gardens. She gave us a warm welcome.

Joss collected the car and drove me to Harley Street, and John McCormack worked on my tooth for ninety minutes. I waited an hour in the waiting room afterwards, as Joss was at a meeting about a film. I did not mind waiting as there was plenty to read, and my mouth was numb from the injections. At 6.15 we left for the National Theatre. We saw Michael Frayn's *Noises Off*, which is hysterical – we laughed and laughed, and so enjoyed the play. As we came out of the theatre we met David, Toni and Emily. We arrived at Little Postlings [Toni and David's house in Kent] at 12.30. Toni made me some soup. A bean stuck in my throat, so Toni squeezed me a lemon – no result, so I had bicarbonate of soda in hot water – and vomited up one bean! I was left with a sore throat.

Got up at 5.30 to go to the loo – no vomiting or cramps. I got back to bed, and Joss and I cuddled and slept till 11 a.m. We went downstairs and Toni made us a delicious coffee. She'd been so busy. The children were at school, the gardener was set to work and the washing line was blowing with fresh sheets and shirts. It's been a lovely peaceful day. On Monday Ursula had noticed one of my good earrings was missing. I was in a mad panic. Ursula contacted Joss, and he had the idea that it might have fallen out in the Rectory. So we phoned. Brenda went to look, and luckily she found it. Thank goodness – what a relief! Brenda also said Simon had moved the kitchen sink, so we'll see a change when we get there. It's all in preparation for the lift, because of my wretched motor neurone muscle waste. Sammy arrives on Friday – it will be so good to see her. Toni fed the children and put them to bed.

Toni drove me to Manuela – the osteopath in Oxted. She was wonderful. At five, Emily, Abbi, Joss and I were driven by Toni to see *The Lion King*. The opening was magnificent, with the African singers and dancers, but the acting was dire! Toni collected us, and dropped Moyra, Joss and me at the Ivy, and took her children home. We had a fun meal. I managed strained soup cup with Rosemary, and then scallops with creamed spinach. We got a taxi back to Moyra's.

Another taxi to the Hale Clinic and Georgina gave me colonic hydrotherapy. She was very good, and Joss watched. Then after a rest at Moyra's we went on to the dentist. Mr McCormick was brilliant and fixed in my crown comfortably. We got to the Queens Theatre, and saw *The Seven Year Itch* which Michael Radford had directed. Michael and Emma and Joss and I went to the Ivy. Toni and David arrived and then Daryl Hannah, who was in the play, joined us. Joss had Welsh rarebit and sausages, and I had strained aubergine soup and cod. Everyone shared four puddings. David drove us to Little Postlings. Bed 3 a.m.

After breakfast we drove to Kirsty's house. Kirsty was very welcoming. Her house is wonderful now – with a huge kitchen. Our couches and kitchen equipment, and our curtains from Floral Street fit perfectly. Kirsty gave us a great lunch of avocado and prawns and cooked peppers and olives. Then Joss and I had a kip for an hour, and went to bed at midnight. Sweated under the duvet and I got very dry and woke and had water twice!!

Kirsty had made thousands of scones at 7 a.m. She was so organised, cooking vegetable lasagne and lamb and chips, and giving us breakfast. Samantha arrived yesterday. She looks very well, and very pregnant with her seventh child. I'm so proud of my daughters. They are all so hard-working and talented. I do wish Toby could find the right girl. We had a delicious lunch and lots of champagne and wine – a lovely christening and Monty was so good.

We drove to Devon. The Rectory is in a mess – filthy, dirty and dusty, and everything in the kitchen is missing, as cupboards have been taken out, and the sink moved. We were so depressed that we opened a bottle of champagne and had a light supper. Sammy started Nico at Clovelly School, and Tommi and Natalie at play school.

After breakfast Joss took Sammy to Barnstable to see the consultant and have a scan. I cooked a chicken for supper. Natalie and Tommi were running in and out, and I was just making their gravy when I blacked out and had a bad fall. I hit my head on the saucepan stand, and my leg on the Aga. I felt dizzy and breathless, so took two aspirin and we dished up. The children ate a good supper and enjoyed it.

We watched the service of remembrance on TV, and I cried. It was so moving. Joss is the most cuddly and sweetest man. I am so in love with him. When I was young I didn't know how love can bloom and strengthen, and reach such powerful ecstatic heights and depths. It does make life so full and precious.

Joss drove me to have a colonic irrigation. It was horrid. [This was to help relieve Rosemary's chronic constipation which was the result of her previous spinal injury.] My stomach was pummelled for hours and eventually they got some result. But the rest of the day I had dreadful pains in my stomach. I don't think I'll go to him again. We had scallops for supper. Joss was sweet. He chopped up the bacon for me, and fried it with garlic and tomato.

Toby rang to say he'd be in Barnstable at 10 p.m. I can't believe it! Sammy very kindly went off to buy Chilli a Christmas present. The house is full of builders who are in the lift shaft, and just a breath away from the loos and the kitchen. Joss went off to Barnstable to fetch Toby, and brought him home. Oh, what joy to see Toby again – looking well and happy. We settled him in his room, and then opened a bottle of champagne to celebrate. Toni arrived. Toby and Toni went to bed at midnight, and Joss and me at 1.30.

Toby was very helpful, washing lampshades, changing bulbs, setting up my ironing seat and helping Joss on the iMac. It is lovely having him to stay. It is a beautiful day.

Toni drove Toby to Tiverton, and then she drove home. I was sorry to see Toby go, as he is off to Australia, and it is so far. Joss and I had a kip, and made the most exquisite love. Oh, I'm so happy and Joss is the most romantic and wonderful lover.

My arms are twitching a lot this evening. Sammy stayed in bed because she felt ill. Joss spent the day trying to decide how Tracy and Paola are to get here. They are leaving Italy tomorrow.

Joss was in a very bad mood all day. I sometimes wonder if I should live on my own, and only meet up occasionally. He would be less harassed. A car came to collect him at four, as he is off to do Dorothy Tutin's *This Is Your Life*. I wish I could have gone. He thought I'd be too tired! Tommi had a family birthday party. It was very sweet. I had a pawpaw and yoghurt for supper, and went to bed at two. Joss arrived at four. It was lovely to be cuddled until late morning.

I had kippers for breakfast which I couldn't eat as the thin bones got stuck in my throat. I coughed them up, and then had yoghurt to try and wrap up the hair bones. We left for Stoke Mandeville, and I saw Mr Derry, who was most concerned about my choking. He is worried about a chest infection.

I had a dreadful night as my legs were so itchy, and kept me awake. Joss went off to the chemist to get me some moisturiser. He phoned Samantha, who feels sick, and is getting contractions. So after lunch they are going to the hospital. We left at 2.30 with Joss in his dress suit, and Melanie drove us to the Hale Clinic. Ursula gave me a very good colonic irrigation, and I feel marvellous. Toni arrived at five-ish to say hi to me, and then left with Joss to go to the church where Joss is reading for Save the Children. Melanie drove me back to her house, and I had a yoghurt and vodka with her. Then she went to pick Joss up from the station. It was wonderful to see him.

Tara was born at 1.20 a.m. at Barnstable. Samantha had a labour of twelve hours. Tracy phoned us. He was elated. We all got up early as Melanie is dropping Joss at the station. He's going to record *Jekyll and Hyde* in Dean Street. When he finished, Melanie and I picked him up at Maidenhead station, and we drove to Devon. It rained heavily. Samantha and Tracy and the new baby were up and smiling. What joy!

I have a bad headache. The baby is no longer Tara. She's Charlie. The midwife came to see Sammy. Yesterday my wheelchair arrived, and Tracy took it in. Sammy, Joss and I had fish and chips for supper together. I had a choking fit and had to cough up saliva, and breathe in the wind outside. Then I was fine. We watched a movie.

It is a lovely sunny day, so went to Bideford. Walking out of doors is impossible for me, as my toes flop and trip me up. Joss shopped, and I waited in the car. Then he dropped me to have my feet done, while he went to buy a chain for Samantha's cross. Toby phoned. He and Angie had two cars stolen last night. Kirsty rang up as she has a bad cold, and she was upset and crying, because she wanted to come down today. I cooked a huge fish pie for Sammy's family and us.

CHRISTMAS DAY: Excited noises from the top floor and staircase – from fourteen little excited voices, as children opened their stockings. We had champagne as we opened all the parcels. The children were so happy and excited – so were their parents. We cooked a huge pork roast, and Ben was very helpful in the kitchen. A lovely day. Ben and Tracy also said it was the best Christmas they had ever had. Toni and David, Tom, Emily, Abbi, Izzie, Georgia and Lettie arrived at 10 p.m.

Joss has a dreadful cold. He went shopping; bought door handles that I can turn, and got antibiotics for both of us. I didn't take mine, as I'm not ill. I made soup with cabbage and carrots, ginger, chilli and garlic for lunch. Later I made pasta for the whole family, as it is our last meal together this year, and they leave early tomorrow.

The house is very quiet. The builders and families have gone. Joss and I are quiet and happy. It's a bad day for my swallowing. I've started my antibiotic as I've got tracheitis.

NEW YEAR'S EVE: The last day of the year. After lunch we had one and a half hours' kip. Then for supper we had caviar and blinis and toast and vodka and mince pies. We watched a movie, and at midnight, we kissed for the entire twelve gongs of Big Ben, and had a glass of champagne and pulled a cracker. A wonderful time we had together. We are so happy, and so deeply in love.

2001

JANUARY

Sammy and Tracy left for Umbria today. Joss and I went to recycle the empties and newspapers. It was very windy, and very difficult to open the car doors. Came back and Joss gave me an enema, and I had a miserable time. For supper I cooked prawns, garlic and scrambled egg. It was difficult to eat. I don't feel well today – I've had a bad time keeping my balance and swallowing. Thank God for Joss being so supportive.

The TV man came to put a telephone in the lift. Simon made a platform by the front door, for wheelchair descent. Sue came and made me try my wheelchair. I felt hopeless! I had a bad fall in the kitchen, and hit my head. It came out in a bump.

Got up at 9.30 – and had an accident getting to the loo. It's so far away now and I cannot rush. Joss was a darling and sorted it out, while I had a shower. I've had a bad day swallowing. Hope it's better tomorrow. Lovely letters – from Samantha, Daisy, Florence, Emily, Georgia and Lettie. I cooked a delicious fish pie for lunch. Joss cooked mashed potatoes, and peeled them. My hands are so weak, I can't peel apples or potatoes, but I can still do peas and carrots. Walking is a great problem, and I need a wheelchair outside. The lift broke down four times last week. Men came yesterday and worked on it for five hours, and they say it is okay now! We'll see. Bed 4.20 a.m.

How wonderful – the sun is shining on our pillow as we wake up. Joss made such magical love to me and I adore him. I am seventy-two today. Joss has given me a beautiful day, and gave me an exquisite diamond and emerald ring. Beverley the speech therapist came. She was so nice, and very helpful. I had cards and presents from all the family. We had gravlax for lunch, Joss made a delicious dish of olive oil and avocado for me and we had lovely champagne. We had a kip for one and a half hours, and then did letters. Terry White sent his son to board the floor for the wheelchair. He has a bad cold. His wife had her breast off today for cancer.

It is a freezing cold day. Sarah and Sue came to see me about my wheelchair. They helped me go up in the lift, and discovered that the wheels are unbalanced. They left, and Joss and I had just sat down to our lunch of trout and avocado, when the district nurse, Elaine Clements, arrived. She was exceptionally helpful and very sweet. Joss and I ate lunch when she left. We had a sleep for two hours, and had just sat down to eat, when Toby rang to say he was nearing Bideford. It was great to see him again. His friend is very pleasant. They didn't want supper, but picked at the roast potatoes. They were very tired and went to bed. Joss and I watched a movie.

Joss had a long talk with Toby, as he was depressed. Later we had a lovely day with him. Joss ordered some organic wine for me, as it is much easier to drink. Then he did my buttons, and put on my pants and shoes, and my beautiful necklace and cross. They are so pretty, and make me feel very special.

Toby popped his head in to say goodbye, and they left at 6 a.m. We went back to sleep and got up at ten. It is a cold, rainy day, and we had a lovely Sunday – we read the papers, watched movies, did the wash, cuddled and were just happy together.

Sarah came and helped me with the electric wheelchair. She was very helpful. Then I made soup with broccoli, carrots, tomato, garlic and ginger. It was delicious and we finished the lot. Had a lovely cuddle and, in the evening, we had smoked trout and avocado. The avocado was difficult to swallow.

Joss is worried as he's lost his driving licence and he can't catch up with things. I feel so bad that I can't help as I used to. I can't even hear his lines any more, as my speech is getting very difficult, as my tongue and lips have lost their power. Bed just after 2 a.m. and I found it difficult to get into bed.

A bad choking day. Nurse came, and brought lots of sponges, a suction machine and pads. Everyone is helping, and Joss is marvellous, and so patient with me.

FEBRUARY

Sarah came, and we hadn't had our breakfast. She gave me a lesson – getting in and out of the lift. Beverley arrived, and brought some thickener, and put it into wine to make it easier to swallow – but it made it worse! Crab and avo for lunch, and then we went upstairs. I was in heaven. Joss is the most wonderful lover, friend and soulmate, and I'm so lucky to have found him in 1951.

It was difficult to eat again. I am exceedingly tired today, so after lunch we slept for two hours.

Ton Ton and Gigi were collected by the RSPCA. So sad – we just couldn't cope with their half-eaten mice and vomit everywhere. It will be our first time ever without a cat. The RSPCA took their beds, dishes and all their food. I started crying at lunch because meals are such a problem. I always looked forward to Joss and I having lovely meals together. Now it's a nightmare. We had a kip, and then we put on sausages for supper. Will I be able to eat them? We had the sausages with scrambled egg – Joss took the skins off, and we had a lovely meal.

Late breakfast, and then we left to see Dr Markham, who was the one to give me a hole in my stomach to help me feed through the tube. I took four Dulcolax, and by 3 p.m. I felt like vomiting, and was in pain. Difficult eating supper, and I feel really ill. Went to the loo at nine, and was retching, and felt so ill I went straight to bed.

Got up at 9.30 and felt like a wet rag. Breakfast was difficult. At two Sue and Sarah came, and I drove my wheelchair around, and Sue was very pleased with my progress. Joss has been offered a film in Moscow, and so we won't be able to go to the palace. [To get my CBE.] It is very exciting, going to Russia. We had crab for supper – lovely.

Joss went to Bideford and picked up Kirsty, who is here for just a few hours. She was so helpful, and it was wonderful to see her.

I took new opening medicine last night, and it hasn't worked, so I took more tonight. My bloody bowels! They ruin my life. We tried to eat the pork shepherd's pie I made, but it stuck in my throat, and

I couldn't swallow. I ended up eating mashed potatoes and gravy and tomato sauce. Bed 4 a.m.

Toni and David arrived. They were incredibly helpful. I asked Toni if she'd look through the clothes that I no longer need. I was so touched, because she chose the clothes I'd worn a lot and remembered me in.

The alarm woke us up at 5.55 a.m. I had a wakeful night, so I was glad to get up. Kirkland's car arrived at seven and drove us to Terminal 4. He was very helpful, and pushed me in my chair. Well, it is now 9 p.m. Moscow time, and we are sitting in first-class. It took ages for Georgina to get our visas. She finally met us at Terminal 2 with the passports, and Joss spent an hour to upgrade us. The lunch looked horrid, and I couldn't eat it, so Joss and I had our trout out of our lunch box, and I had three glasses of tomato juice and a cup of tea. Joss had four glasses of champagne and cheese. I hope when we arrive in Moscow in an hour, someone will be there to meet us!!! Yes, someone with 'Eckland' written on a piece of paper. A jolly girl gave us a grin, and said, 'It's a big car, so you have to walk a little way to reach it.' Joss pushed me through thick snow for two blocks, and there was a huge bus, with a lift for a wheelchair. Joss was furious. At the airport there was no lift, so two men carried me in my wheelchair down thirty-two steep stairs. Then the 'walk a little way to reach it' took for ever, and in intense cold and freezing wind, all the way to the bus. The bus was driven by a cold little man, who cranked me down off the bus, and sped me in my wheelchair along an icy road into a hotel. It was a long time before Joss came in carrying luggage – because he didn't know where I had gone. And there was a problem – no room was ready. So Joss and I had vodka, and then discovered we'd been brought to the wrong hotel. Joss wanted to ditch the film. We didn't unpack. We had room service of ice cream, borsch, bread and the smoked trout we brought with us. We went to bed, and slept. It was 4 a.m. Moscow time.

How wonderful! I was woken up being made love to – so beautifully and ecstatically. We cuddled for another hour, and we got up at noon, went to the bathroom and Joss showered me, so now I'm nice and clean. We went into the hotel restaurant, and I had delicious cream of crayfish soup and sole, and Joss had deep-fried perch. Marit Allen came and gave Joss a costume fitting. At six a girl came and moved us out of the hotel, and drove us in a normal car to the Kempinski. We got in a proper lift, up to a lovely room on the fourth floor. I put my wheelchair behind the cupboard, and Joss and I walked down to the lobby and met Marit for tea. We had a fun time, but my crème brulée was covered with fruit and nuts, so it was very difficult to eat. At eight we came upstairs and had a sleep, and then unpacked our cases. Sammy phoned – sweet girl. A producer had sent Joss a bottle of champagne as an apology. Unfortunately, I was unable to drink it!

A very comfortable night. Got up and went down to breakfast. An amazing spread. Joss had blinis and cream, and pink caviar. He got me a hard scrambled egg, which I couldn't eat, so I had a yoghurt, tomato juice and coffee. Then the Lactoberyl began to work, so I hurried to the lift. But a footballer pulled the lift up to the eighth floor, and got out at the fifth. It all took so long, and when Joss lost the door card – it was too late. Thank God I brought Biotex. Joss as usual was a great help. It is snowing non-stop and Red Square is deep in snow.

What I thought was a snow-covered field outside turns out to be a river. The snow has turned to ice, and the river is breaking up. It is a weird sight. Breakfast was a fiasco. Joss was desperate for me to eat something, in spite of the fact that I've never been able to eat breakfast. He got me blinis with lemon and carrot juice – on which I choked. Then he panicked. The carrot juice came out of my nose. He brought me a slice of turkey breast, which I managed to swallow, and then yoghurt, which was difficult. I do dread meal times. Joss doesn't realise what hell it is for me to swallow normally. Things I loved a year ago, I cannot contemplate now. I hate to see him panic and say hurtful things – which he does. After rehearsal, we went and had a Japanese meal, which cost a fortune, but it was wonderful. Joss had fish and noodle soup and grilled scallops, and I had cream of spinach soup and black eye cod, grilled on a leaf with sage and honey – easy to eat, and so delicious. We both had green tea ice cream. It was a wonderful meal. Joss has shaved off his beard. I miss it.

Got up at 6.45, and I was glad – it was a rough night. The Volga is so different this morning. Last night it was solid ice. This morning all the ice had melted, and the river is running clear, and is lovely. Joss left for filming. He was so sweet – phoning from the lobby as he left. He phoned again at 9.30, and was furious that the staff had not brought up my breakfast. He rang the hotel, and it came up post haste. I read, and then wrote to Sammy and Kirsty. Joss arrived back, and said Harrison Ford was giving a party for the crew to get to know each other. Marit went with us to the nightclub. Kathleen Bigelow arrived, and then Harrison Ford, who was very friendly, but we left early and had turkey and avocado and ice cream, room service.

Poor Joss's back was so bad, and thank God I was still able to massage it. After breakfast there was a message for Joss to go to the set. I was reading when Joss came in at two with his make-up on. He was not needed for a while, so we had a lovely lunch in our bedroom – self-service. We went downstairs for an espresso, and then he was picked up again. I used my wheelchair as a trolley, and washed up lunch, and put away fridge things. Then I brought up half a pint of spittle. Joss came back – he hasn't filmed!

I woke up very dry at 4 a.m. Had a sip of water, and then brought up spittle for hours. I used hundreds of tissues. I read all morning. Sammy phoned, and then Joss called and told me to have lunch, as he's filming two long scenes. I had half a Guinness, two pieces of fish and half an avocado. The river is frozen today – it is icy cold. Joss phoned again at three. They were lighting the next set, and he told me to rest. He was exhausted when he got in at 9.30, and we went downstairs and had vodka. Kirsty phoned this evening.

Finished packing, and then we went downstairs and got in a mini-bus to Moscow airport. It took an hour, and when we arrived we had help through security. There was a mess-up on the plane about the seats and wheelchair again. Our lovely driver met us, and drove us to Devon. Joss did a shop and we got to the beautiful, warm Rectory at midnight.

MARCH

It was very windy all night, and extremely cold. I found it very difficult to get out of bed. My body is getting very much less mobile. I also have a great deal of saliva that is difficult to cope with. For lunch

Joss had oysters on toast and I had Moscow sardines – not easy – and ice cream. Then we went to Barnstaple, to the mobility place, and saw a mini-Jazzi wheelchair, which is interesting – so a demonstration next Wednesday.

Our passports were collected last night. I've decided to go to Ontario with Joss on Saturday, as Toni cannot stay longer than Wednesday because it is Abigail's birthday – and she is arranging a party!! I'm so excited to go.

There was a break here, because pages were missing. Rosemary and I went to Toronto, and on our return, with Kirsty pushing her in her wheelchair, Rosemary was able to come with me to Buckingham Palace when the Queen placed a ribbon around my neck and made me a CBE – an award far more deserved by Rosemary than by me. However, I am delighted to be a Commander of the British Empire, which is easier today, as there is no Empire to command.

As these two months of the diary are missing, there is a break here until we are once more back in Clovelly, and by this time she was losing her ability to swallow. Eventually, when she was no longer able to take anything by mouth, a tube was attached to her stomach. The tube was attached to a machine, which provided her feed from bags. This was done in two shifts – eight hours at night while she slept, and then for four dreary hours during the day. Rosemary was determined to take food normally, for as long as she could, but by now speech was impossible.

Joss was in a panic this morning, as he had to be in Barnstable to do a voice-over. He dressed while I washed, and then he dressed me, and went downstairs and made unnecessary phone calls to the chiropodist and to Elaine. I do wish he wouldn't get so panicky – it does embarrass me. Elaine arrived at noon. She re-dressed my arm and leg – and said my tube was perfect, but she worried about my swollen ankles. After she left, I came back down to do the post. Kirsty gave me a drink of water down my tube. I feel very weak this morning. Joss got in with loads of shopping. Then he cut up the lobster, undressed the prawns and we had the most delicious lunch. I pulverised mine. Joss put two glasses of champagne down my tube! It was heavenly. We washed up and then slept for two hours. Came down and finished the post. Got to bed, and, surprise, wonderful Joss and I made exciting and satisfying love. What utter bliss. We cuddled close and had a peaceful sleep – our souls mingling together.

I woke up bright and fresh. Joss dressed me, turned my tube and made coffee for us. I poured orange juice for him, and he had cereal and I had lemon yoghurt. Then he went to Woolsery and bought the Sunday papers. We had a fun breakfast, reading and eating. Kirsty and Ant cooked a chicken for the rest of the family, and Joss and I had a wonderful lunch of crab, smoked salmon, avocado and tomato. Joss gave me two glasses of champagne in my tube, and I feel so great, and then we had berries and ice cream. I washed up with Joss, and then we had a sleep. Later Joss and I had soup, and we watched a movie. Very scary. Bed at 3.05. During the night I became stiff and uncomfortable, but I couldn't wake Joss up. I was dying to get up, but I can't move without help – and my 'Help' couldn't surface!! Eventually I woke him. His leg was also in spasm, but he managed to push me out of bed. [I would push Rosemary to the edge of her side of the bed, and then get myself out of bed, and go round and lift her to a sitting position, and then lift her on to the bedpan.] I'm finding it more and more difficult to communicate. Life is extremely frustrating.

Toni is exceptionally helpful marking all my drawers, and sorting out my sewing box. Kirsty put Ned into nursery school, and went into Bideford, and bought my Lactulose and Senacot. When she came in, she gave it to me in my tube. She is also a great help. I'm so lucky. My two daughters are such lovely people, and so willing and helpful. Toni drove off in the little Mazda, and then Joss and I sat down to lunch and had another fabulous meal of smoked salmon and crab and avocado – and again he gave me two funnels of champagne. Oh, I feel so good! We finished lunch. Our waiting for the stuff to get down my tube held us up. We had a quick wash up, and then a kip. I'm going to get soup for supper, and Joss is to have tinned oysters!

Yesterday was not a good day. It was a weepy one that I couldn't control. Today we had a brunch of kippers, but they were disaster for me. Kirsty is very helpful. Joss phoned John Lewis for six more bibs for me. My dribbling is so bad; I'm like a running tap. Sometimes I want to die, as I feel I'm such a burden to everyone. I am more and more helpless every day. Joss is doing very well with his iMac. I'm glad 'cause it must be an escape for him – as reading is for me. We had a rest from 3.30 to 5.30. Kirsty and her family left at three. It's lovely to be alone here with Joss. Oh, I just adore him. Funny – the sun is shining all day and I feel positive and happy. I'm not the person I was yesterday. This disease does keep me on a seesaw. I wish I could balance it up much more. At 9.15 we had smoked salmon, crab and avocado, and then raspberries, ice cream, champagne and white wine. I feel really pissed and wonderful. Oh, then America phoned to say Joss has got the part in the film *No Good Deed* by Dashiell Hammett.

When the film was first suggested, I refused, because I would be working most days on the movie, and she would be on her own, so Rosemary, who was unable to speak by this time, angrily wrote that I was mean to turn it down, as she wanted to come with me to Canada. I am convinced that this was subterfuge, because she thought it important that I should not stop working. However, she was adamant – and of course I gave in.

Joss's director, Bob Rafelson, rang at seven, and they talked for thirty-five minutes. I could tell they liked each other, which is good. We got to bed at 2 a.m.

Joss woke me up when he was all dressed and ready. I was upset because I felt left behind. I washed while Joss was downstairs, and so I had to ring a bell to tell him when I was ready for him to dress me. I feel such a burden. It's not fair on Joss. I don't know what to do. I'll need to make other plans to give Joss his own space. The sun is shining, but the wind is cold. We are trying to find someone to help me in Canada. After our meal I had two phials of red wine, which was great!! We watched *Shaft*. It was a horrid, violent film. We got to bed at 3.30 a.m.

A lovely sunny day. Joss helped me in and out of the shower, but got furious with me, because I wouldn't use my wheelchair. He left me on the bathroom chair to dry myself. It took me ten minutes to work out how to stand up from that miserable bathroom chair. Eureka! I did it!!! Then I collected clean underwear from the bottom drawer, and sat down and waited for Joss to get over his aggro, and come and dress me.

It is difficult to find an excuse for this. I have been told I am in a temper even when I am in a good mood – and am told I shout. This is a result of so many years projecting in the theatre. My only excuse is that I reacted here out of tired nervous desperation.

We got down to breakfast at 11 a.m. Joss made delicious coffee, and then we took the trolley upstairs to collect my washing. [Rosemary hated inactivity, and was furiously determined to continue as closely as possible with the way that she had always lived.] After lunch I was stacking the dishwasher when I lost my balance, and fell flat on my back. I hit my head on the table leg, and I have a bump on the top of my head. Joss overreacted again. I had Lactulose, and then we rested, before working in the office. Kirsty and her lovely family arrived. It is great to see them again. I'm so glad they are here – and joy, oh joy – Kirsty can come for a week to Montreal. I'm so relieved.

I had to get up at 8.30, because my right leg was paining. I hate not being able to get out of bed. It takes away all my independence. Joss is very graceless about getting me up. He does not understand how stiff I am, not being able to move, and he complains that I am impatient!! It was lovely hearing the happy children in the garden this morning. It is a beautiful day. After breakfast Joss went out to collect my pension, and post his air tickets. I made scrambled egg and bacon for Joss's lunch. I had soup and granadilla with ice cream, and we had coffee. The lift has broken, so we can't rest. We sat in the office and worked. Then a lovely surprise – when Joss brought me a phial of cranberry juice and some water. That was a really thoughtful thing to do. It's these little things in life that mean so much these days, and make me feel better. I read his new revised script, and enjoyed it. The liftman arrived and could not mend the lift. So there is a problem. Kirsty and Joss helped me climb up twenty-six stairs to bed. I was shaking by the time I got up. Kirsty lifted my legs and Joss let me balance on his lovely supportive arm. He brought up my Lactulose and gave it to me upstairs. We washed but Joss was perspiring, so he had a shower. He undressed me, and lifted me onto the bed. We turned out the light at 12.18. At 3 a.m., I was dry and choking, so dear Joss brought me a phial of water. We cuddled back to sleep.

Poor Joss – my legs were so painful – I had to wake him up to push me out of bed, and let blood circulate in my legs. I took a long walk to the loo [with the help of a push trolley contraption], and then washed – still managing to use the bidet! Joss then dressed me. Kirsty came back from taking the children to school, and Joss and Kirsty helped me walk downstairs.

Joss washed my feet for me. Had breakfast, and then Kirsty helped me pack. In the middle of packing we heard a big bang. Joss had missed the last step and fallen down. Kirsty and Brenda rushed to help him. He has shock, so I told Kirsty to give him a brandy, and put ice on his poor hand. It is badly bruised, and I persuaded him to go to Dr Cracknell, who got the nurse to put on an elastic bandage support. We had a kip. I am very tired today. I think packing is exhausting.

Joss said he had a bad night, worrying about flights. I slept soundly. Got up, washed and Joss dressed me as usual. I spent the morning washing up, answering the post and reading about Milosevic, who is in prison on trial for genocide. Ben phoned – he and Kandy are coming down on Tuesday!

JULY

Joss is in agony with his legs, back and chest. I could see he found it difficult to get me out of bed and dress me. Kirsty came in to learn how to turn my tube and dress me when she is in Canada. Toni helped me get things sorted out, and Joss was doing the computer with her, when he suddenly had bad pains in his chest, so Toni took him to the hospital. Joss had an ECG and his heart is okay! Oh boy, am I relieved. He then saw the doctor who thought it was a reaction to his fall – sore ribs. I am so happy be is okay! What a burden I am. Now I have to wait for Joss to undress me, and get me into bed. Then it is magic, with his comforting arms around me, and his lovely voice in my ear. 'I love you' – repeated till I fall asleep in a dream-like ecstasy of security.

Poor darling Joss got his rag doll out of bed, and then helped me into the shower. I so enjoy a shower. I had a beautiful wash, and then my love helped me out, and gave me a towel to dry myself while he showered. When he was dry he helped me dress. As we finished breakfast the DHS man arrived with changes to my wheel-chair. I then used my trolley to tidy the empty bags in my bedroom, and pack a hairbrush and comb in my bag, and take my washing downstairs. I went into the kitchen and washed up breakfast, tried to clean the Aga and then put on a wash. The film company couldn't get us a flight on Saturday as planned, and so we are flying off a week later.

Joss dressed me. We had breakfast. I didn't have coffee because we are going to Barnstable to get my hair done, and I don't want to pee. Coffee goes straight through me. Margie was waiting, and gave me permanent highlights and semi-blonde gold rinse, cut my hair, and shampooed and blow-dried it. I am incredibly tired today and feel very weak. I think the hairdressing was a strain. We had smoked salmon and crab for lunch, and then went to rest. We slept for three hours!!! When we woke up I had to get to the loo, but my fingers could not grip my pants to pull them down. Panic! SHIT. Joss was stuck with a lift that wouldn't work, and when he eventually got to me in the loo he was so cross. He grudgingly helped me change, and then had to get Ben and Kirsty to help me walk downstairs. My legs were collapsing and I felt sick. I got into the kitchen, and dear, sweet Kirsty helped me to cook supper. We went to bed at 2 a.m. I wonder how much longer I can sit on the bidet. My walking days will soon be completely over.

Joss pushed his rag doll out of bed at 10 a.m. He was very loving when he dressed me, and said how nice my hair looked. He put in my earrings, and put my cross on, and rinsed my knickers. Kirsty was an angel. She pulverised my lobster and boiled garlic for me, before she went to Tiverton to collect Ant. Joss and I had a kip and, after supper, my darling Joss gave me two phials of champagne. Oh, I am so in love with this man I married. He is so much a part of me. I'm so lucky to have found him. My true soul-mate. Kirsty and Ant arrived at 11.15, and had vodka and fresh orange juice with Kandy, and they all went to bed. Joss and I washed up, and then went to bed at 1.30. We got into bed at 3 a.m. It takes us so long to do things. Poor Joss, with his sore hand and nails, is very disabled by pain. After he undressed me he had to go to the loo. I didn't mind, as it gave me a chance to work out how to get on the bed. I didn't want Joss to strain his broken rib. I put my legs up, then lay back, wriggled my bum and feet and managed to get on the bed. My nightie got twisted horribly, though. Never mind, I got a lot of kisses from my honey, which wiped all my worries away.

Sunday – my favourite breakfast time. I love the lack of pressure. Delicious cappuccino from Joss, a lovely read of the *Sunday Times* and discussions of articles. Ha! Ha! I mean Joss reads me things, or comments, and I write an answer, or mime one!!! The poor darling really has drawn the short straw with me being so boring. He dressed me, lovingly, and we came down to breakfast and had the most scrumptious cappuccino. We read the paper – dreadful violence in Bradford between the National Front – the mindless gits – and the Asians.

The film company phoned, and said they were going to put our flight off another week. Shit! We have to change our flight and everything. What a nuisance. At least his visa came in today. We have to rearrange all the girls who are coming to Montreal. I'm so sorry – Kirsty can't come to Canada now.

Joss was so sweet, looking after me all night. He turned me over twice, to prevent bedsores. He's such a honey. I don't feel very well. I have no energy. Joss backed a horse called Everlasting Love and it came in first. We were thrilled. Joss is wondering how to learn the John Mortimer play he tried out in Chichester. I can't help him any more, so we must get someone to hear him. I have a hell of a lot of saliva today. I hate it, as it runs out of my mouth in a stream, and sometimes chokes me. We had such a lovely suppertime. I had some Chablis with my fish, and champagne with my lovely raspberries, blueberries, meringue and ice cream. We went up to bed, and darling Joss and I made the most exquisite love. Oh, I do adore him.

Darling Joss saw me through the night. His loving concern was to turn me, and place my feet on the sheepskin. I'm so lucky. He was up and dressed before I woke up, and he got me out of bed. I went to wash, and he lifted me off the bidet, then turned my tube, dressed me and put my earrings, my cross and bib on me. Oh, what a treasure. I feel so bad taking up all his time. We bad a lovely breakfast and he made a magical cappuccino, which was so fluffy. I washed up and then went upstairs with Kirsty, who was very helpful, locking cases and tidying away things. After a delicious lunch I looked through the culture section of the *Sunday Times*, and took a note of the best children's book. I want to get copies for Paola and Daisy. I love looking through the window at our lovely garden. The trees we planted are growing tall, especially our Rowan tree. I love listening to the wonderful thrushes' song, and all the other birds. Our blue gums in the front are growing stronger, and my nut tree is spreading. At dusk the crows gather their families into their nests, with a great squawking and excited gaggle. They are really very family-orientated. I'm very tired. We started for bed at half past one and finally got there at twenty past three.

Up at 6 a.m. We packed my tubes, and Kirsty put ready-mixed Lactulose and Senacot in it. Kirkham cars arrived at 8 a.m. I waited while Joss looked for his camera and car keys. At 8.40 we left and had a pleasant drive to Heathrow. Penny and family and Toni and family were there to meet us, and were all a great help. So was everyone in Air Canada, and they helped us through to the lounge. After saying goodbye to her family Toni stayed with me while Joss went to Duty Free, and I had a tomato juice. The airport helper came to collect us. Joss wasn't back, so we left, and luckily met him on the way to the gate. Joss had my boarding card, so we were put on the plane. Very comfortable seats and a pleasant flight, but as my feeding tube doesn't work on the plane Joss had to use the plunger to feed me.

Toni came with us, and was to be the first of our family relay team to pass the baton to one another at Montreal airport – usually each one leaving as the next one arrived. It was to be a precise and complicated venture, and very difficult to perform. However, I am proud to say, the baton was never dropped. It is very difficult for anyone with motor neurone disease to cope away from a hospital. As time passes, every nerve, every part of the anatomy weakens and then dies, but the brain remains active and clear. In the majority of cases hospital is the only answer. But we were fortunate, the Old Rectory in Devon was to become Rosemary's world – and the new lift was large enough for her to revolve her wheelchair. This enabled her to inhabit three of the four floors. The steps outside the house were covered with a ramp for the wheelchair, which fitted into the back of our car. There were several friendly day nurses and night nurses to wash and dress Rosemary and help apply the tube to feed her.

But I am getting ahead of myself – those days were still to come, and it was not only Rosemary who was fortunate – as a close family, we were able to be with her.

Montreal.

When the plane landed in Montreal, the production team came to our seats. They were very helpful, and carried our hand luggage. An airport man pushed me in my wheelchair on to a truck, the production manager took Joss off to immigration, and Toni picked up our baggage. We were driven to the Delta Hotel, to our suite, which is huge. Although we were very tired, Toni was stoic and helpful, unpacking essentials, which meant almost all our things. We went down to supper, where the chef had mashed food for me – delicious salmon and avocado. Although it was so late – 2.30 for me – I enjoyed it. Joss put me to bed, and saw me through the night. Oh my precious love, thank you for your night watch.

David woke us up, phoning Toni. I don't know what time it was! Down in the garage we found the car that was left for Joss, and drove to the supermarket where Joss shopped and Toni pushed me in the wheelchair. We spent the whole day shopping. It was lovely. We got in at six thirty, and I had yoghurt. Melanie phoned in tears, because the filming schedule has been changed, and altered the time she had planned here. She wants to come out for only one week. Toni was so gentle with her on the phone. I feel so bad needing help. This fucking disease I have to carry and upset everyone's lives!

Got up at 7 a.m., and took a taxi to the Neurological Hospital. We saw a doctor who examined me, and gave us a lot of information. We got back to the hotel, and a car was waiting for Joss to take him to meet the rest of the cast. After lunch I wrote to Charlie, Brenda, Daphne, Samantha, Emily, Georgia and Lettie, and then I wrote my diary. Toni has been so clever, borrowing a CD player and a trolley with plates, knives, etc. It is twenty past four and Joss not home yet. Toni massaged my feet beautifully, and I sat and read. Joss came in. He'd had an interesting day, meeting the small cast and crew.

Joss collected at 10.30. Toni pushed me out in my wheelchair. I had the most exciting day. She was wonderfully energetic, pushing me over eight-lane traffic, and up a hill. We went into the most overwhelming basilica cathedral of Mary, Queen of the World. As I entered, I cried at the magnificence of the glass windows, and the opulence of it all. We spent an hour touring the cathedral, and I said prayers for Joss and the family.

Toni and I went out. She pushed me in my wheelchair to a most beautiful cathedral in old Montreal. It had blue windows and was so lovely. We travelled around the church, and we both lit a candle for Paul. Then she pushed me around the old harbour. The air was soft and fresh, and there was a host of ships. We got home to the hotel at 6.30. Toni massaged my feet for fifteen minutes, laid the table, hung up my shirt, put my shoes on, helped me off the loo, had a shower, changed and left at 7.15 for the Mozart concert in the church. I settled down and read, and waited for Joss to come in. He arrived at 8 p.m. with some delicious foods – smoked salmon, prawns and mousse of lobster, etc. Joss was very helpful, helping to mash up my food. God I feel so helpless, and such a burden to everyone. I want to die. Toni came back at 10 p.m. – inspired by the music in the church. She undressed me and put me to bed.

Joss helped me get up to pee at 7.30. Then he put me back to bed to cuddle, till 8.30, when he kneed me out of bed, on to the floor, and had to run round and pick me up. He then dressed me and turned my tube. After breakfast he phoned Melanie and Penny.

They told him Kirsty flew to Malawi today. It's another lovely day out – but freezing in the hotel. Joss was collected and then Toni pushed me right up the hill. It was lovely out in the sun and fresh air. We went into the shopping mall and bought some CDs, then had fun shopping for Toni's children. We got home at 4 p.m. I had Lactulose and Toni mushed me up avocado, lots of tomato and smoked salmon, and a whole salmon mousse. As we were in the middle of lunch Joss came in. What a lovely surprise! He joined us for a snack of bread and cheese. While we had a sleep, Toni walked to St Paul's Road and bought a dress and other things. I let Joss read my diaries and we eventually went to bed at midnight. Joss put me to bed, as Toni was very tired and went to bed earlier. Joss and I had lovely cuddles all night and he turned me over and, oh, I love him so much.

Joss has the day off today, so he is planning to take us for a drive. Well, we did!! We drove to St Sauveur des Monts, and found a wonderful supermarket, where we bought lobsters and pork and fresh veg and fruit, etc. Then at 5 p.m. we went to Papa Luigi and had a fun dinner. It was a very jolly meal, and the air up in the mountains was fresh and lovely. The cloud formations were stunningly beautiful. Joss was in pain; his legs were in spasm, so Toni drove us home! She drove very well. A lovely day – and one I shall remember.

AUGUST

Got up at 8.30. Toni lifted me out of bed and helped me into the bathroom. After I washed myself, she turned my tube and dressed me. Joss was collected, and after breakfast Toni pushed me over eight lanes of traffic to the railway health shop. We got back at 12.40, and Joss came in, looking fabulous. He feels a lot better, I'm happy to say, 'cause I love him so. After lunch Toni cleared up and packed. I'm going to miss her so much; we've had loads of fun, shopping and sightseeing. Her energy is boundless. Toni was picked up at 5 p.m. for the airport, and now Joss and I have a lovely quiet weekend together. Joss is hypersensitive about Toni taking me out. I'm so helpless, and the change it makes for me to be pushed out by someone who likes to 'play' is just a bit of fun. It was a rest for me, because she anticipated my every need. [I think I reacted badly because I was not able to spend more time with her – I was frustrated, and probably jealous.] After a delicious supper – I had beetroot and whizzed-up beans – Joss helped me wash. I went to pick up a flannel, and fell and cut my leg in two places. Joss plastered it up, and put me to bed.

We had a long cuddly sleep and got up at 9.30. My right leg was very painful in the night, and I woke up a lot. Joss lifted me out of bed, and I washed. He dressed me and turned my tube, and we went down to have cappuccinos and read the paper. There was an interesting article about euthanasia. I have physical deterioration in a big way – it's a rapid change for me. Last night I dreamt that I said to Joss, 'Don't worry I'll get the paper', and I jumped up, ran down the steps and picked it up. I ran back upstairs and said, 'Voila'. Imagine my horror waking up, unable to speak, and unable to move!

We woke up in each other's arms. Joss got me up and dressed. My tube was stuck up, so he had to use the forcer. Palestine has declared war on Israel. In Revelations it says the East shall rise up and overcome the West. Spooky – it looks as though it is happening. Such a sweet girl is cleaning our room. She's made a bed ready for Melanie. At 12.30 we got in the car and Joss drove to Atwater market. His first port of call was the wine shop. He was so excited, he pushed me in, turned and 'smash' – my wheelchair had knocked two bottles of wine on to the floor. I wanted out of there! So Joss parked me outside, and I watched the world go by for half an hour.

Joss was all showered and dressed by the time he woke me up. It is sad waking up. I rush about as normal in my dreams, and then wake up to this useless bag of bones. Shit. Shit. Shit. I threw cold water on my face, and made up, and feel better. We eventually got down and had breakfast at noon, as Joss had to dress me, turn my tube and massage my feet. He's very sweet, but God, I feel such a burden. At two we left in the car for Atwater. I stayed in the car reading while Joss shopped. He was exactly an hour. It was pleasant sitting in the fresh air, and there was a lovely cool wind. I really enjoyed it. We were in the middle of lunch when Melanie arrived, looking radiant and very pretty.

Joss was picked up for filming. He phoned to tell me Dorothy Tutin had died. I'm so very sorry. She was such a sweet person.

We had a long but disturbed sleep. My ankle on my right foot kept waking me up with pain, when I lay on my left side. I hate lying on my left. I washed, and Melanie turned my tube, dressed me and massaged my feet. Joss has been on the phone all morning. It is now 1.45 and he's talking to Virginia McKenna, who is arranging Dottie's funeral. He also spoke to Sammy, who has a migraine. Now he is trying to talk to Derek, Dottie's widower! It is all so sad. We had supper at 10 p.m., because Joss is night filming.

Joss got into bed at 6 a.m. He turned me over. We cuddled close, and he turned me back at 8.30. I slept till nine, when Melanie magically appeared to get me up. Thank God she is here. We dressed, silently, in the dining area, and went down to breakfast. A transvestite served us! Joss got up at 12.45, and then at we drove to Atwood market. I was in the wheelchair, pushed around and left alone, while Joss and Melanie picked things off the shelves. I hated it. I felt frustrated in a big way. I will not go again. After he returned from work Joss got to bed at 4 a.m.

Joss turned me on my left side at nine, and left me there till I woke him up at 11 a.m. He got me up and I washed – he dressed me, and then dressed himself. He was very sweet and helpful. Melanie looks beautiful today in a long skirt and super black top, with a tiny circle of silver on it. At 6.30 my wonderful caring husband made the most exquisite, sexy love with me, and then we cuddled and woke up at 8.30, just as Melanie got back. She enjoyed her walk.

Shit! Shit! Shit! Joss turned me on my left side during the night, and I was so uncomfortable. He woke up, but is in such pain he can't get up quickly. I told him I needed to go to the loo. He didn't function – and disaster. I feel so helpless. I can't get out of bed, unless I'm helped, and with Joss in my way and not being quick – I despair. I so want to die – I can't bear the frustration of not communicating and moving. There is no point in being a burden to everyone. I can't go on expecting my daughters to look after me, or Joss, when he is in pain too. Melanie cleaned up the place – just like Toni had to – and she gave me a shower, and dressed me. I think it would solve all our problems if I took an overdose. I just don't want to carry on. After lunch I went to the loo again and again. I felt very weak and purged. At five Joss drove us to the island and we had dinner at the Restaurant Helene. It was a very romantic restaurant, full of couples having celebrations and their photos taken. I started with a delicious cream of mushroom soup. Joss and Melanie had rack of lamb and spinach, and I had blended John Dory and purée, and then we all had vanilla ice cream. It was a lovely evening, and just what I needed to lift my spirits. I was incredibly thirsty when I got in the car, and when we got to the hotel I had three phials of water, but my throat was parched – the only relief was from my tooth water spray. We got into bed – or rather Melanie lifted me in – at 11.30.

Joss phoned Penny in Italy, and Sammy answered. She was delighted – she had received the parcels of dresses that I'd sent. Kandy and Penny, Daniel, Inigo, Ella and Nancy and Holly are all there at Podere Antico. It must be very crowded. Toni and David and their children are all going today. They are all gathering for our fiftieth anniversary meal. It's a shame that Joss and I can't be there, but it really would have been too much for me. [We had planned to celebrate our half-century of marriage in Italy with the family, and even though Rosemary and I were unable to go, the family decided to celebrate it for us.] We had a sleep till 5 p.m. Then Joss was plotting where we should go. We got in the car and I took my tube with me. We drove to Hudson. It was a beautiful drive, and we passed wonderful lakes. We went to the Clementines Restaurant – a picturesque building with a great atmosphere, and Louise, the pastry chef, was so helpful.

Joss woke up at 8.40 with excruciating pain in his back and legs.

Melanie helped me out of bed, and I massaged Joss's bum and lower back. I can no longer use the force I used to, and now use my knuckles. Soon he'll have to get someone else to do it. A lovely surprise! Toby phoned, and he's coming for our anniversary – how wonderful! We shall have our eldest child and our youngest child to help Joss and I celebrate our golden wedding anniversary. I hope we can return to Hudson for it.

Melanie and I went shopping. I then read. My life is nothing without Joss. I miss him so much this evening. He phoned at 8.20 – I do so wish I could speak to him. [As Rosemary was unable to speak I would talk, and she would acknowledge with a gentle grunting sound.] Melanie lifted me into bed at midnight. It took ages to fall asleep, as I missed Joss. It was heaven to feel his arms round me about four-ish, and saying in my ear, 'I love you'. Then I could sleep in peace.

Toby is due at 4 p.m. Joss is picked up for filming at two. Another night of filming – I hate it. I need darling Joss so much to help me through the night. Melanie and I went out. I tried hard to find a beautiful pipe, to give Joss for our anniversary, but couldn't, so I got an Indian pouch and a lighter. He can choose a good pipe in London.

We started to put lunch on the table when Toby arrived. The poor boy is so stressed out and grieving, because Angie says she wants to separate. How Toby still loves her beats me. She is out on the town every night. He is so sad. I poured him a glass of champagne, and we 'talked' until six, and then we all had smoked salmon, and Melanie and Toby had cake. Then we 'talked' some more, and Toby phoned Angie, and she was out, and Chantal [Angie's sister] upset him, then I did some ironing, and Toby talked. While Melanie and I ate supper Toby phoned Angie again. She told him she was in love with someone else. He came back to the room in floods of tears. He is beside himself and can't think straight. We 'talked' again, and then at 11.15 he phoned Angie once more. They talked for over an hour, and then he came back in, feeling positive. Melanie put me to bed at 1.15. Joss came in at 1.30. I was ever so pleased to see him. He kissed me beautifully, and we went off to sleep together in a wonderful cuddle.

18 August: Our golden wedding anniversary

Melanie helped me out of bed at 10 a.m., and Joss turned my tube, dressed me and then gave me a most beautiful black pearl necklace, and a sweet model of a girl holding a pig. He said it was him and me!!!! Sammy, Polly, Penny and Toni spoke to us from Italy. There were thirty-one of them and they had a wonderful lunch that went on from one until seven at night and then all had fun in the pool. They enjoyed their lunch at Casanova. They were all very happy, and not a quarrel all day. At 5.10, after a glass of champagne and a twenty-minute kip, we drove to Hudson, to that lovely restaurant Clementines, and it was such a pleasure to have Toby with us on this anniversary. I feel it is a double celebration, our fiftieth and Toby's freedom from Angie. Toby had fish chowder, then ostrich, and no pudding. He drinks very little. Joss had chowder, then deer and then apple mousse cake. Melanie had vichyssoise, and so did I. Then Melanie had fish, and I had the most delicious puréed lamb and gravy, and then 'Cloud' cake. I had two phials of red wine, and felt wonderful. This is certainly my favourite restaurant. We sat on the porch, while Joss had a pipe, and the chef came out to introduce himself, and to thank me for the notes I had left on my empty plates thanking him for such lovely food. Toby drove us home, and we got back at eleven. Joss had some gooseberry tart, and he and Melanie a glass of champagne, and I had a phial. The housekeeping gave us flowers, and we gave the girl a glass of champagne. Then Toby was on to his family for an hour, so Melanie undressed me, and Joss 'threw' me into bed. Toby came and kissed me goodnight and at 1 a.m we turned out the light. (I went to the loo perfectly.) A wonderful fiftieth anniversary.

Lucky me! I had a lovely sleep. Joss, Melanie and Toby all had nightmares. After lunch Toby packed and at 3.48 he kissed me goodbye, Melanie saw him off, and he flew to New York.

Melanie is packing. I'll be sorry to see her go. She's phoning Italy about her train tomorrow. At 5 p.m. Joss took her and put her in a taxi. She is off to Heathrow, and then to Italy. Joss had a shower, and Kirsty arrived at 5.30. She was very tired.

Joss got me out of bed. Kirsty turned my tube and dressed me. Joss was picked up at 12.30. I'm longing for him to have days off. I am looking forward to going back to Devon, and breathe fresh air, and have my own Aga and dishwasher and washing machine. Joss phoned to say he wouldn't be home until 3 a.m. Shit. At 1.20 I started to get to bed. I had Lactulose and one phial of champagne to make me go to the loo! Kirsty put me in bed but I couldn't get comfy. Joss came in at 4.30 a.m. It was wonderful to feel his arms around me.

Joss was picked up for filming. Kirsty and I went out to the cathedral, and then a walk along the riverfront. This morning we heard a tape of Joss's *Desert Island Discs* and I cried and cried. It was beautifully done and very moving. I don't feel very well today. Joss came in at 9 p.m. The poor man had got made up and dressed, and waited till 8 p.m., and then was told he was not needed.

We had a wonderful letter from Samantha today that made me laugh. She has such a talent for letter writing. Her letters are very precious to me, and full of drawings from her darling Tommi, Natalie and Charlie – and today, lovely drawings from Ella and Holly. The grandchildren are such precious people. We drove to Atwater. I hate shopping there, because of waiting outside shops, or being parked somewhere. Still, I mustn't complain. I suppose I should be thankful for small mercies. It is difficult – as I was so energetic and loved rushing around doing things. To have to SIT and wait for everyone else is not easy. I read the paper – dreadful news about Mugabe and what he is doing in Zimbabwe. Joss had many calls to make, so at noon Kirsty pushed me in my chair to the Picasso exhibition, and later Joss drove up and met us there. I thought the pictures were pretty repetitive. Kirsty whizzed up beans for me at lunch, and then chicken, but it wouldn't whiz up much, and was very difficult to swallow. I choked a lot. Then I had pawpaw, and Kirsty cut me a slice too narrow, and not being able to speak, I couldn't make her or Joss understand why that was wrong. I am so frustrated, and Kirsty cried, and Joss got upset – simply because I can't talk and explain. At six Kirsty put me on the bed, and then she went for a walk. Joss came to cuddle me, and we slept till 8 p.m. Yes – the day has improved. Kirsty came back from her walk much happier. We had sturgeon for supper. Kirsty whizzed it up, and it was delicious. Then she whizzed up strawberries and blackcurrants, which I had with the mousse from the cake, and cream. I had three phials of white wine. Kirsty put Sudo-cream on my ankles. She measured my tube. It is eleven inches long. Joss got into bed at 2.15. He was so very loving. He knelt by my bed, and soulfully told me how much he loved me. I do adore him. I know it is his deep love that keeps me going.

Kirsty is packing, as she leaves tomorrow. I shall miss her. Kirsty and I had champagne to celebrate. We had red wine with supper, and I had three phials and got pissed. Kirsty and I got the giggles, and I couldn't stop laughing. It is impossible for me to walk when I laugh. Kirsty was extremely kind and supported me. We got to the bathroom, and she sorted me out. Thank God for my wonderful daughters, and the help they've been.

SEPTEMBER

Kirsty went out for a walk, and returned with the most beautiful sunflowers. They are stunning. I wept, because I hate my girls leaving. They are so sweet.

Kirsty left at 5 p.m. and Penny arrived at 5.50, looking wonderful, and so happy. She gave us a lovely folder of photographs of our anniversary dinner at Casanova in Umbria. She had wonderful news for us. Iain and she are going to get married. They are both going to sell their houses and, together, buy a bigger one. Pray God they keep their present happiness. At supper the berries made me choke a lot. I've had to give up Hellmann's mayonnaise, because it has vinegar in it. Every day I have to give up something else that I can't swallow. The choking is exhausting. I only recover after using my tooth water squirt. It is a lifesaver. Joss helped me into the bathroom, and to undress and do my feet. He got me into the bed with difficulty, and my neck got in the way. He had a shower, and then we made exciting love. Such a lovely surprise. Asleep at 11.15, and we went off together to Never-Never Land.

Penny helped me pack, but I had a great attack of saliva, and had to have a suction tube. I'm okay, really, just a profusion of saliva. After supper I had two phials of champagne, and feel very jolly. Penny massaged my feet and legs. She undressed me, and put me to bed. Joss came in at 12.35, and cuddled up close, and we went off back together to sleep.

Joss phoned to say there was chaos in the studio, and he won't be home till late. Penny whizzed me up a lovely lunch and I had a phial of red wine, because I was cold from the wet wind. I read, and then Penny massaged my feet, and put me to bed for a rest. At 7.40 the phone rang. Penny was not here. She had gone to phone Iain. What I did not know is that her phone card ran out, and Iain was calling her back. The phone rang incessantly, five times, and I could not move to answer it. Then I heard Penny at the door, but she couldn't open it. I was lying there worrying if there was an emergency. Eventually a security guard opened the door. Penny came in, and had just sat me up, when Iain phoned again. He was obviously upset. Of course I toppled over on the bed again, and Penny had to see to me, and said she'd ring Iain back in ten minutes. I hope she sorts things out. It is now 8.25, and where is my love? I miss him so much. Samantha phoned today. She is looking forward to being with us in Devon. Joss arrived at 8.35, looking very tired and frustrated. He'd been hanging about all day.

Joss saw me through the night, turning me and cuddling me.

We had a snack, and packed my cold box with whizzed-up sardines for the plane, and yoghurt and whizzed-up tomato. A car collected us, and drove us to the airport, where they were very helpful, and settled us in the lounge. At 8 p.m. our helper arrived and took us on to the plane. They had a narrow wheelchair on board to take me to my seat. As Penny was a doctor, and accompanying me, they upgraded her to sit with us in Business Class. She was sitting next to an astronaut, and engaged in conversation. After her dinner she massaged my legs for half an hour, then took me to the loo, and helped me. It was an extremely pleasant flight.

There was a funny episode as we went through security in Montreal. One of the actors had given Joss a lighter in the shape of a gun. Joss had it in his hand luggage, and within five minutes armed police surrounded him. It took half an hour of filling in forms, etc, before we proceeded. The gun was confiscated, sealed in an envelope and given to a flight attendant to give to Joss on touchdown. Melanie was at the airport to meet us, and so was our driver. I was carried into his car, and we drove to Devon. We got to the Rectory at 6 p.m. Samantha, Paola, Nico, Tommi, Natalie and Charlie were there. It was confusing getting home, as I couldn't remember where things were packed. I was very tired and was glad to get to bed.

Woke up at 11 a.m. Had yoghurt, and Joss made wonderful coffee. Sammy helped as much as she could, but Charlie is demanding, and so is Natalie. I wept several times with frustration. No one understands how boring it is to have to write down every thought. I often feel I would rather be dead. Poor darling Joss gets in such a loud, shouting temper with his frustration at not being able to communicate. Sammy is looking very tired. I'm worried about her. However, she worked really hard, helping me pack things away. She was not well and went to bed at 11 p.m., Joss and I had a sleep, got up at midnight, had a snack and went to bed at 3.30 a.m.

Poor Sammy still has a migraine. Nico and Tommi are at school. Paola is looking after Natalie and Charlie. Joss dressed me, and we breakfasted with the radio on when suddenly – horror upon horror – planes had been hijacked and driven into the Twin Towers in New York and the Pentagon. The TV showed scenes of mayhem – tall towers, full of people, crumbling and bursting into flames. It was so sad, and mind-blowing. The loss of life is gargantuan. We spent most of the day watching the news, as more reports broke through. America is stunned with the horrendous awareness of all those people, in hijacked planes, at work at the World Trade Center, at the Pentagon, and in the street – oh, it is so very frightening. Those suicide carriers of evil are shocking in their violence. So many firemen and policemen have been killed as the buildings collapsed on them. There is little point in doing much – we are all so stunned.

Toni arrived like a breath of fresh air. I had a shower, with Joss's help. Then Toni dressed me and I came downstairs. Sad news in the paper. George Bush wants war. I think the world would respect America if she didn't use force and war, and instead used the Secret Service and negotiation to get the perpetrators.

We got up at 6 a.m. We had a quick breakfast, and drove to Stoke Mandeville. Joss drove to Swindon, and Sammy took over and drove the rest of the way. I had a kidney and bladder ultrascan first, and then a spinal X-ray. Samantha then blah-blahed about me, and it ended up with the doctor insisting I had tube feeding, or with food going down the wrong way I will get a chest infection and die. I left there – cross with Samantha exaggerating and Joss not saying a word. The fact that I cannot talk for myself depressed me. Stoke Mandeville has got run-down, with toilets out of order, X-ray machines not working, doors broken and long queues waiting in corridors. It is such a disgrace. Darling Joss helped me through the night. He turned me, and put my feet on the water cushion.

Sammy came in to help me out of bed and dress me. Yesterday Joss brought me a self-drive wheelchair and some bars to help me get up. After breakfast there was a lot of post, which I answered, and filled out orders for Christmas. After lunch I was very tired, so I had a kip with Joss, who was so sweet and loving and helpful. We had crab and prawns for supper, which was terribly difficult to swallow. I feel really ill tonight. I sniffed salt up my nose to unblock it. I have too much saliva, and I have a headache. We started watching *Short Cuts*, a lovely film, but halfway through I was feeling so ill that Joss put me to bed, and fitted me up with a feed for the night. It was 3.10. When I woke up to be turned, Joss couldn't work out what I wanted. I had to write it down! My right leg had bad pain and I couldn't get comfy. I felt very near to death last night.

Disaster this morning. I woke up and asked Joss to get me up. He said, 'In one minute – I'm going to put on the heating'. I waited and waited, and then total frustration came over me. I tried to move, and got my legs out of bed, but couldn't move my top. Joss had done the heating, talked to Samantha and gone to the lavatory, while all I wanted was to sit up and go to the loo. I can't bear 'Just a minute' – it means fifteen minutes. I don't think it is fair when I can't get myself up. It only takes a minute to put me in my chair, and then I'm free. He can be as long as he likes then. I came down to breakfast and Samantha dressed me. My tube was blocked; so she had to use the forcer, and then gave me aloe vera and my minerals. I couldn't manage any breakfast, as my throat seems to reject everything. I have such a bad headache. Joss and Samantha are in the kitchen, discussing meals and me!! It's weird for me to sit here and feel out of it already. The doctor came to see me, and put me on antibiotics.

Although I was not aware at the time Rosemary was now beginning to go through a much more depressed stage. As the symptoms grew more debilitating, her confusion became overwhelming, and her moods began to sway back and forth. She had always showed enormous strength and ability overcoming any trouble and misfortune, but now that the disease was rampant, the inability to fight back was totally frustrating.

I feel too ill to write a diary today. I'm coughing a lot. Toni arrived sometime in the afternoon. I was so pleased to see her. The health visitor came – also the dietician – ill – I feel I'm near death. Joss was very much a bully tonight.

I feel very emotionally bruised. Toni and Sammy heard Joss shouting last night. We made sure everything was on time today. Toby arrived this afternoon – it's lovely to see him. Toni cooked sea bass in the oven for all of them. I got into difficulties, and Sammy was an angel to help me, and got me to bed after supper. Toni set up my night feed, and then Joss got into bed disgruntled, because

Sammy and Toni giggled. I had a breathing problem. Lights out at 10.30. Joss turned me at 2 a.m, and back at 4 a.m.

Joss got up at 5 a.m, dressed, breakfasted and left at 5.39. He drove to Tiverton, got the 7 a.m train, and went to London to narrate *Les Miserables*. This has been the worst day possible. I've spent the whole day retching and coughing, and trying to get up saliva. I was so exhausted I went to lie down at three. Dr Cracknell called at six, and Sammy brought him upstairs to see me. He left something to relax my chest. Toby, Sammy and Toni are all very sweet. At seven Toni went out for a walk in the rain. Then I wrote, and at 9 p.m., Sammy called me to give me my antibiotics. She had Charlie in her arms as she poured the medicine out, and then Tracy phoned, so she really wasn't concentrating. Neither was I, as I was coughing badly. Whether she didn't shake the bottle, or stir sufficient water, I don't know, but it got stuck and couldn't go down. Toby and Sammy were in a giggly mood, and tried to force it down. They each had a go at forcing while I was coughing. No luck. [The tube was stuck up, which could be dangerous.] I had to go to bed with no water, no Lactulose – nothing. Bed 10.30. Joss arrived back some time later.

Joss took me, and Toni, to the hospital. We were put in the Surgical Admissions Unit, and my blood pressure, ECG and oxygen tests were done. The doctor tried to manipulate my tube, but blew it – so I waited for the operation. The anaesthetists were so nice, and nurses so kind. They took out my old tube, and gave me a new one. I came round with an oxygen mask on, a kind nurse had tucked me up comfortably in bed and I had a drip fixed. Nurses came every two hours and turned me.

At 7.30 they got me up, put me on the commode and then they bathed me and washed my hair. Toni arrived at eight, and she joined in and dressed me. We waited for the doctor to see me and start my feed. Then we went out front to wait for Joss, but it was Melanie who drove me home. Joss arrived ten minutes later with a load of shopping and scrummy food. It's really a sod that I can't eat it. I was hitched on my peg, until 10 p.m., while the family ate a delicious Thai meal, and in the evening, lovely fish and veg. At ten Toni put me to bed, and fixed me up with a new bottle for the night. Joss got to bed soon after. We were asleep by 11.30.

I woke at seven this morning with Joss crying – he'd had a bad dream. We then had a lovely cuddle. I do love Joss so very much. We've had the most wonderful, exciting, romantic life together, and I really don't want to leave my soulmate. Sammy came in to look at my feed, which was not finished. Half an hour later, Toni shut it off and flushed me out, helped me bidet, and wash and dress. I went downstairs, and had a few sips of coffee and yoghurt, to keep Joss company at his lonely breakfast. Toby went for a seven-hour walk and came back exhausted.

OCTOBER

Joss got up at 7.30, and Hilary the new nurse arrived at 8 a.m. Toni showed her how to shut off my feed, and how to wash and dress me. Another day of people arriving – Mary the social worker, etc. They chatted and chatted, and brought things in for me to try – loo things, bath things – and then Louise came and cleaned my new peg. I got really worn out. Toby said his goodbyes at 7.30, and drove off: I was sorry to see him go. I feel I'll not see him again. Toni left at five. Now Joss and I are on our own, with Samantha being sick upstairs, and five children needing attention. Joss hung up my washing for me, and then got his supper of soup and spare ribs, and I sat with him while he ate it. I got very tired. We went to the kitchen, and Joss gave me Lactulose and morphine. He helped me wash and get undressed, and into my nightdress, and then he had to set up my feed. He had forgotten to listen to all the instructions about tube feeding. He wanted me to write it down. On one's side, how can one write? [By this time I had lifted Rosemary onto the bed. Once she was settled, there was no way that she could move, and, as she was lying on her side, it was not possible for her to use her pen – difficult enough in any position.] Joss can be so impossible at times. He overreacted, said things he didn't mean, and I started crying. I had to get up again, to breathe and re-write instructions. At last the penny dropped, and Joss got the feed going, and fixed it on me. It was okay when we turned out the light.

Joss came back at three. He helped me do a pee, and then got into bed with me. We slept till 5.30, when Dr Cracknell arrived. He was very kind. He saw us in the bedroom, and then we all came downstairs. When he left I had my dose of Lactulose. I suddenly felt very ill. I was icy cold and nauseous. I thought I was dying. I stood by the Aga for a while, and it soon passed. I have another hour to write. The photographs Joan had sent me of school have got me thinking. The photographs were of our last Cambridge class at school, at the beginning of our grown-up life. I must say that all my dreams have come true. I passed the Cambridge with high grades, and got to Cape Town University, which I loved and had a wonderful time. I did perform with the International Ballet Company. I did act onstage. I did marry my leading man. I did have seven children. I did travel extensively. I've had the most rich, loving, happy life, and I am quite resigned to my motor neurone. It's a small price to pay for my exquisite life, and – oh my! – am I so lucky as to have met my soulmate! Joss and I have been so close, so in love, so excitingly together for fifty years. We are so lucky. I'm not going to complain any more. I am so grateful for my happy life. Ros came at nine and undressed me. She was very sweet. I sat downstairs in my dressing gown until 11 p.m., while Joss had his supper. We went upstairs and Joss did my tube. Sammy helped, and then lights out at midnight.

I had a wonderful dream last night. There was a crowd of us travelling to some lovely country. We were in a train, and Joss was in the top bunk. He called down to me, and pulled me up to him, and we made exquisite love, and then arrived at this beautiful place, with flowers everywhere. We joined others, had a lovely meal and we were remarried. It was all very happy. I feel very well today and very much in love with my darling Joss. I wrote out for Joss how to make a fish pie. He's cooking it for Penny, Iain, Daniel, Inigo, Ella and Nancy. They will be here this evening. It is now evening – half past seven – and Penny plus family have arrived with the vicar. Joss gave them all champagne, while they talked. Ros came at nine, and helped me undress and wash, and put me on the bed, and attached me to my feed. I fell asleep and woke an hour later. I felt I wanted to go to the loo. I heard Joss and the children, so I called and called and called. When I could call no more, as my breath gave in, I tried to scream, but no one heard me. I started to cry with frustration. My mouth filled with saliva. I was so exhausted, I kept quiet. I started trying to call again, and finally Joss came up with Penny. Joss put me on the commode. Penny stayed in a kind of panic. I only needed Joss. I was too tense to go to the loo, and Joss put me back to bed, and soon joined me.

Ros arrived just as my meal finished at 8.a.m. I read the paper – all about the Taliban, and the American and British forces and bombing. It is very disturbing. At ten someone came from the hospice, and gave me a wonderful massage with rose and lavender. As she finished, Beverly arrived, and brought a box that says 'Yes' and 'No' for me to use. As Beverly was finishing, Hilary arrived, then Brenda, then Elaine and then oil delivery. Hilary fixed me up to my feed. Joss had scampi and chips for lunch, then strawberries and cream. It all smelt so good – as I'm having my peg. The electricians were busy in the kitchen all day. Poor things had to move everything each time I needed to get my wheelchair through. Joss has a bad cold, and doesn't feel well. My feed finished at 5.30. I dropped a piece of paper, which I need, on to the floor, and spent twenty frustrating minutes trying to pick it up – all to no avail. Shit! I read three chapters from my book, and sorted out things until Ros came at nine. Joss arrived at 1.30, and oh! – what a lovely surprise – he made love with me, and I was so elated – a lovely sexual time. Slept in an aura of love.

NOVEMBER

Pain Pain Pain in my legs all night, and my anklebone. Difficult – sitting on the bidet today. I don't feel very well. Hilary helped me dress, and gave me my aloe vera. The night was a nightmare. The painkillers didn't help. The pain in my legs was excruciating. I could not get comfortable, and Joss shouted at me because he was frustrated, and did not know how to help. He gave me a heavy pad and paper to write on, but lying on my back, I couldn't hold the pad and press hard enough to write. We had a very busy night. Joss had to turn me several times, and move my sore legs. Then he came back to bed. He cuddled me, and saw me through the night.

I feel very lonely today. Toni and David had arrived late last night. I am sitting, attached to my feed. Joss, Melanie, Toni, David and Kirsty are all by the table, eating fish and chips, drinking white wine, laughing loudly, and having such fun. I am very lonely.

Oh pain, pain at night. Joss tried to help, and turned me over several times, but my legs continue to pain. I dreamt I was given a game of lacrosse. I ran into the garden and played it with Toni. We were so happy knocking the balls through the tunnels with our sticks. I was shattered when I woke up, and found I couldn't move. *C'est la vie.* I needed Joss, and he cuddled me, and made exquisite love with me. Oh what heaven – then we had a wonderful deep sleep, and suddenly all was well.

DECEMBER

Joss was an angel to me last night. He wrapped me in his arms, and he is so loving and supportive. I am so in love with him. He is my reason for fighting on. I notice day by day, a little of something doesn't happen. My fingers can't hold a letter. My wrists are so useless that I need two hours to carry a cheque book from A to B. My knees can only stay straight for one minute. A month ago it took me ten minutes to walk to the loo with the walker. Now I can only stand for one minute, while my pants are pulled up and down. I hate being so weak, but Joss's love helps me cope with it all. I wonder how long I can write.

This was a wonderful day for me. I sat with Joss while he had breakfast, then Melanie put me in the car, and Joss drove me to Bradworthy, and we went shopping for Penny's wedding presents. Then Joss drove me to Clovelly harbour for a breath of air. I watched TV until Hilary came back at 9 p.m. Joss watched over me all night. I am so in love with him; he is so good to me and makes me very happy.

A stranger arrived at the dot of eight, and she was very caring and marvellous. She washed me and dressed me. Joss helped her, and put my jewellery on. I read the paper, and sorted out things, and then Joss said be wanted to take me to Atlantic Village. So we went, and came back for my feed. Now I am feeding, but I hate sitting here for four and a half hours, when I could be looking for things. Ros came and was so happy and uplifting and put me to bed at 9.55. Joss came soon after when I was asleep, and I woke up with him kissing me, and we made love so beautifully. I was not moved till 5.30, and he moved me again at 7.30.

What a rotten day! Last night was sheer bliss. Joss was wonderful, and we had a fabulous night. We are so close and loving together. He is the light of my life – the absolute depth of love I feel for him – and I know he returns it. But now – it's a bleak, dark morning. Ros got me out of bed, and took me to the bathroom, and I was holding on to the rail, but my legs just folded. Ros couldn't wash me, and I burst into floods of tears that I could not control. It was horrid. Then I was going through my post, when the physio arrived. She was teaching Melanie and Joss what to do, and so I was given little therapy. When she left I was still tearful. Hilary arrived, and took me to the bathroom. I was able to stand, so I still have a bit of hope. Please legs – keep your knees locked. Thank heaven we have our lovely new Tempur bed – we really have peaceful nights on it. Joss put on a Woody Allen movie for me, which I loved. A lovely day, we saw two movies. Ros came at nine, and sat and watched the end of the film. She was so good; she washed me, and put me to bed. Joss came, and he put his arms around me – so closely – I was in heaven. I felt it was true love, and I slept so happily that I floated away in sheer ecstasy.

My feed finished at 7.40, and Joss flushed me out and gave me a phial of water. Ros arrived at nine, and she washed and dressed me. It took a lot of effort to get my stockings on. Joss went out shopping, and I found my belts that I won't wear again, so I gave Ros my gold belt, my silver belt and my gypsy belt. She was very pleased with them. I'm very stable today. When Joss put the light out it was 10.35. At 11.05 my knees were agony, so Joss turned me. Once my knees were upside down they stopped hurting. But Joss turned me several times, and my knees were very painful, and my thighs went into spasm. Altogether – the night was pain.

Joss, I deliberately don't put on washing until you've finished breakfast. It is now 10.30, and I've had to put it on because, for some reason, you are not fetching the paper, or having breakfast until noon. I can't wait; otherwise my washing won't be hung up till three. [Rosemary had always been industrious – her determination and strength were extraordinary. She felt it was vital that she remained in control and constructive. She refused to give up. This was difficult to watch, but this was her way to fight the disease.] Penny came to talk to me. Joss said, 'Let's open our presents now'. I said no. So that was that. We watched a movie, *Gosford Park*, which was wonderful. The whole of the evening was spent discussing the wedding, and talking to Penny and Iain who are very well suited. They went with Joss to see Hartland Abbey about their wedding reception, and they came in and had tea, and are off to Scotland tomorrow.

CHRISTMAS DAY: Joss said 'Happy Christmas' to me at 2 a.m., when he was turning me in bed. The next thing I heard was from Ros, whose icy hands stretched into the bed and grabbed my legs, which she pulled at right angles to my body. She had my legs strung out, and she bent over me, and gathered up my body to a sitting position. Then she took me in my chair to wash and dress me. I came downstairs, and sat with Joss, while he had his breakfast. I told Hilary to come later. We did presents. Joss gave me the most delicious, exquisite diamond heart and a golden bracelet. I adore him; he is so wonderful, caring and kind. I had a lovely time downstairs; Melanie had decorated a wonderful lighted Christmas tree, and put all the presents around. It was so festive, and Joss gave me lovely pink champagne. I had four phials and felt great. Hilary fitted me with my meal and it finished at 5.30. Melanie flushed me out. We watched TV and Joss had sausage and mash for lunch. Melanie cooked a turkey downstairs, with Sam, Adam and Tomas. Ros didn't come tonight, so Melanie washed me, and put me to bed. Joss came and cuddled me, and I was in heaven.

Ros got me up. Joss had already flushed me out, because the

feed finished early. I felt very ill, freezing cold and nauseous. Melanie gave me some water. My stomach rejected it. At 2.20 I had 150mm of feed introduced gradually. Joss and I had a cuddle sitting here – it was lovely. Then Melanie flushed me out, and gave me vitamin E and water. Melanie is very organised. She is tidying up, and throwing things out. She really is working hard, and getting us clear. I've just seen Joss walk into the sitting room to make up the fire, and a great wave of divine love came over me. He is my reason for living. Ros came, and was feeling whacked. So she sat down with Joss, and had a glass of white wine and some olives. At 9.20 she took me to wash and bed. My honey bun joined me at 10.32, and I was transported to heaven in his arms.

Joss was up and dressed by the time Ros came. I suddenly thought – ME – what was I able to do today. I had to be scraped off the bed, someone had to flush out my tube, wheel me to the bathroom, someone had to put me on the lavatory seat, get me off, clean me up, try to wash me sitting on a commode, dress me, put my stockings and shoes on, brush my hair, put my wash in the washing machine, put the powder in and set it to run. I'm not able to do a fucking thing by myself. I cried, and that upset Joss. Toni and David, and the twins, and Abbi and Isabella arrived, and went out to dinner this evening. Joss and Melanie had dinner here. It was a horrid, horrid day.

I had a bad night. Joss was sitting on the bed, and it crashed down – so Melanie put it on a pile of books. I suddenly felt very sick. I felt faint. I sat on the commode and then started retching. Eventually, I was able to go to sleep, but only without food from the machine. Ros got me up at eight. I am weaker today, and my heart is pounding so quickly. She managed to wash and dress me. I taught Joss how to cook a chicken, and showed him how to make lovely gravy. [As Rosemary was unable to speak this was not easy, however, with the help of pen and paper, she managed.] Hilary put me on my feed, and Joss had his lunch next to me. Oh, how I love my Joss more and more each day. We watched *Daisies in December*. It is such a gem of a film. Hilary watched it and cried. Joss and I had a cuddle for an hour, and I am much brighter now.

I've done a silly thing. I've left out a day. Toni and David went home on Saturday night, and I've written about Sunday, but one day is so like another, it matters little.

NEW YEAR'S EVE: We had a lovely letter from Samantha, thanking us for their Christmas presents. Samantha is a brilliant writer. She should write a book. Usual day. Very difficult tonight as I can't stand, and I am very weak. Then Joss came, and I was so pleased, as his arms went round me and took me to heaven.

2002

JANUARY

Ros got me out of bed, ready to go downstairs. One problem – the lift was not working. So I turned my chair around. Joss brought up my tray, and I wrote for a little while. This new year has set me back somewhat. David gave his attention to the lift and in one hour it was working. I opened letters – or rather, Joss opened letters for me to read. Hilary came back to take me off my feed, and then, upstairs to pee, but no matter how much I tried, I couldn't go. We thought it was the injection that caused it. It was a terrible shock for me. Joss rang Dr Cracknell, who, in turn, got a nurse, who came out and fitted me with a catheter. Success – I was very relieved. Ros came and put me to bed. Joss came soon after me, and we floated off to sleep, wrapped in love.

I slept without moving, and Joss woke me at 5 a.m. He felt he had to move me. He grabbed my legs, and threw them across the bed, as if he was chucking logs on a fire. I must tell him that my legs are very sensitive and, when he grabbed my leg, it set off a nerve pain which was agony. Ros gave me a bath, and once again I have no energy. I am too tired to go on. Joss had lunch with me. He had mixed fish and chips. When my meal was finished Hilary appeared, and turned off my feed. I feel so much better, and wide-awake. Ros came at nine, and washed me well. She put me to bed, and then my love came in, and my life was perfect. He put his loving arms around me, and I floated off to a marvellous, spiritual level of sleep.

A frantic call from Ros at 7.35. She's got a trapped nerve, and can't get here. Joss phoned Hilary, and she came in fifteen minutes. Joss came in with a lovely black skirt for my birthday tomorrow. Hilary is here all morning, and is very helpful, because Joss has someone interviewing him. I think it is Janet Street-Porter. [It was Lynda Lee Potter.] I can't write more now, because my fucking saliva is ruling my poor life. I feel nausea too. So I was glad when Ros came and put me to bed no feed. Joss again saw me through the night, and I love him so.

Bright sunny day. Toni and David arrived last night and, when I got down today, the kitchen was a hive of activity – Toni was emptying her car of herbs and foods for the reception tomorrow. I must say, before I get embedded in food, that I had a wonderful night, because my saliva dried up, and I was able to sleep without a worry of choking. Joss was again sweetly attentive, and he got up at seven, and sat me on my commode, and gave me my bottle to empty my bladder. I got back to bed – or rather he put me back to bed – and I waited for Ros to get me up. Dr Cracknell called, and was telling me to take light meals to help the stomach strengthen. My tummy is distended by air. An electric humidifier has arrived. Joss came in exhausted, and needed a rest. So, after Hilary left, we had an hour's kip. My fucking saliva is bad again. I am so destroyed by it. Toni, David and Melanie are working so hard for Penny and Iain's wedding. Moyra Fraser arrived with Joss at 8.30 p.m. Ros will be here in half an hour – thank God – I need to get rid of my saliva. Joss came to bed remarkably early. He took Moyra home first – she's staying at the Red Lion – and then came into my bed – which was heavenly.

It was a very good night, as my saliva dried up, and I was able to sleep without choking, and Joss was ever present to turn me. Melanie came down to express my tube. Joss got up at seven, and woke me, and my bladder knew it had to empty. Melanie sat with my bottle for three quarters of an hour, and she told me I had filled a Badoit bottle. So at last it is emptying itself!! Joss gave me an early birthday present – the most wonderful silk blouse, jacket, skirt and scarf, so I was able to wear lovely clothes, and I felt good. Everyone was dressing up. Toni and David took me, in my outdoor chair, and expertly lifted me into the church. Joss came in the front, and sat next to me. Everyone was ready – and we had to wait for Penny. At 11.35 she arrived, and walked up the isle on Joss's arm. They both looked so wonderful. Iain stood up, serious and good-looking in his wedding outfit, with a carnation in his lapel. Daniel and Inigo read beautifully, and were perfect ushers. I was really pleased with them all. I thought it was a very moving service. Joss didn't like the vicar, because he lacked humility. But aside from that, it was a lovely wedding, and the harpist (Iain's daughter) played beautifully. After the service Iain's family came home. Toni brought me in my chair. Joss opened champagne, and I met Iain's parents, who I liked immensely. They have their feet on the ground, and are charming. They both wore heather in their coats. It was very homely, and super. Joss was the last to go to the reception. I desperately want him to let himself go, and have a lovely meal. I had a little champagne in my tube, and it instantly gave me a lift. When all had left for Hartland Abbey, Hilary put me on my feed, and we are glad to have a quiet afternoon. It's still very windy out, and the blue tits are trying to eat and keep balance. It's now three o'clock, and I should think the reception is nearly over. I did birthday cards with Hilary. Joss got in at 4.30. This evening I read. Ros came at nine, and put me to bed. I was very tired. Penny and Iain returned. Penny washed and changed, and they left for a secret place. Joss saw me beautifully through a hard night.

At 7 a.m. I said, 'Joss'. Smiling, he came to my assistance. I pointed to my hip, and he thought I meant something else. He smiled, and moved me. I was lying on a painful hip – and tried to say, 'painful hip'. Joss shouted. I cried, and it was bad. Sammy came in, and told Joss my hip was bad. Joss understood, and finally moved it. I read my post in tears. After Hilary left, I sat in the sitting room, and read Sunday papers. It turned out to be a lovely day. Melanie, Sammy, Charlie and Tomas were all sweet, and Joss was a honey. The only bugbear was my catheter, which was so slow. My feed was up by 10.10. and Joss came later, as his dinner was late. I don't mind waiting for him, as he's my best friend, and I adore him.

I'm seventy-three today, and it's been a marvellous day. Bright sunshine and Joss has given me so many beautiful presents. He gave me two skirts, a wonderful jacket, a warm shirt, a soft waistcoat, a lovely statue and two silk shirts. Melanie and Sammy and Joss were such fun. A marvellous physio came, and really helped me, but I got dreadful pains in my stomach. Joss opened a bottle of champagne for me. I had three phials, and my tummy felt better. We did presents all morning, and I feel so loved.

Joss woke up in a good mood, and said we would have a lovely day. We did the post together over breakfast. Then Hilary turned up, and fitted me up with my feed. Joss and I went up to have a rest on the bed, but my saliva was very bad, and kept me awake, as I tried to find a tissue. I tried to get up, and Joss got in a mood, because I couldn't tell him what I wanted. He threw the pad and pencil away, and started to cry in temper, 'cause he couldn't understand. I started to cry as well, and the physio arrived as we were both in tears, but she was very understanding. When she finished, Joss and I both felt better, and he had a vodka. So I asked for red wine, which made me sick, and I brought it all up. Ros came and washed me down, and put me to bed very gently. Why are my spelling so bad? I have a theory. I think I'm talking – so I am writing not as quickly as I'm thinking.

This was the first sign of Rosemary's misspelling and confusion. Gradually, it escalates and moments of repetition occur, and so I have done my best to change the spelling and clarify when it is difficult to understand. As time goes by, day by day Rosemary's confusion becomes more obvious and more critical.

I woke up in a better mood. Joss was wonderful overnight, and kissed me, and turned me many times, and I love him so. He made me a special coffee for my tube, and I had a rush of energy. Then he left by car for Tiverton, to catch the train to Bristol. I pray to God to bring him home safely. Hilary had to stay near me, in case I needed things. Hurrah – Joss got in at five. It was brilliant to see him. He liked my hair. Ros was pleased, as she had washed it. He kissed me again, which I need – I missed him while he was away. Melanie got him some lunch, and we watched a spooky film. It was so scary, I found it difficult to go to bed. Ros got me washed, and into bed by 10.20. Joss came and cuddled me. And it sent me off to sleep in a heavenly mood.

Bad start today. Joss woke me up to turn me. I think it was 3 a.m. Then I woke at seven feeling sick, and by 7.30 I said to Joss – quick, I need the commode. How lucky he got me sitting there in time – that was a great plus. Now how is he going to clean me? He eventually stood up and bent me over the side of the bed. My face was squashed but that didn't matter. When I was clean he collected me up, threw me on the bed and put my food back on. Ros came and fast-forwarded my feed, got my wheelchair steady and, when my food peeped, she turned it off. Hilary arrived. Toni had arrived last night. My saliva was particularly bad all day and I found it got too difficult to manage. Hilary was not waiting, and said, if Toni could do me she needn't come back. Toni said she could. Then our day was free. I wrote to Daphne and Moyra and to John McCormick to thank him for all his work to all of this family. We then had a kip on our chairs. Joss and Melanie had lunch next to me. Melanie and I went through magazines of King-sized covers. I can't see as well as I could so Melanie kindly filled in the shopping and made out a cheque which I could sign. Dr Cracknell just called and he's worried about my swelling and is going to give me a mixture to give me. I'm fed up with saliva and he's looking into the patches. He thought my knees were swollen. Joss got in a temper with his computer. I love him so much that I don't want him to give up work because of my illness. I'll kill myself if he doesn't work because of me. Ros got me to bed by 10.10. Joss then came up, and wiggled me to get my legs even. Then he came to bed, and it was heavenly. I slept so well knowing Joss loved me, and I adore him. We live in that comfort all the time.

FEBRUARY

Ros came in at eight and got me out of bed, washed me, dressed me and she left on holiday for a long weekend at Butlins. I feel desolate. I can't write my diary any more because of my neck. Joss kept making me sit up and it's impossible to write. A huge tall lady, Anna, came to take on what Ros was doing. I was then let her take me to the loo, to wash and undress me. She put a clean nightie on me and I came down afterwards to watch a movie with Joss and Melanie. We watched a film and Melanie put me to bed.

Last night Joss came and made wonderful love to me. It made me very happy and we slept very well. Another morning with Anna, who is very nice but she can't cope with me. She's too tall and can't put me up on my chair. Joss is very tired. Nothing happens these days. I am stuck on a feed, and then have someone to pass things to me, open my letters, because I can't do that. Anna didn't put me to bed, because I wasn't tired and wanted to sit up. She didn't mind at all. We went to bed at 11 p.m. and Melanie put me on my feed. So it's all up to someone else to look after me. I can't get out of my wheelchair or stand up, I can't swallow, drink or eat or talk, and it's getting me down. I asked Dr Cracknell if he approved of euthanasia. He thought about it, and straight away gave me something else for saliva and he gave me an enema. I think you have to say that to make doctors think! Life is pretty hectic these days. We go through the papers and have physios and others. Anna came and put me to bed and that's that.

Joss was on his computer and insisted I came in the office to be with him. It was a bore moving all my things in there and then he goes in the next room to have his lunch. I want to die, so he can be on his own and not to force me out of my usual corner. I don't want to write my diary any more. It is going to get me in a mess. I love Joss so much and I know he loves me. But his personality has changed. He is so much better working and he won't work because of me, so it's a roundabout. I have enough to deal with from my disease. He can have no notion what I have accepted to keep cheerful and what I have to endure. I can't understand when in bed last night we had wonderful cuddles that were unique in their intimate way. Goodbye, dear diary. Oh, I forgot Dr Cracknell came. He was very understanding. I really can't see the point of me trying to get better. I feel so fed up.

Oh, diary, I have such bad news. Last night in bed I messed the bed in my sleep. I am bitterly ashamed of myself and never want it to happen again. I was woken up this morning by three people staring at me. I was really confused as I thought some really bad news was being brought. It was really bad for me, as I've already explained. Ros and Mel were trying to clear my dressing by pulling my nightie over my head. Melanie was so kind to clean everything up. Joss left at ten for London. I hope Joss is okay in London. If he works I'll be very happy. Ros came at nine and washed me and put me to bed. Joss came up to me at 9.30, and was so loving and I was so pleased to see him. He had his supper and came up when I had my saliva, which was drying up because I stuff my mouth with a flannel to concentrate. It was a wonderful night and I slept until 3 a.m. Joss and Melanie put me on the commode, and then Melanie lifted me to face Joss's back, and I enjoyed rubbing his back a little as we went to sleep together and we were so in love.

Ros woke me up to an empty bed. Joss had got up about seven, and he went into the kitchen and made me a wonderful coffee and one for Melanie and Ros. He was dressed for his film and looked so good. I do love him so and I like him filming because it's his life. He left, and Melanie and I wrapped parcels up for birthdays. Joss came in at five when he had finished filming. I so pleased he's back because I'm very much in love with him; although I am keen he gets to film, I miss him terribly when he is away. My love for Joss outweighs all my problems which go with MND. I am only sorry I'm letting him down.

Joss gave me two phials of coffee which down well. The rest of the day was horrid. So many people came round and I was dead tired all day. I'm very confused with all this coming and going. Hilary is always being busy at home and I can't use her as much as I need. Luckily, Ros came and took me upstairs. She washes me beautifully and puts me cosily to bed. Joss came to bed later. I always love to see him. He is the one stable person. He is my soulmate and he does his best to see me.

Melanie was more than helpful. She brought all the things

downstairs to me. Kirsty arrived and Melanie had managed to wrap everyone's presents up. They arrived and all the children had their presents and adored them. They all are quite little and Kirsty is pregnant and I was surprised she drove down with five children all by herself. I am so sorry for her. I felt like a schoolgirl coming out of class, when my feed stopped. But my saliva is getting me down. Thank heaven Ros came and got me away from the crowds, and she took me upstairs: Joss came up and cuddled, and all my troubles were over. How I adore him.

Joss and Melanie stayed with me when I had my meal. I am now free – my tube switched off – and so its goodbye, diary, I'll try later. It is now 5.15 so I have a few minutes. I love Kirsty. She's so sweet. We had a good chatter and I am now free. I am so happy that I love Joss and we may be going away some time. I very happy today 'cause Joss is always with me. I may go with him as he may not accept work if I don't go with him. I love going and I'm not giving up because of being helpless.

It was such a lovely day the sun got so strong and it came right through our window and I wrote several cards and Joss and I had a short rest together. We got up in twenty minutes. I love Joss so much. He's my best friend – my best companion and I'm so grateful he still loves me when I'm so helpless. I try very hard to do things that I should do. And I can't. I tried to pick up a basket in my wheelchair, and I couldn't. Another thing I can't do is pick up things from the floor. I am totally helpless.

There were a lot of goodbyes to say and I am thrilled with Kirsty having a new baby. She expects in the first week in August. When they left – the house returned to its quick and quiet domain.

Joss gave me an enema, and since I was upstairs, I stayed there and Joss lay down with me. Ros came at nine, and I was blissfully happy to go to bed. Ros is a stable girl who is so profferfella [professional], and I immediately put my trust in her. Well, Sunday is over, and Joss made exquisite love with me, which is a big plus to my energy and the total love I have for Joss. We had wonderful day and night together.

I went to push the button and it was no good, I can't push the button on! I have to rely that there is always someone here to help. Hilary came at ten to put my feed on early. We went to Barnstable to get Joss another computer. Then we stopped at a big store and I sat in the car all that time. I don't care. We drove back home and they [Melanie and I] left me in car for another fifteen minutes. They forgot I'm a person and thought of me after they'd taken the shopping in and both decided they were missing me. I was collected like a lost heavy parcel and Joss couldn't understand why I was upset. I had a bit of my medicine up in my bedroom. I'm so cross. Then I came down and it cheered me up. How I pulled myself together and got through the day, I don't know. I'm okay now. At 9 p.m. when Ros came and she gently washed me and undressed me and put me to bed. I was wafting into sleep when Joss came in and told me he and Melanie had fixed a changed itinery. I was so cross that they planned it without me. I thought Joss was taking advantage of the fact that I can't talk. I got out of bed and tried to get in my electric chair and go down the stairs and Melanie stopped me. I went into the bathroom and I was eating a paper tissues to choke me. I had a paper to write to Joss about how upset I was that he hadn't consulted me. It's a great hardship for me to write at all now. It's going to be difficult now. Eventually, Joss got me to bed and by the morning I was okay but still feeling bruised.

We had a lovely day today. Melanie is packing up parcels for me and I adore Joss's coffee. I apologised for the horrid night, and we had a good day.

Ros got me up. She flushed me through and gave me vitamin E and I tried to look at Joss. He started to cry. I had to leave my feed, to go into his office to try and calm him. He was so cross to see me writing all day, and choosing things. I got upset when Hilary tried to fix me up to my feed; I had to stop my feed. I was trying to choose which brassieres were to go to Melanie and Hilary. [By this time Rosemary had become obsessed with giving presents to everyone around her. She spent much of her time perusing shop catalogues, marking items of clothing to be ordered, which then arrived by post. It was a difficult situation, because one did not want to deflate her enthusiasm.] I came back to my feed, but she had to flush me out while I was in Joss's office and I had a blackout. I've now come back to my feed. I'm still sorry to say I was weeping when Dr Cracknell came and I couldn't stop. I have to come back to my feed and I finished it at 3.30. It is now ten to seven and I'm still on my own. Melanie is with Tomas and Joss is with his computer. He's brought in his pudding – so I'm okay. I am only surviving because Joss is very important to me. I love Joss very deeply and I don't seem to do the right thing. I expected Ros to come and I did not say goodnight. I am very confused and I hope everything will turn peaceful.

Another day I hope the Lord will help us through. Joss and Pam help me through the night. It is bliss to have Joss to cuddle and I adore him. His strength and his love cover me all the time. Night becomes a joy – to have Joss put his wonderful body and arms to touch me, I have a beautiful sleep and the worries fall off us as we cuddle. That was last night and today Ros came. She takes her job seriously. Joss and I drove to Bideford to get a present and then Joss went to Bideford pannier market. Hilary helped us out of the car. She'd made a super fire for us to come into. I have had a very good, happy day. Ros came at nine and wash me and put me to bed. My darling sweetheart came to bed at once. My favourite time begins in bed. We have such lovely things.

Another day to take in and I'm in the basement, I can't reach anything. Just as I started my diary, Joss selfishly wants me to move upstairs. Thinking back — the luckiest thing was when I met Joss.

Before that – university.

Andy, a medical student, proposed.

I never even contemplated.

David – proposed – I never thought of it.

Lionel – proposed – a mistake.

Thank God Joss arrived on the scene. I adore him and don't like to be away from him. He is my reason for living.

MARCH

My sight is getting very bad, and I am very confused these days. I feel my mind is going mad. I think this has happened because I can't walk or talk and it's a strain for me. I feel rotten today. I came downstairs feeling refreshed. I am so in love and we answered letters, and read papers. Anna came and put me to bed. Then I told them to go, and asked Melanie to give us twenty minutes, and Joss and I made the most beautiful love. I am so in love with him. I adore him. After fifty years of managing our love has grown, and we are deep souls. Melanie came back. She put cream on me, and got me to bed.

Joss is making an effort to fix something for our trip and I am excited to go to Italy. I've had enough on this page. I'll finish tomorrow. Goodnight. Monday is over for me once I have the pleasure of Joss beside me in bed. That's really the highlight. Goodnight, diary. Ros came and washed me and put me beautifully to bed. Joss came in. He must have had a very quick meal.

I am very confused today. I can't believe we are in our home. Dr Honen said it was the medicine I'm having. Well I suppose I just have to accept it. I was very pleased when Ros came at nine. She is quiet and sober and she does what she is trained to do. Joss also got to bed at the same time. Ros put me comfortable and Joss didn't have to see to me. He got to bed and cuddled me, and I went into a deep happy sleep. Poor Joss was in pain and couldn't sleep.

I am not able to get anything done with Joss giving me things to do. The worst thing I experienced today was to see Joss falling on the floor by the huge bookcase. Melanie carefully helped him up, and he has a nasty bruise on his left leg. It is very frustrating to sit around him and not being able to help. I've read the Sunday papers, both full of bad news about Jews and Palestinians, and the people in Zambia. Poor Africans. I have to sit here all day to be fed. Food has no interest to me now. I have lost interest now that I am so useless. I don't want to write to my diary any more, because it will be boring trying to write. I am totally fed up with my helpless state. I am helpless, and as I don't speak, I am not a very clever girl.

I am so sorry for Joss. I am no good match for him. He should put me into a hospice for helpless people, and then feel free to accept work in films or theatre. I'm so glad to see Ros here to take me to bed. Toni and Tom arrived. Toni is very sweet and she has a lovely son. Ros got me to bed, and Joss followed at once. I had a lovely sleep with Joss.

I am so fed up with Melanie and Hilary making arrangements – Joss is my lifesaver. I came down to Joss with a happy smiling face, only to be attacked by him saying that he didn't want helpers. He said I didn't love or trust him to do things, so I get him to take me to the loo. He made me very unhappy by calling me stubborn. He wants to help me, but he can't because of his back. He was in such a bad mood, and he made me so unhappy I wanted to die. Being totally hopeless is more than enough to worry me, without Joss getting cross with me. I'm trying to please him. He gets in the bed and cuddles me, and we went to sleep.

Joss is in a better mood now. We did catch up with things. Dr Cracknell made me talk to him and I told him all our troubles and he said that I should have a lot of fluids and he gave me a quick look and left. Joss and I had a wonderful quiet day together.

A hell day. The nurse Dawn came, which confused me. I love Joss so very much. He is my best friend as well as my lover, and my life has been so happy because he takes me with him to any country he has to work. I adore him and he's the reason for me to live. I can't live without you, darling Joss. I'm so lucky you have married me. Dawn put me to bed. Joss came to bed and I slept very well with Joss's arms around me.

Ros came at 4 a.m. to get me out of bed and to wash me and

dress me and to go downstairs. Joss drove us some of the way and Melanie drove for the rest of the journey. The airways were so kind and helpful. Three people helped us with all our luggage and my chair was wheeled straight on to the plane. We had a good flight to Rome. Darling Sammy met us at the station. She looked so pretty and was so welcoming. I was really very proud of her. We were driven to Tracy. What a lot of lovely children. Tracy was wonderful. He carried me upstairs. Sammy, Melanie and Joss had lunch on the patios and Melanie set my feed up. I felt sick. I'm very tired and someone put me to bed.

APRIL

Hello everyone. The days are all exciting in Italy. One day is much like another day. But it depends on who wants what. My saliva is so bad, I can't cope with it. I love Sammy and Tracy, and their children are so pretty. We had a late lunch. Everyone said the lunch was delicious. Melanie came and set me up on my feed. Everyone excluding Melanie and Joss drank a lot. Joss and I had a kip but I don't like sleeping in the afternoon. It is 6 p.m. I don't know how the days go.

Our last day in Italy. Poor Melanie – she has to dress me – then she flushed me and gave me vitamin E. Then she kept me with my diary. I feel I am a burden to everyone today. Just a minute – I think I have a point to make. HELL. To be parked in a chair that has to be pushed and left in a draughty place and forgotten while everyone else is next door and laughter comes through and I can't call. So I sit and pray to God to help me take it all and smile. Thank you God, I really know you are with us.

Back in Devon.

Joss was obviously tense and that was not good – I do love him so much and I'll do anything to please him. It was not a happy day. My saliva was so troubling. Some how the day went by. Joss made me so happy, cuddling me beautifully all night.

During the night Joss made love to me. Ros came at eight and we woke. I am so glad my husband was making love to me last night. Ros dressed me and gave me a wash. I've had a very fine day. Joss is sitting so close to me. I love Joss. The day has been so good – Melanie put my feed on and Hilary was sitting next to us, and so I got on with you, diary. Dr Cracknell came so I can't write much. Joss wrote me a beautiful letter. I adore Joss and his body is so constant and I am so happy.

Ros came at eight and Joss and I were both exhausted – with reason because Joss and I made exquisite love... I am having a bad day with saliva and so many people came today. Then Joss was also trying to get a helper. I do love him so. Ros came. Joss turned me.

It was a lovely day. Joss got very cross with me. Joss thinks I'm naughty and stubborn and he keeps shouting at me. My saliva is very big. Joss forced me into going into bed and looking at him. I was so upset because of my saliva with no tissue. I couldn't tell Joss because I can't talk. I had to suffer on my own. I couldn't tell Joss that he was suffocating me and I nearly died on the bed. He says he loves but today he hates me. I was pleased to see Ros who calmed me down and put me to bed.

Shocking news of what is happening. So many children have been killed by these Hutus. It is a part of this disease, that we can't shop like others do and it's a moment of feeling good. I can't read what I have written. I have no idea. This is a day I don't want again.

I am very sorry for you, darling Joss. I won't order any more. I won't worry you, Joss, or order anything. [By now our drawers and cupboards were full of clothes and presents and we had to call a halt.] We all went out shopping today and enjoyed the scenery. Then Ros came and put me to bed and that was that – my darling Joss came and gave me a loving cuddle and he moved me all night.

MAY

My days are getting harder and harder. We all went out to the shop. I got into my wheelchair and Joss wheeled me too fast to see anything. He did a lot of shopping. It was a happy day. Polly was so kind and helpful. It was lovely to see them all. They left at two. Joss is asleep by my side. I love so much.

I woke up the happiest girl. Joss made wonderful love to me. He was so happy 'cause we both spent an hour making love. I haven't had such love since we were just married. That was last night. Now this morning Joss made me a lovely coffee and after breakfast we went into the car and shopped a lot longer. I hate being pushed. I exhaust too. I still have to wait for reading glasses. It so difficult with a lot of reading.

Joss left for an important thing in Kent – a Bible reading. He made orange juice for the girls and coffee for me. I am so in love with Joss, I hope he's okay. My feed went on at 12.50 so it won't be finished for four hours. I never feel good at this time. I miss Joss but am sensible about it. I love him and I am so glad to know he's working. Elaine came, took my blood. I very glad that's over.

Joss left for work early to London at 7 a.m. Melanie drove me to the chemist and suddenly there was a woman run over by a car. Melanie got out and ran to help them. She spent half an hour talking to the police and she got the woman into an ambulance. I hope Joss is okay and keeps well. I love him, and the weather is one minute cold and one minute hot. I long to see you. I love Joss so much. I'm sorry you haven't phoned – you can't know this.

JUNE

Today began rather sad – nobody was in the kitchen. Then they came in, and I had my lovely coffee with Joss. I can't lotion now. I feel sick and hot so I will con if I can't. I take it up. I part all after the I had a picture of the family.

Rosemary was now finding writing very difficult – so I bought her some pastel paints and brushes. And from that moment on, with her brush in a clenched fist, she spent each day painting non-stop.

I was very dire but I batter [battle] on and it was a good day.

Ros returned yesterday. We had a breakfast was okay. Then Joss shout and shout many times and cry and cry. MND it is difficult and I kept crying. Grace gave me some juices and water for my tummy. Joss called Toby and Kirsty. I love Joss and we stayed in death. We're so busy I couldn't get round to my diary enough to say we had a happy day.

Joss, Grace and Connie went shopping and I am sitting here with Melanie and she's setting my feed. [Grace had been employed to help and Connie was her friend – Grace soon left, but Connie stayed on – as our friend.] I felt very good today. I hope it lasts today. I can't think. I do need to do painting. So my diary will finish. This afternoon Joss and everyone got back at 3 p.m. He's gone now, to get coffee I suppose. I worry about Joss. He's unpredictable. But I love l him more and more and I need him by my side. Then I am happy.

Melanie and I went upstairs to pack for Oxford. We come downstairs to have my feed and juice and I talked to Sammy. I'm now sitting while Joss is eating his lunch. If I make a little move he thinks I am ill and shouts at me. When my feed finish I can go out. I feel in PRISON when he keeps me in. [We were about to go to the Acland hospital where Rosemary was to have Botox injections for her saliva problem which had now become serious, and also to see about a better neck brace for her wheelchair.] Ros gave me a lovely hot bath and dressed me. She took me downstairs. Joss had given me coffee. It was a house of panic. Any way I'm trying to survive. I'm a bit sorry to be left alone. Joss is staying with me and that's all that matters. I had a weep. But I'm fine. The nurse put me to bed.

I sleep very well and nurses came to give food. It's still very strange. I have to adapt more. I'm sure it will be okay. It's a lovely sunny day. I am sure I am waiting for something to happen, they are kind and trying to help me. I hope something happens. No one else is with me. My pharmacy went very well and now Joss asleep and Melanie is having lunch and me on my feed. Nobody there and me waiting for somebody to take me to the doctor. The girls come and put me to bed. One day over and I spent it most crying.

Somebody came to get me up washed me and dressed me. Melanie was here and she left me. I haven't had a wheelchair that drives so I can't move. It's appalling no one came. The doctor left me. We drove all the way from Devon and he left me. So now it's Wednesday and I haven't seen one and I'm so upset. I haven't got a chair that can move.

I got out of bed with help from the good nurses who look after me. The girls are helping me pack. We are going home today, so it's a busy day. My feed was late so I'll be stuck here with my feed for another three hours. Joss is having his lunch. My saliva is causing a lot of problems. Joss is waiting for our girls. It's a long journey for them. I can't see them arriving before my feed finish. We've had a very disappointing week. [Very disappointing because the Botox injection, which had been suggested would remove the saliva problem, was now considered too dangerous.] We got home at half past six.

Back in Devon.

Connie is looking after me. She is so kind. I am trying to manage my Jazzy after what I had in hospital. That was a wonderful electric chair. I wonder if I can get one. The birds are singing beautifully. I had a little crying this day to think that life is hardly what I need to survive. But that's okay. Now I've hope, and I'm determined to get on with my life and enjoy what we can.

Today it's busy. I painted three pictures and Joss is sleeping by us. We kept very quiet but the phone was waking him. I was very tired and waited for Ros at nine.

We had a good breakfast reading the Sunday papers. I want to help Joss to get out. Melanie pops in and out, I feel sorry for Joss. He left at 5.30. I hope he is doing okay. Dear God, look after my husband. I am so in love with him, and I need him. I don't want to be left. I'll go with Joss where he go.

I am so content Joss has appeared. Please let me think. Meantime, I need to think. I love Joss, but his body is so big that he crushes me and he makes me squash. He gives me his front and makes it difficult to breathe. I have now had a solution and I came back to write my diary.

We had a lovely time at breakfast Joss made a lovely coffee and took me to the loo. Then we all went to the shops and never got back till 3.30 when they put me on my feed. I'm stuck here for three hours. At 7 p.m. my lunch finish. It is a lovely day. My saliva is bad and Joss gave me a suction. Happy day.

JULY

Ros came and wash me and dressed me. There is a feel of panic here. Everyone is in a funny panic. I am silent because I can't talk and I can't write because I don't want my fingers get dirty, but I would like to comment. Never mind I always miss all the fun because I have to feed. Connie got to get my feed on. Joss and Melanie have their lunch. I don't know what is going on. I am sitting here as Joss goes on the telephone and we are going to Oxford and it is late. We arrived at the Acland hospital and it was a hell. [Melanie and I had driven Rosemary there for her to have the Botox injections which were now considered necessary and a neck brace to put on her Jazzy wheelchair and we had to leave her in the hospital for the night. I wanted to stay with her, but this time was refused permission.] They can't cope with me here. They dropped me when they put me to bed and then forgot to let me pee. [The Acland hospital is one of the most expensive hospitals in Britain – despite the name I'm glad we have no connection.]

Thank you Joss for coming. Joss and Melanie came with me to see the doctor. This week I'm going to write. The doctor came, and we then got in the car and drove home. The doctor gave two injections, and we got home at 10 p.m. Ros washed me and put me to bed. This has been a horrid time. Long drive by two injections.

I had head massage. The wheelchair people brought my chair. I did not like it for it was not comfortable. It did not have a headboard. Joss said he doesn't like it either so I was back in my Jazzy. Toby and Angie and the babies came while I was asleep.

Ros came at 8 p.m and brought me downstairs. I was so happy to see Toby and Angie and all their children. Joss tried on his costume. [Rosemary was determined that I would continue working and do another movie. When I was offered the movie *I'll Be There* I, eventually said yes – on condition that I only shot one day at a time. This meant I would never be away from Rosemary for more than one night at a time, and the company agreed.] I am having my lunch. Joss and everyone have had lunch. I love Joss so much and I shall miss him. No trouble. I am so very glad he's going back to film. I am thrilled he's working.

Ros came and put out of bed. Joss left at 6 a.m. Melanie came and dressed me. The nurse came to redress my right leg. I miss Joss already. I have been painting all day. I have done several pictures. I was so pleased to hear Joss on the telephone. I miss Joss so much. But so pleased he is working.

Ros came and I was taken to the kitchen. We had coffee which Melanie made. Then I had my head massage and hand massage.

I am on my feed now. It went on at 12.30. It is a funny day, hot one minute and overcast. Any more news. I miss Joss so much. [I was doing my first day's filming.] I can't help crying for him. I can't speak of it because it would stop Joss working. I am really glad he is working and I hope he does more filming.

Joss and I had a lovely day. We all had a lovely time in the garden. We were free so I could go. The rest of the time I had my feed. The rest of the day I was painting. And I have nothing to add

I had a very good night. Only once Joss woke me to pee, and called Connie once to turn me over. Joss came and got me up and I haven't ideas what next.

Joss and Mel got me up and Joss took us to Rosemoor. Thank you, Joss – I got what I want to get flowers. It was tiring however. Jill came and gave me a lovely head massage and managed my hands and fingers. Then Beverley came and brought me a small typewriter to try.

Melanie washed me and dressed me and I had a lovely coffee. I loved my day. I spent the day painting with Connie. Grace and Melanie took me to bed. Joss and I had a hard night. We used the bell on the small typewriter to call Connie.

It had been a very hard night. In the small hours Rosemary tried desperately to ask me something, but, no matter how I tried, I couldn't understand, and she was unable to point to any letters of the alphabet to explain what she wanted. After some time I called Melanie and Connie, but they could not understand either. Eventually, an hour later, we finally realised that Rosemary was trying to tell us that she wanted to raise her head, because she was starting to choke. It was a long, exhausting night, and the next day Rosemary painted, but all she wrote was –

Washed and dressed. I was sleeping all morn. I had a lovely coffee. I was sleeping all morn–

Rosemary's diary ends here.

So the next night I put a chaise longue, with a raised end, next to our double bed, and lay at the side so that I could hold her hand. When Rosemary and I first learnt that she had motor neurone disease, we had made a vow that we would fight it together. At five o'clock that morning, I whispered, for the very first time, 'Don't worry, darling, when you go, I promise I will follow'. Rosemary smiled, and squeezed my hand. Exhausted, I closed my eyes. A few seconds later I opened them, and she had gone. But the smile remained.

EPILOGUE

I hope to God that I can keep that promise. It is several years now since the day that Rosemary closed her eyes for the last time. When she went my, heart went with her and now only part of me remains. When Rosemary and I joined together in marriage, we became one. She truly became my better half, and we had a wonderful life together. Nothing fazed her. She accepted poverty and disaster in much the same way as she accepted success and achievement, so we were able to keep our heads. Her quiet strength, her balance and her great love helped us to conquer poverty, disaster and tragedy, and gave me the impetus to keep working non-stop. She gave me strength.

Apart from visiting our children and close friends, I no longer travel, because it was her pleasure that I experienced as we moved around the world – it was her excitement and her enthusiasm. After she died I have only been to the theatre once, because without her sitting beside me I felt guilty, because I was missing her joy and excitement, and if I cannot go to the front of a theatre, working on the other side of the curtain would not be possible.

It has been a full, exciting life, and I am very grateful. We have a vast tribe of children, grandchildren and great-grandchildren. All I want now is to see them tread a peaceful, successful path, and help drive this planet forward an inch or so.

During the last years of Rosemary's wretched disease my life was isolated, and, like Rip Van Winkle, it took me some time before I was able to catch up with the outside world. When I did it was much changed. The predictions of H.G. Wells and George Orwell have been uncannily accurate. 'Things to come' have indeed now come and – even though a few years later than anticipated – so has elements of Orwell's *1984*.

It is possible to have two lives – I know because I have had two. The first began in 1928, and is still going. My second life began in 1951 when I met Rosemary, and it ended fifty-one years later. Rosemary was my second life. Today I still breathe – I still love and enjoy our vast family – and even though time would be easier to cope with had I never found such love – I still live. I am back in my first life, and life's lustre has gone, but that does not depress me too much, because I anticipate flames rekindling when I depart.

I can die with that, because when I go through that door, you know who I mean to join.

POSTSCRIPT

During our lifetime together, it was vital that I kept working. Starting married life as we did, we were always uncertain of what was around the corner. The fear of a bleak future was always there, and with our vast family, there was too much at stake. After so many disasters on our tightrope of life, I dared not take the risk of dropping off – not with so many mouths to feed – possibly more than any other living actor. I had a partner who always faced every obstacle with calm and courageous optimism, and so I played almost anything that I was offered. Here are just a few of the recognisable roles that we took on – fact and fiction. I say 'we' because, in spite of her accidents and disasters, Rosemary was always our backbone. I was fortunate, because with so few repertory theatres, there is little demand for actors to play diverse roles, and consequently little demand for actors. This is sad for the young today who are asked to play nothing more than an extension of themselves.

Recognisable theatre roles include:

After numerous parts in repertory companies at Stratford-upon-Avon, the Embassy Theatre, Buxton, Croydon, Salisbury, Windsor, Chesterfield, Coventry and Oxford, playing roles ranging from Buttons to Bottom and Banquo to Jesus, I stayed in London and played Belcredi, Belch, Caliban, Northumberland, Pistol, Aegisthus, Lord Froth, Captain Bluntschli, Justice Squeezum, Galileo, Kirilov, Long John Silver, Blind Pugh, John Jorrocks, Captain Brassbound, Mitch, Frederik Egermann, Eustace Perrin State, Juan Peron, Falstaff (three times), Mr Darling, Romain Gary, Captain Hook, Clarence Darrow, Captain Shotover, Weller Martin, Gaev, John Tarleton and Alfred III at Chichester and only toured during the last fifty years as Sir in *The Dresser* and as Petruchio in *The Taming of the Shrew*.

Movie roles include:

Don Masino Croce, Joe Gargery, Ambassador Andre Lysenko, Jock Delves Broughton, King Arthur, General Bergdorf, Henri Matisse, Winston Churchill, Black Rabbit, The King (in *The Little Prince*), D'Artagnan's father, and many more.

TV roles include:

D'Artagnan, Kipling, Peggotty, President Ford, President Carter, Moulton Barrett, Jerry Westerby, Herman Goering, Aristotle Onassis, Danton, Chebutykin in Checkov's *Three Sisters*, Menenius in *Coriolanus*, C.S. Lewis in *Shadowlands*, Lewis Serrocold, Isaac, Terence Fielding, Tolstoy, Alan Holly, and many more.

Radio roles include:

God, Macbeth, Falstaff, Lophakin, Beethoven, Verdi, Bach, Beau Nash, Stravinsky, Danton, Flashman, Socrates, Big Daddy, Honoré Lachaille in *Gigi*, The King (in *The King and I*) and many more.

THE ACKLAND FAMILY TREE

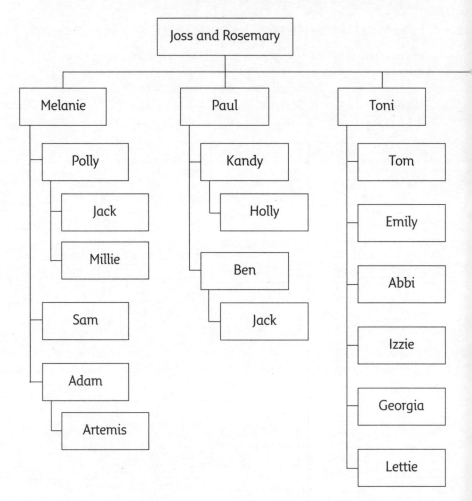

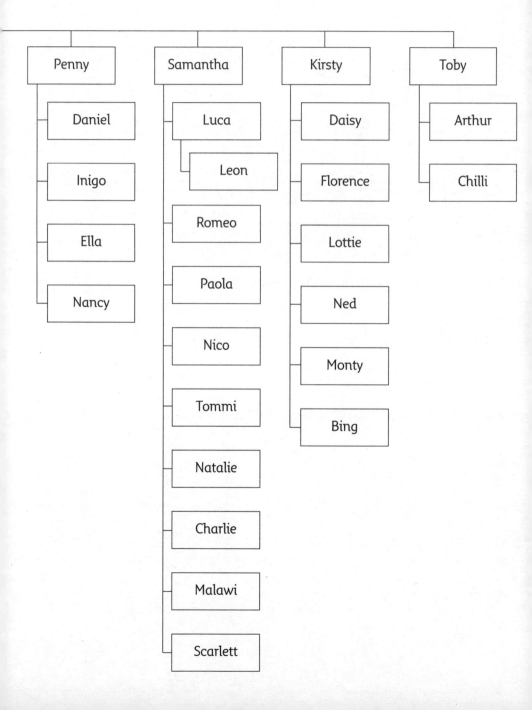

motor neurone disease
association

The MND Association supports those living with motor neurone disease and promotes research into treatments and the search for a cure for this devastating disease.

For more information go to www.mndassociation.org or call 08457 626262.